I0816078

# The South Carolina Militia in the Revolutionary War

## *Captain Henry Felder & the Backcountry Defense*

John Brian Eleazer

*Foreword by Chris Weatherhead-Felder and Clarence Felder*

Published by The History Press
An imprint of Arcadia Publishing
Charleston, SC
www.historypress.com



First published 2025

Manufactured in the United States

ISBN 9781467158527

Library of Congress Control Number: 2025931880

*For the descendants of Captain Henry Felder,*
*American Revolutionary War Patriot.*

# Contents

# Forewords

I met Brian Eleazer when our company was holding screenings of our docudrama *All for Liberty*, about Captain Henry Felder and his family as they fought for freedom in South Carolina during the American Revolution. He is a descendant of Henry Felder and has researched the life of Captain Felder for many years, as well as the extraordinary militias that joined the battles and skirmishes.

However, the sacrifices and bravery of militia leaders and their followers in the colony of South Carolina were largely not reported in the general historical record from 1780 to 2024. This is due largely to a focus on the generals, officers and battles in the northern colonies.

It is often true that the shopkeeper, farmer, blacksmith or dairyman who put down his work to go fight for the freedom of all is not heralded in history books because higher leaders are chosen first. But without these people, who had much more to lose in many cases, victory could not have been achieved. The militias comprised these hardworking men who turned the tide of the war of independence in 1781. I would add that they also had the support of their wives and elder family members, who fought in their own way.

I am gratefully married to a courageous descendant of Captain Henry Felder, Clarence Bates Felder. Together, we researched our story of Captain Felder for a docudrama. It's important to mention that Henry Felder was a leader of his community long before the war and was asked to serve in the first and second Provincial Congress. He was appointed to make gunpowder and gather munitions. His seven sons and his wife during that period supported his fight against the tyranny of King George and his power-hungry minions in North America.

Mr. Eleazer took the story of Captain Henry Felder and expanded his research to cover the entire war in the colony of South Carolina. It is an honor to support the vast research and objective observations you will find in this book. It provides much-needed recognition for a large segment of heroes who gave us victory in America.

CHRIS WEATHERHEAD-FELDER,
Director, Co-Producer, *All for Liberty*

Well, fellow patriots, since you are reading this, you have made the wise decision to consider this book. My respect and admiration for author Brian Eleazer is a continuing process. He and his lovely and generous wife, Marilyn, have demonstrated that they are not "fair-weather patriots" but rather strong comrades in fair weather or foul. Brian and I are proud descendants of Captain Henry Felder of the Orangeburgh District of South Carolina.

You will learn in this exciting book about many forgotten men, lost in the fog of war, without whose blood, sweat, tears and toil America would not have become an independent constitutional republic. My talented wife, Chris Weatherhead, and I were blessed by divine providence to make a movie about Henry Felder and his brave family who gave their all in the struggle for American freedom.

A favorite memory was when we were filming a scene between Governor Rutledge and Henry Felder. Rutledge was seeking help from Felder to recruit men to fight from his region to stop Lord Cornwallis, whom he compares to an alligator that will "gulp down the whole colony" in one bite if he is not stopped. Yet Rutledge was a little concerned that Felder's backcountry militia would not be up to the task and would be easily removed by the British with their training, bright uniforms and bayonets attached to their Brown Bess muskets.

Felder and most of his men were sharpshooters, who depended on their accuracy with rifles for hunting animals to feed their families. For decades, the Cherokees had also taught these men the "strategy of the wolf," which they had used on the Europeans. It was a deadly tactic of never giving up until the enemy is too tired to go on. Felder winks and reassures Rutledge, "I am committed to this effort to gain our liberty, you know that—My men, they do not shine like the King's men, but, they are fierce—I shall get about it."

And he did, along with hundreds of other men you likely have never heard of until now. Enjoy the lessons of the "land of the free and home of the brave."

Clarence Bates Felder,
Executive Director, Actors' Theater of South Carolina

Author at Liberty Tree Tavern. *Photograph by the author.*

# PREFACE

This book represents a public version of my continued research into the South Carolina militia and Henry Felder and his sons. This work will continue as long as new information is uncovered and discrepancies corrected. A researcher is a combination of archaeologist, historian and genealogist, while sometimes acting an interrogator of information presented as fact. My objectives are to assemble the information, present the sources and effect a greater appreciation for their sacrifices for our liberty. Footnotes are important, but it's impossible to cite every statement, so this work is a balance of footnote, comments and readability. My ancestor Henry Felder was one of many similar Patriot militiamen, caught up in South Carolina growth and the fight for independence. His story is their story, and their story is the story of the South Carolina militia—distinctively different from any other colony's militia. Their story is unfinished. Comments, explanations of inconsistencies and additional sources are always welcome.

# Acknowledgements

Over many years, I have been inspired by my grandfather Dr. Lin Shecut Felder's initial research and the collection and stories of my mentoring mother, Carol Felder Eleazer. I extend my appreciation for the encouragement from and conversations with many Felder descendants. I express my gratitude to the always helpful caretakers and staffs of several archives and libraries, most importantly Orangeburg County Historical Society Archives, Orangeburg, South Carolina; the South Carolina Archives, Columbia, South Carolina; and the Southern Revolutionary War Institute and Culture and Heritage Museums, York, South Carolina. Special thanks to my brother, Buddy, for his help in imagery and framing. Without this encouragement and the future assistance of others, this story of our South Carolina militia sacrifices could not have been shared.

# INTRODUCTION

*There is a time in everyone's life when a situation, an event, a moment is thrust upon you. You may run from it; you may ignore it…or you could seize it. Whether desired or not, that event may characterize you, or your actions define you by that moment. What you do becomes your lasting testament…who and what you are. Your legacy.*

*Every man has that moment in their life when they must choose. If chosen poorly, it becomes a moment of regret and a missed opportunity, potentially a haunted memory for the rest of their life. If they choose rightly, it is a Moment of Magnificence. A reward in their soul that will carry them.*

All of us will be tested. We ask ourselves, are we ready? Do we have the fiber, the strength and the mettle to step up at whatever the cost? We believe we are ready…or pray that it does not happen. Like the student in the classroom who hides in the back of the class hoping, "Please don't call on me." Others may raise their hands in the classroom to seek moments for self, attention, wealth or fame.

In the early 1770s in the North American colonies, some men remained loyal to the Crown, while others fled. In the beginning, a few colonists rose in reluctant and calculated support, but their ambitions weakened and their motivations shrank, as they could not risk their privilege, their social position or their wealth. They faltered when the tides of revolution threatened their very fortunes and lives. In the end, fortunately, others quickly lined up against tyranny as patriots with a thirst for liberty. These men and women boldly and fearlessly rallied to this great cause and supported the colonies in any capacity called on—as leaders, delegates, militias, wives, providers or regimental soldiers to combat Loyalists and British troops. These colonists bravely seized their moment, and many unselfishly gave their all.

When I was young, I remember my mother telling me the story of my ancestor Henry Felder, a Revolutionary War Patriot killed by British Loyalists while fleeing his burning home, disguised in a lady's dress. This was a story I could never forget. An older gentleman racing from the back of his cabin, flames licking across the cabin's roof as he dodged the hail of Loyalist bullets carving up the split-rail fence around him. As he ran, his wife's homespun light tan dress or cape flew in the wind, exposing his brown trousers and boots. He had nearly reached safety when a cursed lead musket ball found our hero. Even as he was mortally hit, Henry limped and crawled into hiding, away from the king's men. Over the years, my mother collected many family stories; in turn, I apparently inherited the same consuming passion to research and share these stories. As I pulled together various sources and information fragments while traveling across South Carolina, I accumulated additional insight from people, sites, libraries and archives to bring context to our journey. Historical research revealed some inconsistencies in dates, names and places. Insignificant details may be debated, but one undeniable fact remains true: Henry Felder and his sons and South Carolina's earliest government during the American Revolutionary War are historically and personally linked. A family tree alone does not provide an appropriate tribute to Henry Felder's involvement or the context in which the Felder family lived and died. Moreover, a biography of Henry Felder's deeds, along with pertinent dates and places, could never provide the depth and breadth of the significant moments of men and women like Henry Felder who charted our early American history, the South Carolina militia and their pursuit toward liberty.

This was Henry Felder's journey, a chronicle within the perspective of parallel events that shaped our colonies' quest for liberty and, ultimately, a new free and independent country. Genealogies are marvelous accounts but are sometimes weak in context—an insufficient link to an ancestor and the challenges they faced, as well as, in this case, the significant events elsewhere in the colonies. How does an early Patriot, a militiaman called to arms, continuously motivate himself to the cause while totally deprived of knowledge of the successes or failures far away in the colonies? Their motivation and their perseverance must have been something much more than the rumors and whispers and fragments of dispatches that would find their way into their commander's tent and the militia camp.

Linking specific Felder services to each battle is nearly impossible except in rare instances. On greater occasions, Revolutionary War petitions provide some clues in context of time, place and unit. As I portray the Felders' involvement in the great cause, South Carolina's backwoods militia involvement is parallel to the changing landscapes, the emerging inner conflict between Loyalists and Patriots, the dependence on England and the struggle of several of our patriotic actors. These were desperate times, uncertain times, and freedom was never assured. For the Felders and most South Carolinians, a stark contrast existed between their backcountry roots and those of Charlestown citizenry; the motivations of reluctant leaders and our soldiers sometimes conflicted, as between the South Carolina's militia commanders they knew and trusted and those of the Continental Congress–appointed generals unknown to them. These appointed leaders were often out of touch with the Carolina militia leaders, dismissive to the Carolina militia's in-depth knowledge of South Carolina's unique geography, mostly indifferent to their special skill as rifleman hunting game, their in-depth knowledge of the trading routes and the Native Indians, their militia experience in the Cherokee Wars and, finally, their familiarity with the local settlements and sentiments.

Many books on the war elevate the central Revolutionary figures while being dismissive to other actors, overlooking relevant and significant information. As one author argued, "Bluntly put, much of the history of the American Revolution suffers from distortions and omissions tied to the twentieth century's excessive immersions in 1776 as a moral and ideological starting point."[1] In this book, Kevin Phillips focuses on the significant activities of the preceding year, 1775, similar to writings focusing on only the founding fathers in Philadelphia or selective to the Northern Campaigns rather than the events in individual colonies that influenced, shaped and arguably turned the war. This fixation ignores extensive facts on the militia regiments in the Southern Campaign.

All writers have their heroes—strong views on specific events with selective references to support their perception. In our current world, this phenomenon is further compounded by history revisionists. Unfortunately, many articles and books are affected by unintentional bias and preference. On dates and places we readily agree; however, on other aspects we may disagree. Older written material concerning the Revolutionary War—the actual letters written at the time of the event and the corresponding actions of our Patriotic leaders—is more reliable than after-war memoirs, fascinating folklore and many American history books written in the past fifty years, at least when the book relies on another contemporary book or source. We should always interrogate sources. As one common example, a few well-known heroic figures wrote fine testaments of their grandeur during the Revolutionary War, although their own correspondences and their actions or movements during the actual events sometimes do not corroborate their memories. I have read eyewitness accounts by fellow Patriots, interviewed years after the conflict, that cannot be completely accurate when compared to the known actions at the defined moment. This is not meant to impugn their recollections, only to note that their memories are not perfect. With this said, these memoirs and eyewitness accounts provide credible insights and references requiring an additional "dig" into our past.

Autobiographies and recent history books are most valuable when you survey the original source footnotes while weighing the writer's interpretation of the information. For illustration, search the interpretations of General Benedict Arnold's actions at Saratoga—either direct and dangerous insubordination or daring, heroic leadership that won this key turning point of the war, depending on the author. Most historians and many others use his name as synonymous with treason with little to nothing noted about his contributions before this infamous incident. He did commit treason, but his bold exploits on the battlefield, especially at Saratoga, marked him as one of the greatest generals of the Continental army. General Arnold was always in front, leading his men, and he suffered greatly as well. Some authors offer inferences as analysis based on a singular instance and their one premise for what motivated the actors, like Henry Felder and his sons. Certainly, Henry Felder's motivation emerged early and was unshaken to the end. He did not choose his circumstances but rather responded to the challenge—his moment of magnificence. Moreover, what motivated scores of volunteer backcountry gentlemen farmers, hunters and merchants to act? For me, this makes my investigation fascinating. This spirit to live freely transcends time and is never ending.

Historians have provided many reasons why and how the American Revolution was won, and my conclusions may be debated by some and approved by others. To me, the truth is simple. Patriots' individual decisions and unwavering convictions to a great cause can neither be coerced nor conscripted. When denied and abused, their property seized, liberty's embers grow brighter. An arrogant king and reluctant leaders can never quell the fire to defeat tyranny. As tyranny rages, even the meek and fence-sitters are forced to take the side against suppression. No large army won this war, and neither was the victory due to a better-supplied and trained army. The victor did not have superior weapons. A large army, supplies and advanced weapons are essential in most situations, but even these advantages could not be brought to bear against the lasting perseverance across all colonies, settlements and terrains. Each individual's eternal spirit and determination, regardless of the sacrifice, won the American Revolutionary War. Many may be surprised to learn that the Patriots and the militia already controlled most of the colonies as the Continental army was being established.[2]

In Charlestown, the South Carolina backcountry was largely ignored before the 1760s. Nevertheless, these unimportant "backwoods nobodies" were not passive to the abuse. Settlement by settlement, district by district and colony by colony, these self-supplied, unpaid nobodies and volunteers were not to be denied. The stories of Henry Felder and countless other individuals rising to the challenge echo across our history. From our nation's humble beginnings, individuals and their sacrifices are what makes this country great. A citizenry being ignored, a government that disrespects its people, politicians' refusal to represent their constituents—these will ignite any population, and eventually they will rise against tyranny. Regrettably, neglectful governance is a timeless condition, and we must always be vigilant against despotism. When self and selfishness blind the greater purpose, matters on the ground are seldom resolved from a distance.

Chapter 1

# In the Beginning of Our Colony

At the dawning of the American Revolution, South Carolina was one of the wealthiest colonies in America, mainly attributed to a few large and vibrant plantations in the Lowcountry and around Charlestown. South Carolina's port city was one of the top five largest cities in the colonies and the only one in the South. Charlestown would not become formally "Charleston" until 1783, at the close of the American Revolutionary War. South Carolina was distinctly divided—Charlestown, the seat of government and influence, in contrast to the rest of South Carolina, which was referred to as the "up country" or "backcountry." The backcountry was populated by some of the earliest South Carolinian settlers on plots of land deeded by the Crown. One such family was the Felders, established by a Swiss German man, Hans Heinrich Felder, in the newly formed township of Orangeburgh.

In the three to four years leading up to the Revolution, American colonists struggled with their loyalty and convictions. South Carolinians were no different. Many were faithful to the Crown as appointed representatives, as merchants with dependent trading ties to Britain or as affluent aristocrats with English schooling, families and professional ties. Most of the backcountry colonists were loyal to Britain, as their lands were deeded by the Crown. Allegedly in an 1815 letter regarding the war, John Adams once opined that one-third of the colonial population was Loyalists, one-third was Patriots and one-third was indifferent and neutral to the great cause. Regardless of the quote or the precise mathematical division, those committed to the great cause were the minority opinion and less willing to fight and die for independence. As our founding fathers met, debated and initially sought only agreeable terms to remain a loyal British colony, a few Patriots across the colonies fueled a fire of liberty, separation and, ultimately, independence. By late 1773 and early 1774, that pivotal moment had arrived for many colonists as the British placed increasingly punitive and unreasonable taxation on a free people.

History remembers the Boston Tea Party in 1773 as an early catalyst of the Revolution. At the same time, South Carolinians held their own demonstrations, rallied around their Liberty Tree and conducted their own Charlestown tea party thirteen days prior to Boston's, although more peacefully diffused with the barrels sequestered to the dungeon at the old Exchange Building. By January 1775, South Carolina had effectively supplanted the British Common House of Assembly dominated by British appointments and Charlestown electorates and created their First Provincial Congress, with delegates from across all South Carolina's parishes and communities. Henry Felder was an early influential member with an appointment to enforce the Continental Association's boycott of British goods. He was a volunteer member of the newly established Orangeburgh militia, and in 1775, he joined the South Carolina Provincial Congress.

As a prominent member, Henry Felder and his no-nonsense, backcountry South Carolinian representatives held strong desires toward freedom, self-governance, liberty and the seeds of independence. These Patriots were fully committed and "determined with our Lives and Fortunes to support, maintain, and defend it," as Felder wrote in his grand jury commission's declaration ratifying a separate governance for South Carolina on May 20, 1776.[3] His Address and Declaration was signed forty-five days prior to John Adams and Thomas Jefferson's Declaration of Independence.

Numerous "intolerable acts" had been destructive to the economies of the American colonies from 1764 to 1774. The War for Independence became inevitable when the Crown refused to even read the Continental Congress's Olive Branch Petition in August 1775.

During the course of the Revolutionary War, more than two hundred battles and skirmishes occurred across South Carolina, more than in any other colony. South Carolina's conflicts accounted for more than one-third of all battles fought in the colonies. In the last two years of the war, more than one thousand Americans died in combat on South Carolina battlefields. More than 20 to 30 percent of all Americans combat-related casualties occurred in South Carolina during eight-year war despite few grand-scale battles being fought in South Carolina.

Tracking Henry Felder and sons' Revolutionary War activities is difficult because militia skirmishes and personal accounts are incomplete and often inconsistent. Adding to historical complexities, local district militias operated as small units, as reconnaissance, foragers, scouts and as detachments to larger South Carolina colony regiments or Continental forces. In my research, Revolutionary War petitions list only a few individual detachments or brigades engaged or specific names and units. Smaller skirmishes are harder to recount in messages and dispatches and sometimes appear with variations in unit, dates and location because these accounts were hurriedly written to superiors and misidentifications were frequent.

As petitions testify, the Orangeburgh militia was used across the colony under many Patriot leaders, including General Benjamin Lincoln, General Horatio Gates, General Thomas Sumter, General Francis Marion, Colonel William Thomson, Colonel William Washington and, lastly, General Nathanael Greene. These South Carolinian militia units crippled supply routes and garrisons, bedeviled and prostrated the British troops and supplied the colony militia and the Continental army regiments.

The conflicts involving members of the Orangeburgh militia reached as far west as the Florida border and to the eastern part of the colony in Camden and Georgetown. They fought from the coast at Sullivan's Island and to the most northern South Carolina Indian settlements. Captain Henry Felder and several sons served in the Orangeburgh District Regiment of Militia under Colonel William "Danger" Thomson, Colonel Christopher Rowe and Colonel Charles Heatley, formed in February 1775. When Colonel Thomson was appointed commander of the South Carolina 3rd Regiment of Rangers, Colonel Thomson maintained influence over his Orangeburgh militia, and the rangers and militia detachments often scouted and fought together.

One of the earliest engagements was the Battle at the Breach and Fort Sullivan, where Colonel Thomson and militia held a larger British brigade in check between Sullivan's Island and Long Island (present-day Isle of Palms) as Colonel William Moultrie at Fort Sullivan withstood a bombardment onslaught protected by the now famous palmetto logs.

Henry Felder's patriotic involvements prior to the battle makes it probable that Henry (and plausibly one or more sons) were present at this historic moment for independence. Records acknowledge that several of Felder's sons served in battles from the early Siege of Savannah to the last major battle in South Carolina at Eutaw Springs.

Multiple sources stitch together the militia and regiments movements during the time the Felder family served. From Patriots' petitions archived after the war, Henry's sons John, Jacob, Abraham, Frederick, Samuel and Henry Jr. served in the Orangeburgh militia and, after the fall of Charlestown, augmented South Carolina colony regiments or served in district militias as the lone resistance in South Carolina against the Loyalist and British occupation.[4] Henry Jr. served under Colonel Charles Starke Myddleton's 2nd South Carolina state dragoons, a lightning-fast mounted division conducting guerrilla warfare.[5] Frederick served during the Florida and Georgia Expedition and at the Siege of Savannah.[6] Another son, John, served with and associated with Lieutenant Colonel William Washington's 3rd Regiment of Continental Light Dragoons and was killed near McCord's Ferry trying to escape after being captured while on "special and dangerous services" for Colonel Washington.[7] Samuel served in the Upper Craven County Regiment, predominately Francis Marion's brigade.[8] Jacob was also with the same brigade.[9] Abraham is listed as an officer in Colonel Thomson's 3rd Regiment of Rangers and with Captain William Dukes, Berkeley County militia.[10]

The militias were invaluable for knowing South Carolina's unique terrain and the disposition of the communities and towns. As exemplified by General Francis Marion, no Continental army group maneuvered through South Carolina's rivers and swamps effectively without the aid of the South Carolina militia. And as General Horatio Gates's disaster at Camden attests, ignoring and distrusting the militia's familiarity with the communities and rivers led to major problems. Prior to the battle, Gates had marched blindly toward Camden with neither the ability to forage supplies nor cavalry reconnaissance—a major and catastrophic mistake.

## Chapter 2

# Coming to America, 1720s–1749

Many of the earlier settlers of South Carolina interior had stories similar to Henry Felder's migration to the colonies. Second and third generations of Swiss German and immigrants from the Switzerland and southern Germany region—families fleeing suppression and oppression. Most of the future South Carolina militia evolved from this colony's interior, and their perseverance and thirst for freedom came from the same foundation.

At the time of Henry's birth, Switzerland's social and economic conditions favored increased migrations to America during the 1730s and 1740s. In Bern, Zurich, Basel, Luzern and Fribourg, the Swiss ruling classes bore heavily down on city and country folk, enacting laws such as forbidding artisans from carrying wares to their markets so that the upper or ruling class were unobstructed and unrestricted when market shopping. Similarly, the vegetable markets were closed to the public until after the noble class picked through the vegetables and produce. Meanwhile, the Swiss noblemen found profitable business in equipping and leading regiments into foreign wars as mercenaries. Their armies were recruited from the lower class and countrymen across Switzerland and lower Germany. Many young Swiss men were recruited, served in foreign wars and were never heard from again. In 1740, an estimated sixty-nine thousand Swiss mercenary soldiers served in the foreign armies.

In parallel events, King George II bought the colony of South Carolina in 1729 from the Lord Proprietors, and the king appointed Robert Johnson as royal governor. By 1731, with the mass growth and continuous threat by the Spaniards and Indians, Royal Governor Johnson devised the Johnson Township Plan. The plan was specific to entice European Protestants to settle on mapped-out establishments along major waterways, existing forts and routes in South Carolina's interior. The plan outlined townships about six miles wide with a reserved three hundred acres central for schools, churches and public and financial buildings. Each family would receive fifty acres per family member. The planned settlements would provide a "buffer" between interior threats and the coastal cities. The Johnson Township Plan envisioned approximately eleven settlements across the interior South Carolina colony, and this plan caught the attention of Swiss Palatine (German) adventurist Jean Pierre Purry, also known as John Peter Purry.[11]

In 1724, Purry, from Neuchatel, a western Switzerland township about seventy-five miles from Wattwil, came to England and brokered an agreement with the Lord Proprietors to grant him twenty-four thousand acres and the passage for six hundred Swiss Protestants to settle in the Carolinas. Unfortunately, the Lord Proprietors failed to comply with the requested transportation costs. With a new opportunity provided under the 1731 Johnson Township Plan, Purry renewed his proposition to the royal governor. After the governor favored the proposal, Purry spent much of 1731 in Charlestown to secure the necessary expenses from the General Assembly and an escort to the Savannah River basin. At the Savannah River basin, Purry marked the location of the settlement, to be named Purrysburgh Township, on the northern banks of Great Yamasee Bluff.[12] In September 1731, Purry wrote a descriptive pamphlet of the new land that was distributed throughout Europe.[13] The pamphlet's remarkable accounts of the Carolinas encouraged many Swiss settlers to travel to the new land's appealing townships, and perhaps the senior Hans Heinrich Felder was persuaded as well. In addition to a complete description, Purry also provided a humorous warning about insects, gnats and "muscatoes," as well as the seldom-seen serpents named "Rattle-Snakes." In 1732, Purry established his colony of Purrysburgh, South Carolina, with ninety-three colonists; several hundred would later migrate there. The settlement had a prosperous beginning in comparison to other South Carolina townships. Purrysburgh is also noted in colonial history for experimenting in silk growing and manufacturing.[14]

In addition to Purrysburgh Township, the other South Carolina townships planned included Fredericksburg (near Camden), Edisto (renamed Orangeburgh), Kings Town or Kingston (later Kingston County and

Conway), Williamsburg (later Williamsburg County and Kingstree), Amelia (later within the Orangeburgh District and the present Calhoun County), Congaree (renamed Saxe-Gotha and also within Orangeburgh and present Lexington County), New Windsor (near Aiken County) and Queensborough along the Pee Dee River, near present-day Florence.[15]

In a response to Swiss settlers' increasing desires to leave, the Swiss government attempted to deter its citizens from migrating to America by imposing as much as a 10 percent immigration tax on property carried by those likely interested in leaving for the New World. On November 3, 1734, the Zurich government passed a law forbidding travel to the Carolinas and forbade would-be immigrants from selling their property so they could afford the trip. By January 29, 1735, a similar decree had been posted with sterner punishments, which included taking away land rights to own property forever if a Swiss citizen sold or bought land from potential travelers. During this time, several Swiss cantons started to require the recording of immigrants' baptisms, family members and professions for the few who were granted waivers to travel. While this is helpful today for genealogical purposes, the cantons were determining their impact in lost tradesmen and professions migrating to the Americas. The waivers were short-lived. On February 3, 1735, Switzerland's Great Council decided not to grant any additional waivers.[16]

Fortunately, a migration party of 322, including Hans Heinrich Felder, was reconsidered and was granted special permission on March 2, 1735. The records indicate a payment of £500 required to defray the expenses and provide support for any children left behind. The trip down the Rhine River to Rotterdam was over six hundred miles and may have taken as many as fifty-three days according to some accounts due to weather delays and bad water. Upon arriving in Rotterdam on May 19, the immigrants found an additional money exchange rate higher than anticipated, at 7 percent tax. Additionally, each adult paid 30 crowns (7½ pounds of sterling or approximately 150 shillings) for passage to the Carolinas. A common laborer may have made 25 to 40 shillings per month, thus three to six months of wages for many Swiss immigrants. Nine weeks later, aboard the ship *Samuel*, Hans Heinrich, Ursula and their young son, John Henry Felder, arrived in Charlestown, South Carolina, on July 13, 1735.

The *South Carolina Gazette* of July 19, 1735, announced their arrival:

> *On Sunday last arrived here Capt. Hugh Percy in 9 weeks from Rotterdam and 6 from Cowes, with 250 Switzers on board, who are come to settle a Township on the King's Land in this Province upon the Encouragement*

*granted to other Foreigners. Amongst them are Ninety fit to bear Arms, and it is not doubted but their settling in this Province will much contribute to its strength, and by their Industry and Laboriousness tend to its great Advantage; there being in some parts of this Province very good Land for Wheat and Corn, they may probably upon proper Encouragement furnish us in time with a good Quantity of that necessary and so much wanting Commodity, which now we are obligated to purchase at what rate soever from our neighbors.…They are to settle a Township upon Edisto River, which is thought the best Ground for Wheat, Corn, Hemp, and Flax, as also for planting of Vineyards.*[17]

From Saturday, July 12. to Saturday, July 19. 1735.

*CHARLES-TOWN,* July 19.

ON Sunday laſt arrived here Capt. *Hugh Percy* in 9 Weeks from *Rotterdam* and 6 from *Cowes*, with 250 *Switzers* on board, who are come to ſettle a Townſhip on the King's Land in this Province upon the Encouragement granted to other Foreigners. Amongſt them are Ninety fit to bear Arms, and it is not doubted but their ſettling in this Province will much contribute to its ſtrength, and by their Induſtry and Laboriousneſs tend to its great Advantage; there being in ſome parts of this Province very good Land for Wheat and Corn, they may probably upon proper Encouragement furniſh us in time with a good Quantity of that neceſſary and ſo much wanting Commodity, which now we are obliged to purchaſe at what rate ſoever from our neighbours.

The Province of *Pennſylvania*, to which theſe ſeveral Years paſt many thouſands (ſome will ſay above 70,000) of perſecuted Palatines and Switzers have taken their refuge, is thereby brought in ſuch a flouriſhing Condition, that between the 25th of *March* 1734, and the 25th of *March* 1735 from thence is exported [illegible] 195,028 Buſhels, 1300 Tierces, [illegible] 10,464 Buſhels, *Flour* 37,231 Barrels, [illegible] Half-barrels; *Bread* 3232 Tierces, [illegible] rels, 693 Half-barrels and 681 Qu. Casks.

On Thurſday His Honour the Lieutenant Governor being petitioned by thoſe Switzers that they might be qualified, in order to enjoy the ſame Privileges and Liberties [illegible] born Subjects of the King of *England*, [illegible] Council, and directed [illegible] and *Henry Gibbes* Eſqrs. three of his Majeſty's Juſtices of the Peace to [illegible] ſo many of them as deſired it the Oath of Allegiance and to let them ſubſcribe the [illegible] according to a Law made for that purpoſe; when accordingly in the Afternoon the ſame were read to Seventy-[illegible] (ſome being ſick [illegible]

Fourteen) in the *German* Tongue by an Interpreter ſworn to that purpoſe, and having explain'd to them the meaning of it, and they [illegible] being willing to take this Oath, the ſame was again read in Engliſh by one of the aforeſaid his Majeſty's Juſtices, and interpreted by ſhort Sentences, which they all repeated, and at the Concluſion ſubſcribed to the aforeſaid Oath and Teſt.

They are to ſettle a Townſhip upon *Edisto* River, which is thought the beſt Ground for Wheat, Corn, Hemp and Flax, as alſo for planting of Vineyards.

The Ship *St. Andrew*, Capt. *Peter Robinſon* came out the ſame Time with Capt. *Percy* from *Cowes*, having on board about 200 Palatines, and is expected here every Day.

Laſt Week were preſented to the Grand Jury at *Savannah*, Bills of Indictment againſt *Thomas Mellichamp* and *Richard Turner*, for Counterfeiting current Money Bills of this Province, and iſſuing the ſame knowing them to be Counterfeits: That againſt *Mellichamp* was returned *Ignoramus*, the other *Billa vera*, the Evidence being full it's thought he will be found Guilty by the Petty Jury, [illegible]

*South Carolina Gazette*, July 19, 1735. *Courtesy of South Carolina Archives.*

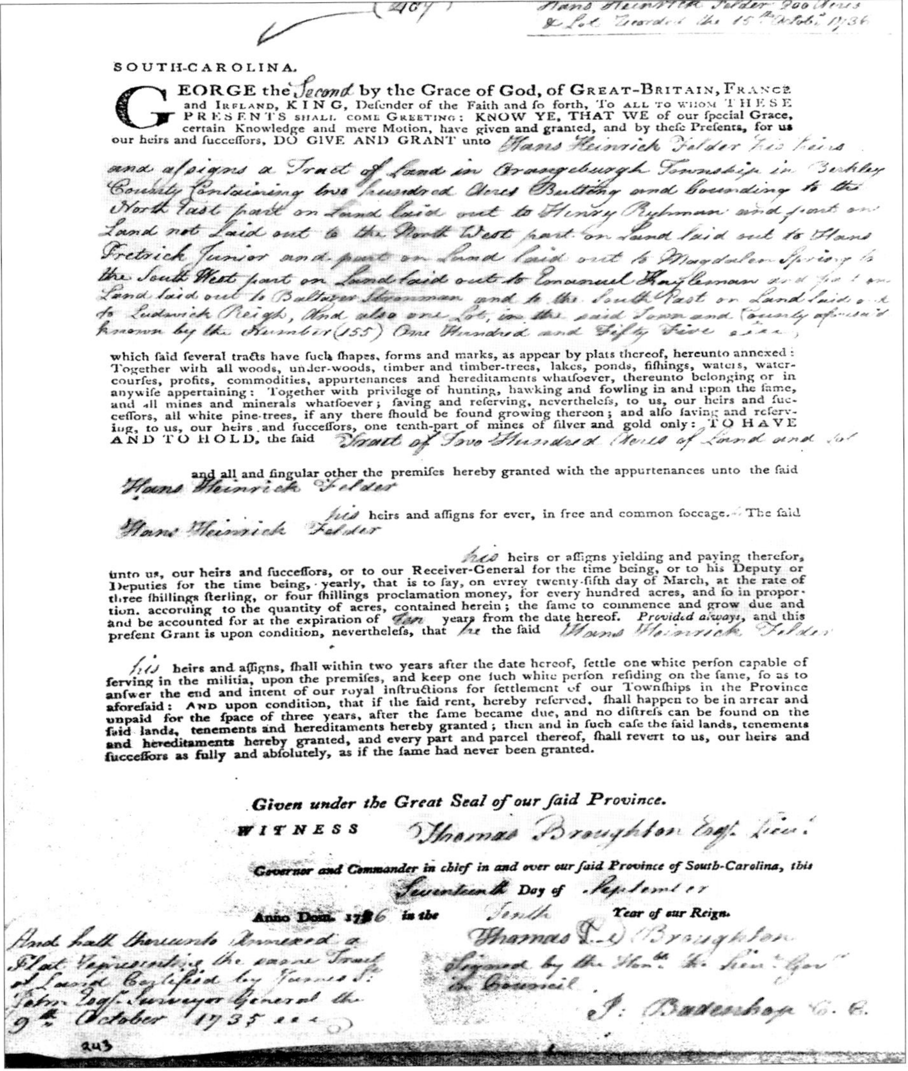

(467) Hans Heinrich Felder 200 Acres & Lot Recorded the 15th Octob. 1736

SOUTH-CAROLINA.

GEORGE the Second by the Grace of God, of GREAT-BRITAIN, FRANCE and IRELAND, KING, Defender of the Faith and ſo forth, To ALL TO WHOM THESE PRESENTS SHALL COME GREETING: KNOW YE, THAT WE of our ſpecial Grace, certain Knowledge and mere Motion, have given and granted, and by theſe Preſents, for us our heirs and ſucceſſors, DO GIVE AND GRANT unto Hans Heinrick Felder his heirs and aſsigns a Tract of Land in Orangeburgh Township in Berkley County Containing two hundred Acres Butting and bounding to the North East part on Land laid out to Henry Ryhman and part on Land not Laid out to the North West part on Land laid out to Hans Fretrick Junior and part on Land laid out to Magdalen Spring to the South West part on Land laid out to Emanuel Hagleman and part on Land laid out to Baltazer Stroman and to the South East on Land laid out to Ludwick Reigh, And also one Lot, in the said Town and County aforesaid known by the Number (155) One Hundred and Fifty Five

which ſaid ſeveral tracts have ſuch ſhapes, forms and marks, as appear by plats thereof, hereunto annexed: Together with all woods, under-woods, timber and timber-trees, lakes, ponds, fiſhings, waters, water-courſes, profits, commodities, appurtenances and hereditaments whatſoever, thereunto belonging or in anywiſe appertaining: Together with privilege of hunting, hawking and fowling in and upon the ſame, and all mines and minerals whatſoever; ſaving and reſerving, nevertheleſs, to us, our heirs and ſucceſſors, all white pine-trees, if any there ſhould be found growing thereon; and alſo ſaving and reſerving, to us, our heirs and ſucceſſors, one tenth-part of mines of ſilver and gold only: TO HAVE AND TO HOLD, the ſaid Tract of Two Hundred Acres of Land and Lot

and all and ſingular other the premiſes hereby granted with the appurtenances unto the ſaid Hans Heinrick Felder his heirs and aſſigns for ever, in free and common ſoccage. The ſaid Hans Heinrick Felder his heirs or aſſigns yielding and paying therefor, unto us, our heirs and ſucceſſors, or to our Receiver-General for the time being, or to his Deputy or Deputies for the time being, yearly, that is to ſay, on evrey twenty-fifth day of March, at the rate of three ſhillings ſterling, or four ſhillings proclamation money, for every hundred acres, and ſo in proportion, according to the quantity of acres, contained herein; the ſame to commence and grow due and and be accounted for at the expiration of Ten years from the date hereof. *Provided always*, and this preſent Grant is upon condition, nevertheleſs, that he the ſaid Hans Heinrick Felder his heirs and aſſigns, ſhall within two years after the date hereof, ſettle one white perſon capable of ſerving in the militia, upon the premiſes, and keep one ſuch white perſon reſiding on the ſame, ſo as to anſwer the end and intent of our royal inſtructions for ſettlement of our Townſhips in the Province aforeſaid: AND upon condition, that if the ſaid rent, hereby reſerved, ſhall happen to be in arrear and unpaid for the ſpace of three years, after the ſame became due, and no diſtreſs can be found on the ſaid lands, tenements and hereditaments hereby granted; then and in ſuch caſe the ſaid lands, tenements and hereditaments hereby granted, and every part and parcel thereof, ſhall revert to us, our heirs and ſucceſſors as fully and abſolutely, as if the ſame had never been granted.

*Given under the Great Seal of our ſaid Province.*

*WITNESS* Thomas Broughton Esq. Lieu.

*Governor and Commander in chief in and over our ſaid Province of South-Carolina, this* Seventeenth *Day of* September

*Anno Dom.* 1736 *in the* Tenth *Year of our Reign.*

Thomas (L.S.) Broughton

Signed by the Hon. the Lieu. Gov. in Council

J. Badenhop C. C.

And hath thereunto Annexed a Plat representing the same Tract of Land Certified by James St. John Esq. Surveyor General the 9th October 1735

243

Grant to Heinrich Felder, September 17, 1736. *Courtesy of South Carolina Archives.*

Shortly afterward, on July 24, 1735, the Felders arrived in Orangeburgh Township and settled on an initial two-hundred-acre plated lot granted through Royal Lieutenant Governor Thomas Broughton and by King George II of England. The land was plated on October 9, 1735, and granted on September 17, 1736. The allotment of fifty acres per individual indicates that the Felder family numbered four: Hans Heinrich, Ursula, young Henry and a fourth member. The identity of the fourth member has been debated but likely could be Johannes Felder, the youngest son, born in 1733, who died around October 1735.[18] However, he survived long enough to count as a member toward an allotment:

> *South Carolina. George the Second, by Grace of God, of Great Britain, France, and Ireland, King, Defender of the Faith, and so forth, To All to Whom These Presents Shall Come Greetings: Know Ye, that We of our special Grace, certain Knowledge and mere Motion, have given and granted, and by these Presents, for us, our heirs and successors, Do Give and Grant unto Hans Heinrick Felder his heirs and assigns, a Tract of land in Orangeburgh Township in Berkley County…and one Lot, in the said Town and County aforesaid known by the Number (155) One hundred and Fifty Five…17 September 1736.*[19]

The settlement had been established five years earlier in 1730, and the Swiss German community was founded in the present-day city of Orangeburg in 1735. For context, South Carolina's first successful newspaper, the *South Carolina Gazette*, was first published in January 1732 by Thomas Whitmarsh in partnership with Benjamin Franklin. Neighboring Georgia was first settled by James Oglethorpe in January 1733, with the initial two settlements being Savannah (1733) and Augusta (1736). At the time, Charlestown's population was around 6,800.

Not all travels from Switzerland were uneventful. A pastor in Oberwinterthru, Salomon Ziegler, recorded a warning in a March 23, 1744 letter:

> *Felden, A year ago two persons left here with an official pass. Hans Ulrich Freyhofer, a weaver, thirty years of age; and Verena Freyhofer, his niece, twenty-four years of age, together with two relatives of theirs from the parish of Elg, at the request of a cousin who lived in Germantown in Pennsylvania, who has gained considerable means and has no children. I received letters from them two weeks ago saying that they had arrived safely after a difficult and dangerous trip. They advised no one to undertake this journey unless it was necessary, for on their ship and one other, over 200 Swiss people died because they could not endure the sea-sickness. They reported further, that if anyone is sick upon his arrival, he is not permitted to leave the ship, so that many die in the harbor because of poor care. They also report that the present war has made the trip dangerous* [a reference

> to King George War with France and Austria]. *Because of this report many have been kept back who otherwise were intending to follow them* [Elg is neighboring canton of St. Gallen].[20]

After their arrival, some Swiss immigrants would flourish and others would not. In a letter written to a relative in Zurich, one settler warned:

> *With regard to the colonies in Carolina. I cannot advise anyone to go there! The land is good but it is entirely overgrown with forests. The heat is very great there and those who go there suffer a great deal. The last which I have had from Carolina, report that they have enough vegetable and garden truck, but neither meat nor grain. Moreover, everyone who goes there has to pay 5 pounds sterling passage money.*[21]

By 1738, the senior Hans Heinrich Felder had acquired 350 acres of land, some under the initial King George grant and some land he bought himself, including a 50-acre tract that was granted to Daniel Goltzer (Geltzer) on September 17, 1736. Regrettably, Heinrich died in 1738, and his wife, Ursula, died the following year. Ursula's estate left young Henry, then thirteen years old, 350 acres under the care of Henry Wurtzer until Henry reached the age of twenty. Ursula Felderin's last will and testament, recorded on November 8, 1739, lists the son as John Henry Felderin (an American-style name rather than Johann or Hans and Heinrich Felder). The name Felderin is the feminine form of the name Felder. After this time, the young son Heinrich (Henry) would be subsequently known only as Henry Felder. According to several sources, he was educated in Zurich, Switzerland, prior to immigrating to America. This would have likely been a formative primary education, as Henry was nine when he arrived in America. Like his father, Henry dealt in red or brown leather (cordovan) and as a cordwainer (cobbler). And at some point, Henry established a store of dry goods and merchandise, as well as raised cattle.

Young Henry was somewhat enterprising. Starting on May 10, 1751, Henry purchased an additional two hundred acres from Abraham and Mary Husenhood, extending his agricultural estate to more than five hundred acres near St. Matthews Parish. Between May 1751 and 1775, he continued accumulating land, as a number of deeds confirm many purchases and additional grants, bringing the total acres to more than five thousand acres and a number of free laborers managing his farms around the Orangeburgh and St. Matthews districts. Tradition and archival information suggest that

Henry was opposed to slavery, as he used freemen on his lands and became the district magistrate.

On December 15, 1747, Henry Felder married Mary Elizabeth Shaumloffel, daughter of John Shaumloffel, and they would have seven sons. After the death of Mary Elizabeth, Henry remarried Catharina Magdelena Schell (Snell) in 1763 and added another seven children to his household. Catharina Schell was the daughter of Adam and Margaret Schell and sister of Johann Adam Schell. Henry's son John Felder and the younger Adam Schell (Snell) were captured together by the British during the war.

Henry engaged in community affairs early. On May 27, 1749, Henry and other community members signed the Giessendammer Petition to His Majesty's Council to South Carolina, endorsing Reverend John Giessendammer as Episcopal pastor to "promote True Religion and Virtue."[22] Their church was built before 1750, making it the earliest church in Orangeburgh Township.

Archives reveal that Henry Felder represented and introduced many settlers before Reverend Giessendammer and the church; he also stood as a godparent for many baptized.[23] A plaque located at the Old Pioneer graveyard on Bull Street, Orangeburg, represents the location of this early church. Some sources indicate that Henry's father, Hans Heinrich Felder, was buried at the Old Pioneer Cemetery, thus suggesting that the cemetery dates to the earliest settlement of the township, as early as 1738.[24] As the original grave markers were wooden, the grave is long lost. A stone marker exists today, listing many of the earliest graves at Old Pioneer Cemetery, but it does not list a Felder.

# Chapter 3

# Rise of Discontent

## *Regulators of South Carolina, 1767–1769*

At the conclusion of the French and Indian and Cherokee Wars, the divide between the royal colonial administrations and the settlers in the Carolinas backcountry widened. In earlier South Carolina history, Royal Governor Robert Johnson purposefully encouraged several interior settlements as a buffer to the larger coastal cities, and these interior settlements rapidly grew and soon outnumbered coastal population two or three to one.[25] Based on educational, social and economic differences, the colony evolved into two distinctively different classes of people: affluent lawyers, merchants and large plantation owners of the coast in contrast to the less educated farmers, tradesmen, hunters and settlers across the middle and upper Carolinas. With the sudden population growth, the backcountry settlements' representation in colony affairs, judicial affairs and matters of protection were nearly nonexistent, encouraging a resentment that endured up until the Revolutionary War. This friction was one of the factors that led to the Regulator movements in South Carolina and North Carolina, each growing from similar matters of representation, administrative corruption or nepotism appointments. However, the movements and the final resolutions were vastly different between the two colonial neighboring colonies.

The North Carolina Regulator movement was fueled largely by corruption from the royal governor's administrations, mostly Royal Governor William Tryon. From the earliest revolts in our northern neighbor, the rebels seized courthouses and engaged in several violent and armed incidents. Armed violence was not to be tolerated in the colony, and the royal administration quickly responded. The North Carolina Regulator rebellion was ultimately crushed by Governor Tryon's militia, and the rebel ringleaders were arrested. When these leaders were hanged, the other Regulators fled into hiding, thereby ending the rebellion.

In contrast, South Carolina's Regulator movement was born through necessity and saw a resolution through the actions of key settlement leaders like William Thomson of the Orangeburgh District and Richard Richardson of the Santee High Hills and, ultimately, the judicial appointments of respected backcountry citizens such as Henry Felder. As a result of the Cherokee Wars, many homes and farms were destroyed. The suppressed economy provided opportunities for organized bandits, outlaws and runaway slaves to conduct scavenger raids and steal livestock and supplies from settlers on the Carolina frontier.

At the same time, the controversial British stamp tax went into effect in October 1765, and the Charlestown citizens went after the two British stamp tax officials without success. Christopher Gadsden drafted a formal response to the stamp tax, stating that "in taxing ourselves and making laws for our own internal government...we can by no means allow our Provincial legislature to be subordinate to any legislature power on earth."[26] While the Charlestown merchants debated the stamp tax and temporarily closed ports, the struggles in the Carolina backcountry unraveled with little notice inside Charlestown. Outlaw gangs organized and preyed on the settlements, terrorizing areas such as the Dutch (Deutsch) Fork and Saxe-Gotha settlements above Orangeburgh District. Cattle and supplies were stolen, torture was common and women and children were abused or kidnapped. Because the settlements did not have organized militias after the Indian Wars, few bandits were captured, and some districts were intimidated. By 1767, without support from the royal government, the communities had organized their own militia protections and appointed sheriffs led by prominent settlement property owners to confront the threat and dispense their own forms of justice. These community leaders formed the initial Regulators with only the desire for "good order and harmony" and petitioned the Charlestown assembly for courts, judges, jails and schools.[27]

South Carolina's Royal Governor Montagu condemned their lawlessness while initially doing little. As the movement continued, the Regulators established two companies of rangers to restore order to the frontier. With "authorized" rangers, the Regulators were able to chase down and punish criminals by whipping, hanging or branding. Some of the worst criminals were dragged to Charlestown for trial, although this was difficult in terms of cost, time and potential for escape. As the Regulators' power grew, so did their boldness in extending down to social issues of wayward women, orphans, malcontents and loiterers. The Regulators' enthusiasm forced acting Royal Governor William Bull to take action in 1768, attempting to address backcountry demands and tamp down the Regulator's strength.[28]

Some Regulators became twisted by their own power. They expanded their activities and control, interfering in lower district elections. For example, in the election of 1768, hundreds of Regulatory supporters marched into three Lowcountry polling places and demanded to vote. In the subsequent year, John C. Calhoun's father, Patrick Calhoun, traveled from the upcountry to Prince William's Parish with a group of armed men. Calhoun was promptly elected to the General Assembly. He and his family had suffered greatly during the Indian Wars and felt strongly about the lack of British support. Meanwhile, Governor Montagu returned to South Carolina and toured parts of the backcountry to view the discontent firsthand. To his credit, when the General Assembly met in June 1768, Governor Montagu urged several measures to bring relief to the people. He informed the South Carolina Assembly that the British Board of Trade had rejected the initial district court's act based on its disagreement on the proviso that allowed judges to be appointed based on good behavior rather than through the governor.[29] However, the governor continued to pursue the matter with Britain.

In March 1769, Governor Montagu was able to establish and reintroduce the Circuit Court Act. With the Crown's approval, a commission of magistrates and militia officers created a structure within the interior of the state. The act authorized appointment and funding for judicial districts across South Carolina, including the Orangeburgh District, with newly formed grand juries. In time, the new leaders constructed courthouses and jails in Beaufort, Camden, Cheraw, Georgetown, Orangeburgh and Ninety Six.[30]

Although authorized, the new district circuit courts were not functional until 1772. During this transition period, several Regulators attempted to preserve their power. While bandit gangs were less frequent, the Regulators continued arrests and beatings, along with reprisals against their enemies. In most cases, these Regulators were able to work with or manipulate the South Carolina administration in Charlestown. While many of the Regulators desired to uphold safety and protection, others took the law into their own hands.

To counter this continued disorder, Governor Charles Montagu ordered his own authorized enforcers, a new group of Moderators, to bring the extreme Regulators to justice. The governor dispatched a "silly fellow" named Colonel Joseph Coffell (or Scouil)[31] from Orangeburgh District to remedy the situation.[32] In short order, this man was deemed unfit in the eyes of his Orangeburgh neighbors, leaders and Regulators. Not to be deterred, Colonel Coffell arrested two alleged Regulators and imprisoned them in Charlestown, much to the dismay of the district.

The self-appointed constable Coffell became more brazen by appointing known criminals in his company to attack his personal enemies and perpetuate further arrests. Future Revolutionary War leader William Thomson reported that Coffell's band was imprisoning "women and children as well as men and going from house to house taking their provisions." Coffell's band would emerge during the war as a particular nasty Loyalist army, crossing the Savannah River and raiding mostly undefended settlements between Augusta, Georgia, and St. Mary's River. The Scouilites would aid the British at the Battle of Midway Meeting House, Georgia, and the British success at the Sieges of Savannah and Charlestown. As result, the backcountry settlements resented the Moderators as much as they sometimes felt suppressed by overzealous Regulators.[33]

In the same month as the approval of the Circuit Court Act, March 1769, the opposing Moderator and Regulator forces squared off for a battle near Bush and Saluda Rivers. Fortunately, and unlike North Carolina's armed conflict, the battle did not materialize, as two very prominent and future Revolutionary War leaders—William Thomson and his Congaree River neighbor Richard Richardson—were able to enact a truce. Thomson became the commander of the Orangeburgh militia and South Carolina's 3rd Regiment of Rangers, and Richardson would become a general in the state militia. Prior to the war, Thomson was appointed sheriff of Orangeburgh District in June 1772. Within two years, the circuit courts started to function, trusted justices were appointed and the Regulators and Moderators faded into history—but not their leaders.

However, the Charlestown wariness of the backcountry did not dissipate, and the divide remained. The assigned Regulators became settlement leaders and delegates, and the Moderators evolved into Tories and Loyalists. Despite the likely contempt across the two South Carolina classes, the Circuit Court Act of 1769 provided three significant elements to the future unity and natural growth of an organized militia to defend South Carolina during the American Revolution.

First, the act elevated the often-ignored and dismissed backcountry people to importance to South Carolina, no longer as a vast wilderness of uneducated "beggars" and vagrants, as quoted by John Rutledge and Henry Laurens. Second, the act brought the Lowcountry and backcountry together into a circuit of courts and judges. The Lowcountry lawyers and judges expressed their amazement at the "up country men, who, they said, with proper advantages would make as fine a population as any upon the earth."[34] And third, the act was the first governmental recognition of the interior settlements as having administrative standing with the older Lowcountry parishes. This made South Carolina stronger for the years ahead, with its first independent South Carolina provincial government established in 1775.[35]

In 1775, as consequence of the new district circuit court, Henry Felder was appointed to serve as justice of the peace and as a magistrate justice for the quorum in the Orangeburgh District, one of the largest districts of South Carolina.[36] At the time, the Orangeburgh District included present-day Orangeburg, Calhoun, Bamberg, Barnwell, Lexington and parts of Aiken and Allendale Counties. Given the Circuit Court Act, the magistrate played a significant role in dealing with minor crimes and law transgressions without other courts or appointed juries. Major crimes were preliminarily heard and, as warranted, referred to the courts in Charlestown. Henry was also appointed inquiry officer and collector with the responsibility for overseeing, brokering and receiving rice and flour for the Orangeburgh and St. Matthews area.[37]

Chapter 4

# Early Charlestown and the South Carolina Backcountry, 1770s

By the early 1770s, Charlestown was a thriving city in the colonies, doubling to nearly twelve thousand residents in thirty years. Charlestown was rich with nearby indigo and rice plantations, splendid homes and plantations. Northern visitors referred to Charlestown as a jewel, while others considered Charlestown as a bit arrogant. Like no other city in the colonies, Charlestown had a large gap between the privileged wealthy and the lesser citizenry of tradesmen, apprentices, freemen and slaves.

Part of the gap was driven by schooling. Charlestown had no institution of higher learning like in Boston, New York, Philadelphia, Williamsburg and other colonial towns. The absence of locally provided education was by design from the wealthy class. Henry Laurens and George Austin questioned the value of any classical education in the Americas, with Laurens declaring that children must be sent abroad for their A, B, Cs and Latin. While a few schools for the lower class and orphans were started with private donations, well-to-do families refused public funds to support these schools. Therefore, male offspring of Lowcountry aristocracy traveled to England for higher education, and most sons studied law. This formal education not only prepared these wealthy elites to practice but also secured careers as merchants, planters and politicians, with strategic connections to British merchants and business.

In 1770, a bill for establishing a local college was introduced in the General Assembly, but the affluent representatives were worried that "learning would become cheap and too common, and every man would be for giving his son an education."[38] The educational divide between wealthy and lower class, as well as the Charlestown elite's educational connections to England, were another source of hesitancy to separate from England in these years.

South Carolina founders Arthur Middleton, Edward Rutledge, John Rutledge, Thomas Heyward Jr., Thomas Lynch, Charles Cotesworth Pinckney, Charles Pinckney and John Faucherand Grimke were educated in England. These men amassed great wealth and influence, and one of the most prosperous merchants was well-known Charlestown resident Henry Laurens. Many of these early founders spent May to October each year in northern colonies, as the Middletons and Rutledges occupied homes in Newport, Rhode Island. Except for Christopher Gadsden, none of these men were interested in discussing independence and felt that any separation from Britain would be disastrous to their way of life.

In earlier years, Charlestown represented the Lowcountry and had little to do with South Carolina's backcountry. The backcountry was described as dangerous, illiterate, lawless and populated with orphans, outcasts and Native Americans. The backcountry frontier consisted of several settlements and small communities (mostly along the major South Carolina rivers and trade route intersections) and a few forts—reminders of the earlier Spanish threats and the Anglo-Cherokee Wars between 1758 and 1761. Churches, markets and taverns were central congregating areas, where news was shared, goods sold and any judicial proceedings conducted. Outside these settlements, travel routes could be dangerous and lawless.

In the Orangeburgh region, the Swiss German settlement grew, and settlers who were more English in origin migrated farther north into the Broad River Fork and Dutch (Deutsch) Fork[39] areas, along the Saxe-Gotha Township within the northern extreme of the Orangeburgh District. Due to geographic separation and alienation by Charlestown and Britain, most of these backcountry settlements were fiercely self-reliant and ever watchful of Indian raids.

The region formed its own social and religious tenets and law enforcement and was arguably almost independent from British and Charlestown influence. As the American and British struggle began, many settlements felt that the conflict was Charlestown's problem; some struggled, as they did not desire to be on the wrong side of the outcome. Several backcountry communities had sympathies toward Britain and were havens for Loyalists, such as Ninety Six, Fort Granby on the Congaree and Camden. During the Revolutionary War, allegiances in these areas would shift one way and then back again until the lands were abandoned by the British forces.

What maintained Loyalist devotion and sympathies toward Britain? One reason was resentment, as some Loyalist officers were bitter for being passed over by the Provincial Congress for appointments. Second, many men were offended to be forced to sign and submit to oaths of patriotic allegiance (although the British also forced allegiances after the fall of Charlestown in 1780). Third, some militia Patriots deserted their service after the appointed Continental generals' misuse of their militias. Fourth, some simply remained loyal, as Great Britain had provided them with the deeds to their lands, and in the beginning, they had no quarrel with England. As time passed and tyranny grew, the settlements felt the brutality of the British and Loyalists. Many changed sides. However, strong unity to the cause did not materialize until much later.

Respectable members of the Charlestown leadership never endeared themselves to the backcountry. John Rutledge, in 1771, referred to these poorer classes scattered across the backcountry and hinterlands as a "pack of beggars" and nobodies. Likewise, the Charlestown government assembly provided these South Carolinians little representation. In the years to come, John Rutledge would likely retract his comment about these backcountry beggars as these freedom-loving ruffians would take a prominent role in South Carolina's involvement in the great cause.

Chapter 5

# Indian Tribes of the Carolinas

When the early settlers arrived in South Carolina, the colonists found the Edisto, Cusabo, Chicora, Santee, Pee Dee, Waccamaw, Catawba, Creek, Cherokee and no fewer than twenty-eight Indian nations.[40] The Edisto Indians occupied areas between Savannah and Edisto Rivers until the late 1600s. By the start of the eighteenth century, most of the Edisto Indians had melded within other tribes of the region, such as the Cusabos. The Cusabos were a group of American Indians who lived along the coast of South Carolina between Savannah River and Charleston. During the Yamasee War of 1715, the Cusabo group were one of the few tribes that fought as a colonist ally.

After the war, most of the Cusabos migrated or lived among the colonists. Several Siouan-speaking tribes were located along the Pee Dee River, in both North and South Carolina. Chicora Indians were situated around Winyah Bay and the Pawley's Island region of South Carolina.[41] Unfortunately, many were captured by the Spaniards and kept as slaves in the earliest settlements (late 1500s). Santee Indians were a small tribe along the Santee River, around present-day Lake Marion. Like the Chicoras, the Santee Indians were victims of the slave trade. By the early eighteenth century, they were virtually nonexistent as a distinctive tribal unit. Several other tribes suffered similar fates. Hostile tribes, settlers' encroachment and smallpox decimated these tribes. The remaining bands were consumed by other Siouan peoples. By the mid-1700s, the Pee Dee and Waccamaw people were slowly settling among the Catawbas or Cheraws for protection against the Cherokees. The Siouan-speaking Cheraw Indians formed settlements along the Pee Dee River in the Carolinas. As the Cheraws dwindled, remnants of the Cheraw tribe amalgamated within the Catawba tribes. Cheraw and Catawba warriors were known to have fought alongside General Thomas Sumter.[42]

The Muscogee-speaking Creek Indians primarily lived in regions around Alabama and Georgia, with some settlements east of the Savannah River. Much earlier than the Revolution, the Creeks established treaties with Georgia and South Carolina colonists and the British government against their common Spaniard enemy. However, during the Revolutionary War, the Upper Creeks sided with British Loyalists in the capture of Savannah (1779) and Siege of Augusta (1780).

With Cherokee villages in upper South Carolina, the Cherokees traveled across the state, preying on other tribes or unsuspecting colonist settlements. Just before the Revolutionary War, the Cherokees and the Catawbas were the most prominent and largest tribes in South Carolina. Both tribes were allies to the British during the French and Indian Wars (1754–63), with few military engagements in South Carolina. The lasting remnant of the French and Indian War was the establishment of several forts in the upper parts of the state, such as Fort Prince George on the Keowee River near Indian settlements. As constant neighbors, the Indians and colonial soldiers developed a distrust leading to conflict. Their retaliation led to the Cherokee Wars or Anglo-Cherokee Wars (1759–61).

A massacre at Fort Loudoun in August 1760 was the most tragic event. More than 142 soldiers and civilians from Fort Prince George were tortured and killed by the Cherokees.[43] News of the massacre created panic across the colony. Before the British and colonists defeated the Cherokees, fifteen towns and fifteen thousand acres of crops were destroyed across South Carolina, North Carolina and Tennessee. The following excerpts provides an insight of the times:

> *During the years 1759 and 1760, the people of Saxe-Gotha suffered greatly from the savages of the Cherokee war. During the time that the French and English were at war with each other in the colonies of America, which however did not reach as far South as the Carolinas; the French instigated the Cherokee Indians to make war upon the peaceful settlers of the two Carolinas who murdered the white inhabitants at midnight, whilst they were wrapped in their peaceful slumbers, and committed atrocities at which humanity shudders. The Congaree and Fork settlements were then mostly exposed to the fearful inroads of the savages, as but few settlers were*

> *living further in the interior than the Germans were at that time. Bolzius* [Boltzius] *informs us, that many were compelled to take refuge among the Germans at Ebenczer* [Ebenezer, Georgia] *and Savannah, whilst others fled for safety to Charleston, Purrysburg, and other places, until those Indian hostilities were ended, and peace and security was again restored.*[44]

Prior to the British tensions with the colonies, both the British and colonial governments had a strong yet sordid trade history with the Indians, largely involving supplies and gunpowder. As hostilities increased, the British became more aggressive in supplying the Cherokees with gunpowder and arms to compel the Indians to raid the colonial settlements, just as the French had done during the French and Indian War. From William Tennent and William Henry Drayton's 1775 journals comes this report:

> *Gentlemen:—Being on my return from the frontiers of South Carolina, where the Honorable Mr. Drayton and myself were sent by the Council of Safety of our Province, I think it my duty to acquaint you that there exists in those parts a most dangerous conspiracy against the lives and liberties of these Colonies. Encouraged by Government and by the Tories* [Loyalists] *in your town and in Charlestown they have gone to great lengths. They do not hesitate to boast that they are furnished with ammunition and that even artillery are at their service any day. This I have by a trusty friend from Cunningham's mouth. I have great reason to think that they are mistaken when they boast of many thousands ready to come down at the* [royal] *Governor's signal—but that they have some hundreds actually enlisted, if not under pay, I make not the least doubt. That they depend upon the Cherokee nation to join their camp when it forms, and have great hopes of the Creeks, they do not pretend to keep any longer a secret. I am in possession of an affidavit by which it appears that the malcontents on the frontiers expect to gather into forts and suffer* [permit] *the savages to pass on and massacre the associated inhabitants.*[45]

In response, the newly formed South Carolina militias conducted campaigns to the upper regions of the state to suppress and break up Cherokee Indian settlements in August 1776. As an example, Major Andrew Pickens fended off an ambush party of 180 Cherokees in the Ring Fight near Tamassee. After the early part of the Revolutionary War and after the heavy loss of more than two thousand warriors, the Cherokee tribes were no longer considered an essential or direct ally in British Carolina engagements.

Nevertheless, independently, the Cherokees continued to raid vulnerable travelers or small detachments along the South Carolina and Georgia border. A treaty in 1777 led to a ceasefire and cession of much of Cherokee land to the colonists, although raids continued as the Cherokees remained a fierce threat. On several occasions, Loyalists turned Patriot prisoners over to the Cherokees, whereby the Indians tortured and killed many of the prisoners. As late as December 7, 1781, Loyalist Captain John Crawford attacked White Hall Plantation on McCord Creek, near present-day Abbeville. After capturing the Patriots, Crawford fled north into Cherokee territory. Subsequently, Crawford turned the prisoners over to the Cherokee Indians. The Cherokees tortured and killed all the prisoners, including John Pickens, the brother of General Andrew Pickens.

Counter to the British-Cherokee alliance, Catawba warriors were a steady support to the Patriots, largely with General Thomas Sumter's state militia. The Catawbas had shown particular loyalty to their allies. After the earlier French and Indian War, King George III rewarded the Catawba tribe with large tracts of South Carolina land, comprising approximately 144,000 acres, for their loyalty to the Crown. Prior to the war, South Carolina representatives sought the Catawba people's support. When William Henry Drayton, president of the South Carolina Council of Safety, traveled the backcountry from July to September 1775, he was able to negotiate a favorable agreement with the Catawba:

> *The following letter was written by the President to Joseph Kershaw, esq., laid before the Council and approved of. Charles-Town, July 25th, 1775. "Sir—The Council of Safety have ordered me to acknowledge the receipt of your fovour of the Nth instant, and to return their thanks for your assiduity in training with the old men and head warriors of the Catawba Indians. Your assurances that those people are hearty in our interest, and your hopes that forty or fifty of them will cheerfully enter into the service of the Colony, affords the Council additional satisfaction, and the design of uniting them to the Regiment of Rangers* [Colonel William Thomson's 3rd Regiment of Rangers] *is a measure which they although approve of, but to…under the particular direction of a white man, agreeable to a resolution of the Congress in their late session. The Council request you to give them immediate notice when anybody of the Catawbas are ready to march in order to join the Rangers, and that you will recommend a white man well qualified to lead them in scouts, and in action. Transmit your notice by the hands of such a*

> *one. The Council will give him a commission and dispatch him with a letter…Col. Thomson, in whose camp he will meet the Indians."*[46]

William Henry Drayton offered the Catawba warriors ten shillings per day, the same standard rate for a militia soldier. As the warriors fought, the Catawba women and children moved into North Carolina and later to Virginia for protection against the Cherokees and the British. In retribution, the British under Colonel Francis Rawdon burned their homes and crops in South Carolina. When the Catawba people returned to their settlement, they found all their lands destroyed. In war, the Catawba warriors were primarily used for scouting and foraging and fought aside General Sumter's troops in several battles.

In early 1776, then Colonel Sumter, 2nd Regiment of riflemen, heavily recruited Catawba warriors as sharpshooters. Sumter's methods and tactics taught his young militia to be riflemen instead of engaging in bayonet combat, a tactic identical to Daniel Morgan's Virginians. These riflemen were employed at the Battle of Breach Inlet.[47] When Sumter was compelled back into service after the fall of Charlestown, he immediately reassembled his old regiment and was able to recruit more than two hundred Catawba warriors.[48] After General Gates's disaster at Camden, the Catawba were present in several key events: the ambush of Sumter at Fishing Creek (August 1780), the siege at Rocky Mount (July 1780) and the victory at Hanging Rock (August 1780); Sumter militia were also reestablished at Clem's Creek (September 1780) with more than forty additional Catawba warriors enlisting in the militia.

At this moment in history, the aid from the Catawbas was vital, as not a single Continental unit existed in South Carolina from August 1780 to April 1781 with few exceptions, such as Daniel Morgan's short but vital battle at Cowpens.[49] The enlisted Catawbas were effective scouts for General Sumter and fought within Captain Thomas Drennan's (or Brennan) company under Sumter's state militia.[50]

Overall, the contributions of the Native Carolina tribes were mostly selective, and sadly, American Indian nations greatly suffered under the European growth and as casualties during the Revolutionary War. After the war, the South Carolina government awarded decorative medals or gorgets to the victorious Catawba warriors who fought for America's independence.

Chapter 6

# Royal Government of South Carolina, Prior to 1774

Before the time of Henry Felder's involvement in South Carolina legislation, South Carolina was controlled by the royal government. Until 1774, the early governmental system in South Carolina, as modeled in the other colonies, was patterned after the English political system. At the top was the Crown-appointed royal governor representing the interests of the king. Assisting him with his executive and judicial duties was a Britain-appointed twelve-member council, or Upper House. Rounding out the governmental system was an elected representative assembly, or Lower House. The Lower House was empowered to enact the laws of the colony as long as the laws were consistent to British Parliament's wishes, and legislation was also subject to the Crown's approval.

By 1761, these assembly members were elected once every three years; however, only men of wealth and societal distinction need apply.[51] The minimum requirements were ownership of more than five hundred acres and ten slaves, or the equivalent in Charlestown properties. Due to privileged education, Charlestown roots, aristocratic connections and wealth, the city's elites dominated the assembly. They were largely motivated by political ambitions and prosperity and served as guardian stewards of the life, liberty and property of the people.[52] The assembly was controlled by rich planters such as Thomas Lynch, Rawlins Lowndes and William Wragg and powerful merchants like Christopher Gadsden and Henry Laurens, as well as influential lawyers like John Rutledge, Charles Pinckney and Peter Manigault. Writers and observers at the time likely deemed these men spirited, unpaid representatives who exchanged their time and energy for an equal manipulation of the political landscape for their personal rewards of esteem and admiration.

From the late 1760s and into the 1770s, the relationship between the Crown and the colonies seriously eroded, and the Crown's hold on the government waned. In these early years, seeds of separation or perhaps independence were sown and started to take root.

As early as 1768, Charlestonians gathered around an old oak, referred to as the Liberty Tree, in Mr. Mazyck's pasture (near present-day 80 Alexander Street). The early passionate Patriots spent hours toasting the "mischiefs over the Stamp Act" and anti-Crown sentiments. While many assembly members remained somewhat submissive to the Crown and worked only toward reconciliation as free British citizens, an early liberty-minded leader, Christopher Gadsden, spoke of "a free assembly, freely representing a free people" and was one of South Carolina's first strong advocates for independence and an escape from the strangles of the Crown's tyranny. Henry Laurens characterized Gadsden as "rash, head strong and leading people into quarrels."

Although future Patriots Henry Laurens and William Henry Drayton considered Gadsden a hothead or a lunatic, in time they changed their allegiance, as both Laurens and Drayton were personally humiliated by the royal government. By 1775, each had awoken to the realization that the Crown was suffocating the colonies through endless taxation. As Gadsden and his "Liberty Boys" demonstrated, British taxation, declining trade and boycotts were inflaming the average Charlestown citizenry.[53] Such sentiment did not escape the South Carolina backcountry. Taxation stifled availability of British goods to the scattered settlements, including a limitation on the British gunpowder trade to the dependent South Carolina Indians. Consequently, the number of Cherokee raids increased from the midlands to the mountain settlements.

In the case of Henry Laurens, his sentiments turned against the Crown based on quarrels with the Upper House–appointed judge Egerton Leigh. Laurens and Leigh maintained a close relationship, as Laurens courted higher appointments, until Laurens's ship *Ann* was impounded due to carrying goods without proper papers in 1767. British custom collector Daniel Moore impounded two of Laurens's ships, and Judge Leigh attempted a compromise by dismissing charges on one ship and seizing only the *Ann*. This did little to appease Laurens, and he successfully sued and fined the British officer George Roupell, who had illegally seized the ships' manifests.

As payback, the British port officers seized more of Laurens's ships, and Laurens attacked Judge Leigh in public print. Judge Leigh responded in kind, attacking Laurens personally. (In a parallel event in Massachusetts, a similar British impoundment of John Hancock's ships drove him to boldly support independence, although Mr. Hancock was smuggling gunpowder and other pirated goods before and during the Revolutionary War.) In 1772, Sir Egerton Leigh disgraced Henry Laurens more personally. Around this time, Judge Leigh impregnated Henry Laurens's niece, Judge Leigh's wife's sister. During delivery, at sea, Leigh prevented her coming ashore and also denied her a midwife, causing a situation that led to the infant's death. The public adultery and indecency of this incident resulted in Leigh losing his judgeship and further prompted Henry Laurens to change his loyalties and turn against the British-appointed members, referring to Judge Leigh as "the most wicked man and greatest fool that ever I heard or read of, in a man of tolerable education and sense."[54]

Meanwhile, the colonies suffered from more taxation. Needing funds to maintain its army and navy after the French and Indian War, Britain manipulatively increased taxation on the growing and prosperous colonies. Several tax acts stand out. Like the Molasses Act of 1733, the Sugar Act of 1764 imposed a tax on sugar and molasses to generate revenue for England. The Stamp Act followed in 1765 and imposed a tax on every piece of printed paper, ship's papers, legal documents, licenses, newspapers, publications and even playing cards. Without the stamp, papers were considered null and void, lacking legal standing. This was repealed in March 1766. The Quartering Act of 1765 required the colonies to provide any needed accommodations in beddings, utensils, firewood, beer, candles and food to the British soldiers in the area, often without repayment. The Townshend Acts of 1767 mandated an importation tax, or duties, on paper, paint, lead, glass and tea; it also restricted the colonies to only import these items from Britain.

The colonies responded with a non-importation act against British goods. In South Carolina, Charlestown called for an assembly consisting of artisans, planters and merchants, forming an independent Committee of Thirty-Nine, including thirteen representatives from each party.[55] This gathering provided one of the first opportunities when the lower class had a voice, and this unnerved the affluent leaders. Wealthy planter William Wragg feared his freedom being endangered. William Henry Drayton was more specific, saying that men educated in liberal arts should not have to "consult on public affairs with men who know only how to cut up a beast…

cobble an old shoe…or build a necessary house."[56] Specifically, Drayton called the laboring class "*profanum vulgus*," a derogatory Latin phrase for the common masses.

As a leader, Christopher Gadsden was more pragmatic and vocally recognized both the growing power of the lower class as well as his dependence on these same workers as a shipping merchant. He foresaw their necessity for unity against the common enemy of tyranny.[57]

The breaking point came with the Tea Act of 1773, which granted the British East India Company a direct monopoly on tea imported to the American colonies. The colonists viewed all these acts as continuous taxation without their consent or recourse. After years of higher and heavier taxes, the colonists were on the brink of an open rebellion.

In South Carolina, a power struggle ensued between Royal Governor Charles Montagu, the Upper House and the Lower House. Over time, the popularly elected assembly expanded its grip in most matters, extolling the earliest principle of democratic politics. As a practical matter, the assembly slowly stripped and used the "power of the purse" from both the royal governor and Upper House by controlling money matters and expenditures. More specifically, the royal governor and Upper House made policy and laws and appointed senior executives. However, the Lower House decided on which laws to enforce or actions to fund. The clash continued until Royal Governor Montagu returned to England in less than high esteem, as did his key council, Judge Egerton Leigh, in 1773. At this point, the royal government and the assembly existed only in name and ceased to function as an organized legislature. The aforementioned Committee of Thirty-Nine became the de facto government of South Carolina.

While Charlestown elite struggled with the royal government, British taxation was directly affecting markets in the backcountry's trade, and neither the elected Charlestown representatives nor the Britain leaders provided aid or security to the backcountry towns and roadways. As with the previously discussed Regulator movement, the British role as a supposed protectorate was largely ignored, as Indians and unrest continued to pester lands and roads north of Orangeburgh settlement. With their pleas ignored, the people of the backcountry derogatively referred to the assembly as "rice-birds."

Chapter 7

# Tea Parties and the First Provincial Congress of South Carolina, 1774–1775

The tea parties and the First Continental Congress actions drew Henry Felder directly into the conflict. Thirteen days prior to the infamous Boston Tea Party, Charlestown staged its own rebellion against tea. Between December 3 and December 22, the Sons of Liberty led a resistance against the British ship *London*.[58] Arriving at Charlestown port on December 3, the ship attempted to unload its cargo of 257 chests of tea. Gadsden's Liberty Boys printed and distributed handbills protesting the cargo, and a mob soon accumulated at the wharf. Although South Carolina's tea party ended when Royal Governor William Bull II ordered the tea unloaded after the expired twenty days in port and stored unopened in the cellar of the Old Exchange Building, England was displeased by Charlestown's "most unwarrantable insult to the authority of the Kingdom."[59] According to William Gilmore Simms, the first tea cargo were stored and rotted in storehouses.[60] Notably, South Carolina's tea party did not end there. In June 1774, the ship *Magna Carta* arrived with tea. However, with fears that his ship would be burned, Captain Richard Maitland moved his ship to deeper waters as the protest continued. Maitland appeased the crowd by promising to return all the tea to England, but the protesters felt that the captain would renege on his promise. Subsequently, protesters boarded the ship, and seven chests of tea were thrown in the Cooper River. And in November 1774, Captain Samuel Ball sailed the British ship *Britannia* into the harbor. But the three Charlestown merchants who commissioned the tea were forced to dump their seven chests of tea into the Cooper River.

The British responded to the tea parties with a series of restraining acts. Known as the Coercive Acts, the first measure punished the offending colonies and created stricter controls on the colonial ports. Largely historically overlooked, the fifth act, the Quebec Act, served as a warning and hostile threat to the thirteen colonies' freedoms. The specific Coercive Acts passed in May and June 1774 against Americans' disobedience included the following:

- The Boston Port Act, which closed the port of Boston until damages from the Boston Tea Party were paid.
- The Massachusetts Government Act, which restricted Massachusetts democratic town meetings and turned the governor's council into an appointed body.
- The Administration of Justice Act, which made British officials immune to criminal prosecution in Massachusetts.
- The Quartering Act, which required colonists to house and quarter British troops on demand, including in their private homes.
- The Quebec Act, which favored the Roman Catholic religion and its representation in Quebec territories. The act expanded the French province into lands considered British, including lands that would become Illinois, Indiana, Ohio, Michigan, Wisconsin and Minnesota. The neighboring colonies viewed the Quebec Act as a direct threat to their security, religious freedoms and future western growth—the exact freedoms that had led the early European settlers to America in the first place.

The acts were quickly renamed the Intolerable Acts by the colonists and elicited denouncement from once loyal Crown sympathizers Henry Laurens and William Henry Drayton. Many noted that William Henry Drayton's conversion during the boycott debates was like a religious experience when he denounced the acts as "exercise despotism over America," and Drayton was a catalyst within Charlestown as he would take progressively stronger roles in the great cause.

After the flight of the royal governor and Upper House in 1773, South Carolina eventually and formally established a standing "General Committee" to function as the executive branch of government. A general meeting of the standing committee was called on July 6, 1774, to address these latest intolerable acts and provide a formal condemnation of the Coercive Acts.

This would be the first time that representation from every South Carolina parish and community was in attendance. Representatives included 15 merchants, 15 artisans and 69 planters with sharp differences in loyalties and views toward the Crown and colony relationship. In the First Provincial Congress, 55 of the 187 representatives were allotted to the backcountry, although many of these backcountry representatives physically resided in Charlestown.

The committee elected Charles Pinckney as chairman, with five delegates to attend the First Continental Congress in Philadelphia. All five delegates—Henry Middleton, Thomas Lynch, Christopher Gadsden, Edward Rutledge and John Rutledge—were born in Charlestown or Berkeley County and were wealthy and socially prominent. Henry Middleton owned fifty thousand acres and eight hundred slaves. Christopher Gadsden was an eminently esteemed merchant, ship owner and land speculator. Thomas Lynch owned rich rice plantations along the Santee River. The Rutledge brothers were English-trained lawyers with a flourishing law practice. All had been critical of British policy after 1763, with Gadsden deemed by the other delegates as outspoken and the most radical. In August 1774, the five South Carolina delegates departed Charlestown for the First Continental Congress.

The First Continental Congress met from September 5 to October 26, 1774. With new American leadership, most representatives remained loyal to the Crown and desired only their rights as Englishmen abroad. The majority voted to condemn the Coercive Acts, adopted the Declaration of Resolve, listed the rights under the British constitution (October 14, 1774) and agreed with the "Continental Association" to boycott import or consumption of British goods while sending a strong formal grievance to the English government (October 20, 1774).

All agreed to meet again in May 1775 if conditions were not resolved. Thomas Lynch and Christopher Gadsden were recognized by other Continental delegates as "solid," men who carried themselves with force and conviction to the cause. Gadsden was considered "violent against" any British Parliament powers over the colonies.[61] However, John Adams specifically distanced himself from the other South Carolina delegates and stated his distrust of John Rutledge, saying that Rutledge "maintains the air of reserve, design and cunning."[62] According to John Adams's notes on the proceedings, John Rutledge argued that the colonies had neither authority nor rights based on the law of nature; instead, he insisted that they had an obligation and allegiance to the British constitution. In direct disagreement, Patrick Henry felt that the reluctant delegates, including those from South Carolina, would "ruin the cause for America."[63]

After the initial language was agreed on, the South Carolina delegation refused to sign the non-importation agreement, stating that it would have a devastating financial risk to Charlestown. All the South Carolina delegates except Christopher Gadsden walked out in protest of the Continental Association agreement. John Rutledge said that the association's compact would lead to ruin for all South Carolina rice planters, stating, "The northern trade will be little affected by the association and he saw no reason why ours should be ruined for nearly all our indigo, and two-thirds of our rice went to the mother country."[64] Eventually, Rutledge forged a compromise for rice planters—a waiver to allow the continuation of the rice trade.[65] Once agreed, the South Carolina delegation returned and signed on October 20, 1774. The association boycott was implemented on December 1, 1774, taking the initial steps toward severing ties with the British Crown.

Upon the delegates' arrival back in South Carolina, the General Committee converted into the First Provincial Congress of South Carolina on January 11, 1775. The First Provincial Congress quickly approved the Continental Association and created committees of safety and observation to enforce the non-importation and non-exploration agreement of the association.

In January 1775, the provincial government of South Carolina appointed parish committees, including one led by Henry Felder to enforce the Continental Association boycott—"A Committee for Effectually Carrying into Execution the Continental Association and for Receiving and Determining upon Applications Relative to Law Processes for St. Matthew's Parish and Orangeburgh Township." The committee selected twelve St. Matthews citizens, including Henry Felder and Colonel William Thomson.[66] The enforcement was supported by force, as necessary, with the Orangeburgh District Militia, established the following month in February.[67]

The non-importation boycott was soon tested in South Carolina, with the early transgression in February 1775. On the thirteenth, the two-masted snow *Lively* from Falmouth and Teneriffe, captained by William Carter, arrived with two tons of potatoes that the captain elected to throw overboard rather than return them across the Atlantic. Three days later, the ship *Charming Sally*, captained by George Fortune, arrived from Bristol with bushels of salt, cauldrons of coal and 40,500 tiles. This cargo was also dumped in Hogs Island Creek. Then, on March 4, the ship *Katherine*, sailed by Captain Frazier, arrived from Angola with nearly three hundred slaves.

As the Continental Association's Article 2 enjoined to "wholly discontinued the slave trade," the cargo was sent out of the colonies.[68]

To distribute and foster support, the Continental Association representatives took the agreement across the Lowcountry, requiring all men to sign an oath or be labeled an "Enemy of the Cause." Whether driven by supply shortages or anger toward the king, anxiety and tempers increased. Although supporting the association boycott, Henry Laurens opposed the growing rebellious and violent displays and disagreed with the forced oaths of allegiance and attitudes forming in the Lowcountry. Contrary to Laurens, William Henry Drayton, now the appointed chief justice, forced action by rounding up signers and dragging those who refused before the committee. Violence and tar and feathering occurred in some instances as anger intensified. While no known case of death from tar and feathering occurred during this period, the proceedings left the victims permanently scarred.

The Robert Smythe incident in March is an example of the seriousness and severity within Charlestown. The affair occurred when the merchant ship *Proteus* landed in Charlestown on March 14, 1775. As the ship arrived, a small representation of the General Committee approved an exception to the Continental Association boycott, allowing Robert Smythe's personal property of Thoroughbred horses and furniture to be unloaded at the docks. A crowd quickly formed, and angry partisans were ready for action if the animals came ashore. The clash continued as assembly members rushed to chambers to negotiate a settlement. The wealthy class argued for an exception to the boycott, while representatives from the lower class argued for the "peoples' wishes" and zero allowances. Gadsden argued that such an exception would alarm the northern colonies and anger the citizens of Charlestown. Further, Gadsden added that the previous vote of a small quorum of committee members was illegitimate and must be reversed. The conservative Crown supporters John Rutledge, Edward Rutledge, Rawlins Lowndes, Thomas Lynch and Thomas Bee rebuffed Gadsden on the grounds that a reversal of the original vote would force the smaller quorum to "lose face." They argued that exceptions were practical—a necessity for supplies like guns and ammunitions—and that the boycott was never intended for personal items.

This was a moment seized by William Henry Drayton, arguing in support of Gadsden. Drayton announced that "the people are ever in the right." After a lengthy debate and refutes, the vote was reversed on the narrowest margin, thirty-five to thirty-four. This huge, monumental moment was not lost on the previous government. Acting Royal Governor Bull quickly warned Parliament officials in England—increased tensions had led "the people" to supersede the "Men of Property," and "the common masses" were no longer submissive to the upper class nor led by their former leaders. Parliament's response was direct, dispatching more British troops to Charlestown. At this moment, Drayton and Liberty followers felt compelled to act.[69]

## Chapter 8

# Prelude to War and Readiness, 1775

At this point throughout the American colonies, each colony had started to secure its own gunpowder and weapons in anticipation of the coming conflict. As if synchronized, three colonies acted to secure gunpowder and military supplies within three days of each other: Massachusetts, Virginia and South Carolina.

On April 19, 1775, the Battle of Concord and Lexington occurred when the Patriots secured most of their hoard of weapons and gunpowder against a British seizure. On April 20, the royal governor of Virginia ordered the seizure of twenty kegs of gunpowder in Williamsburg before Virginia Patriots could capture the scarce supplies. Meanwhile, the next night in South Carolina, William Henry Drayton entered the Hobcaw and Cochran's magazine at the statehouse and successfully spirited off gunpowder, guns, cutlasses, flints and military stores. On May 8, Charlestown received word of the Lexington and Concord battles, and the merchants and planters, rich and poor alike, realized that the fight was inevitable.

The alarm had sounded, and the South Carolina inlands had more concerns. Rumors spread quickly to the Carolina backcountry that the British planned to incite Indian attacks and slave rebellions across South Carolina to force obedience to the Crown.

With the conflict escalating, the Second Continental Congress convened on May 10, 1775, in Philadelphia. Most of the delegates remained reluctant toward the struggle for independence and offered an alternative compromise via the Olive Branch Petition and similar desires for a treaty and peace.

In South Carolina, the First South Carolina Provincial Congress reconvened in Charlestown on June 1, 1775. With the initial act, the First Provincial Congress encouraged militia to hold their men in readiness to support the forming government and prepare for defense of South Carolina. The second act was the approval of the Continental Congress Declaration and Resolves, also known as the Declaration of Rights and the precursor to our American Bill of Rights. On June 6, the Provincial Congress initiated payment for and establishment of three regiments of regulars to supplement the nearly dozen organized militias across South Carolina:

- 1st South Carolina Regiment of infantry, under Colonel Christopher Gadsden
- 2nd South Carolina Regiment, commanded by Colonel William Moultrie
- 3rd South Carolina Regiment of mounted rangers, led by Colonel William "Danger" Thomson, formerly the commander of the Orangeburgh District Militia. Colonel William Thomson was also the Provincial Congress representative from the St. Matthews and Orangeburgh Districts. He was an indigo planter whose estate, named Belleville, was located near Fort Motte.

Captain Henry Felder and his sons served in Colonel Thomson's militia, and they would augment Colonel Thomson's mounted rangers during several impending conflicts. Other ranking South Carolinian officers emerged with military experience from the French and Indian War (1754–63) in the northern colonies and the Anglo-Cherokee Wars throughout the Carolinas. Such officers included Francis Marion, Thomas Sumter, Henry Laurens, Andrew Pickens, Thomas Middleton and William Moultrie.

In other actions, the South Carolina Congress sent Patriots to acquire ten thousand pounds of gunpowder from the Caribbean in the summer of 1775. In parallel, a detachment of South Carolina 3rd regimental mounted rangers led by Major James Mayson captured Fort Charlotte on July 12, 1775, as South Carolina's first revolutionary encounter, although it was bloodless and achieved without a shot fired. Fort Charlotte is in present-day McCormick County and fifty feet under Strom Thurmond Lake. They seized one thousand pounds of gunpowder and eighteen cannons. Unfortunately for Major Mayson, he was arrested, and some of the supplies were seized outside of Ninety Six by Loyalists Joseph Robinson, Robert Cunningham and Patrick Cunningham. Men were choosing sides, and these three

Loyalists were angered when they were not selected for higher militia officer commissions. The Cunningham brothers were cousins to William "Bloody Bill" Cunningham, another Loyalist leader. The remaining captured and unseized ammunition and cannons provided much-needed initial supplies for both the rangers and local militias.

Fort Charlotte and similar raids allowed militias such as Henry Felder's to obtain cannons, although logistically they were difficult to transport and utilize. In connection, on November 24, 1775, the Second Provincial Congress authorized Captain Henry Felder to "grain the damaged gunpowder lying in Fort Charlotte."[70]

Shortly after Fort Charlotte, Colonel William Thomson escorted Chief Justice William Henry Drayton and Reverend William Tennent through the backcountry to recruit and persuade settlers to sign on to the great cause. An interesting story follows. One of the important regions was previously known as Saxe-Gotha Township near Fort Granby, current-day Dutch (Deutsch) Fork and the Cayce area. At this time, Saxe-Gotha was northern territory of the Orangeburgh District and was mostly a British- and Loyalist-leaning German Lutheran community. In some areas, Drayton was initially successful, and in other instances pressures were applied to remain a Loyalist community.[71] At a particular tavern near the Broad River, present-day Spring Hill, William Henry Drayton stopped and attempted to recruit a few Patriots until the probable tavern owner, Evan McLaurin, stopped the proceedings:[72]

> *16 August 1775. Report to the S.C. Council of Safety by Drayton. King's Creek, near Enoree.*
>
> *GENTLEMEN:...On Friday last I left the Congaree store and proceeded to a Dutch Church about ten miles higher up Saluda* [River]. *I here gave a discourse to the congregation consisting entirely of Germans, in which I thought it prudent to mix many texts of Scripture showing that our breaking off all trade and communication with non-subscribers* [non-Patriots] *was not any force put upon them. To my great surprise, only one of the congregation subscribed the association. I found that some of the non-subscribers on Wednesday last had been very active to prevent these people from associating, and had even perverted those of the fifteen who on that Wednesday had heard me and told me they had no doubt but they should subscribe at the church. Upon this, I declared that no miller who was a subscriber should grind wheat or corn for any person who was a non-subscriber. This gave an immediate shock and has given a general*

> *alarm among the Dutch, from which with some other operations I expect a desirable effect.*
>
> *Hence I proceeded the next day, being Saturday* [August 12, 1775], *into the Fork between Broad and Saluda river to McLaurin's, where I had a pretty large meeting of Germans also, and some who had already heard me twice without the desired effect. Here I did not procure one subscriber…*
>
> *On Sunday I intended to have been at another place of Divine worship, but when I got near, I found Summer* [a Loyalist], *to avoid being present at the discourse, had gone to another place of worship. I now reflected that as he was a leading man in this neighborhood and by his absence manifested his dislike to what I came about, and also that most of my hearers on the day before were from this part of the Fork, I thought I might save myself the mortification of preaching to a people who were obstinate and would not hear. Mr. Kershaw, being of my opinion, we made the best of our way from that stiff-necked generation to this place. Thus, I may pronounce, the Dutch are not with us.*[73]

After his less than productive recruitment meeting, Drayton recommended to the council a ban against all goods delivered to McLaurin's establishment. Possibly in attendance, a Patriot in Spring Hill owning property adjacent to the tavern did rise in support of the great cause. Although this man in his fifties was too old for the militia, records indicate that he provided food and supplies to the Patriots and their horses in several campaign paralleling skirmishes, including the Snow Campaign (1775), Muddy Springs (February 1781), Tarrar's Springs (November 1781), Friday's Ferry (May 1781) and Fort Granby (February and May 1781).[74] After the fall of Charlestown, this older Patriot's son, Jacob, fought in the militia. After Drayton's ban and McLaurin's inability to receive goods, McLaurin left the area and was involved in many Loyalist activities. The tavern was likely abandoned or passed through several owners. A Spring Hill tavern, eventually transferred to this elderly Patriot's grandson, remained in his family until around 1975. Built between 1751 and 1770, the tavern stands today as a home and is likely the oldest functioning structure in upper Lexington and Richland Counties. This Patriot's name was Johannes Stephen Eleazer, and his sons were Simeon and Jacob Eleazer. Johannes Stephen Eleazer (1720–1784) is my fifth-great-grandfather and was a Revolutionary War Patriot.[75] A nomination to the National Register of Historic Places was filed for this historical landmark.[76]

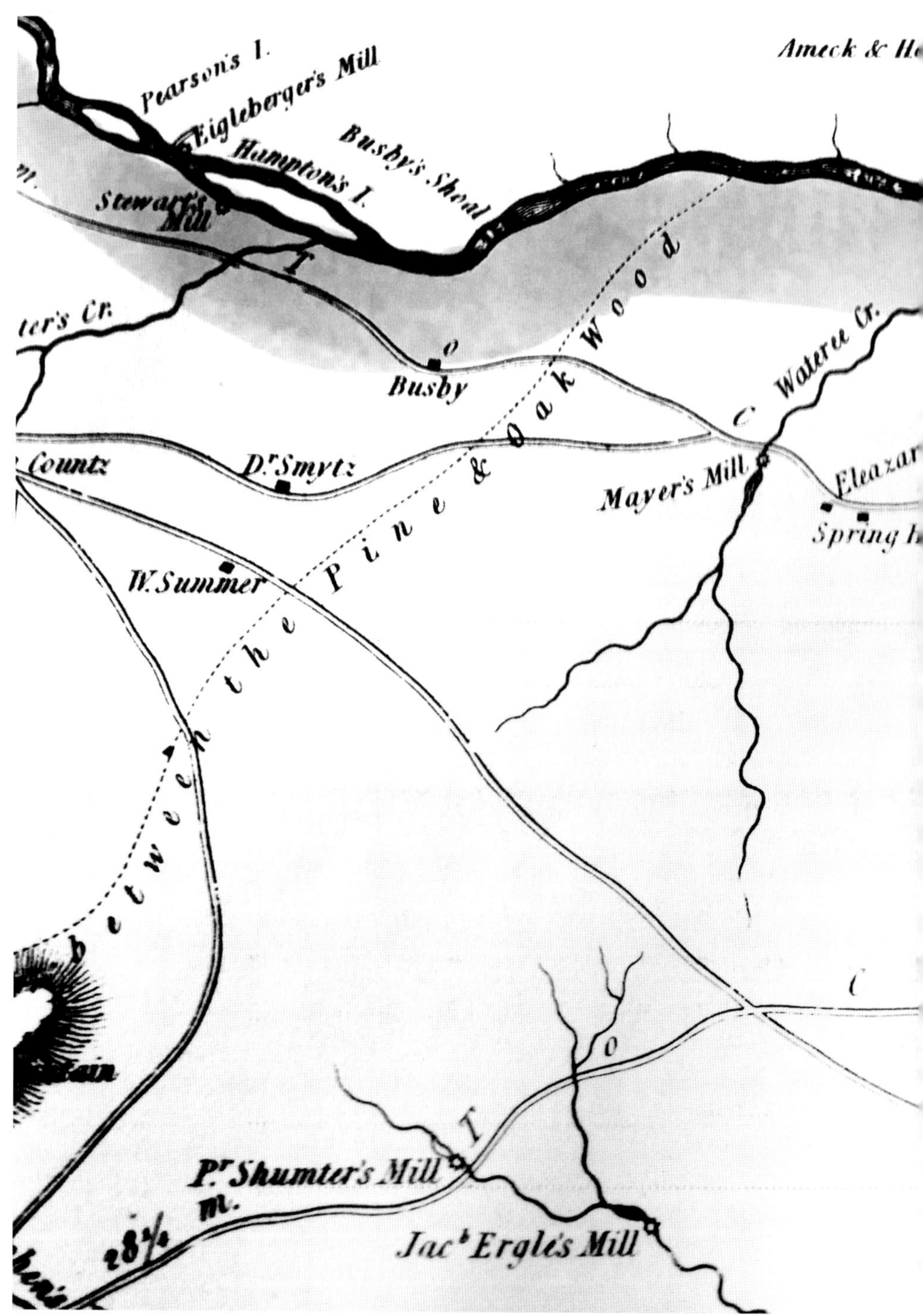
Pearson's I.
Eigleberger's Mill
Busby's Shoal
Hampton's I.
Stewart's Mill
Busby
between the Pine & Oak Wood
Wateree Cr.
Dr. Smytz
Countz
Mayer's Mill
W. Summer
Pr. Shumter's Mill
Jacb Ergle's Mill
28¾ m.

Eleazer Tavern map, from the *Robert Mills Atlas*, 1825, with inset image of historical marker for Spring Hill. *Courtesy of South Carolina Archives.*

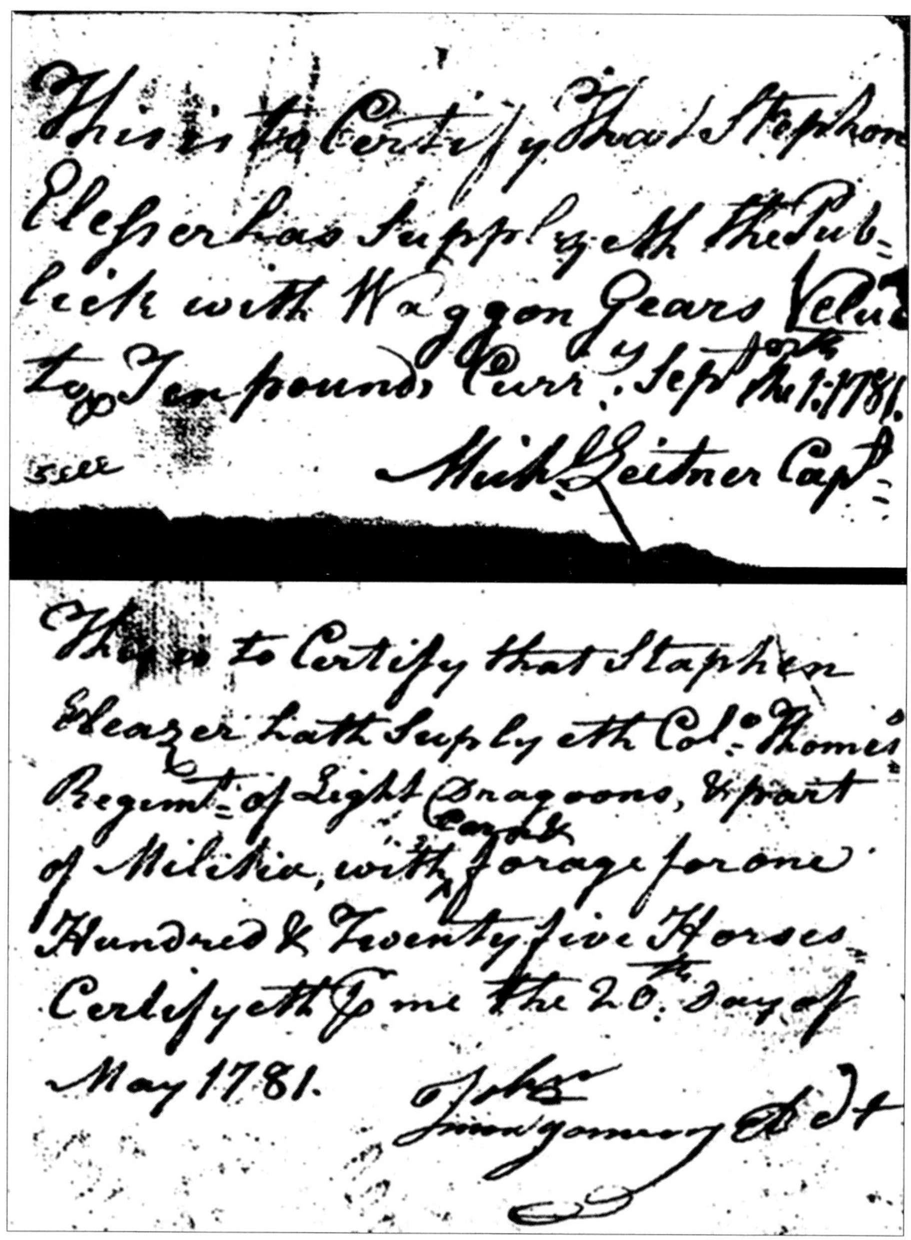

This is to Certify That Stephen Elesser has supply'd the Publick with Waggon Gears Valuety Ten pounds Curr. Sept the 1: 1781.

Mich. Leitner Capt.

This is to Certify that Staphen Eleazer hath Supplyeth Col. Thomas Regemt. of Light Dragoons, & part of Militia, with Forage for one Hundred & Twenty five Horses. Certifyeth by me the 20. day of May 1781.

John Montgomery Adt

Johann Stephen Eleazer supplied militia detachments throughout the great cause. Receipt providing 1st Spartan Regiment supplies prior to Sieges of Orangeburgh, Ninety Six and Eutaw Springs. *Courtesy of South Carolina Archives.*

Around the same time, the Provincial Congress turned its attention to the defense of Charlestown Harbor. On September 14, 1775, Colonel William Moultrie and Captains Charles Cotesworth Pinckney, Barnard Elliott and Francis Marion seized Fort Johnson at the mouth of Charlestown Harbor. They raised the first Patriot flag of South Carolina, the blue flag with silver crescent designed by Colonel Moultrie. Of note, the palmetto tree would be added to the South Carolina state flag in 1861. On October 19, 1775, detachments from the 1st and 2nd Regiments of volunteers aboard the *Defence* sailed to place obstructions in the Charlestown channel near Hogs Island and the Cooper River. The 1st and 2nd Regiments adopted the first Patriot uniforms of blue coats and waistcoats, breeches trimmed in scarlet and black felt hats emblazoned with the silver crescent moon.

Meanwhile, Christopher Gadsden designed the legendary "Don't Tread on Me" Gadsden flag as a member of the Marine Committee of the Continental Congress establishing the Continental navy. Before the first mission of the new Continental navy, Commodore Esek Hopkins received the yellow rattlesnake flag and proudly displayed the flag on the *Alfred* mainmast on December 3, 1775. One month later, on January 20, 1776, British Major General Henry Clinton took command of the British Southern Expedition Force and sailed from Boston with 1,500 men bounded for Cape Fear off the coast of North Carolina.

With events threatening, South Carolina Royal Governor William Campbell fled to the ship *Tamar* in Charlestown Harbor the following day, permanently ending the royal government's physical presence in South Carolina.[77]

Chapter 9

# Second Provincial Congress of South Carolina, 1775–1776

As British and Charlestown forces maneuvered in the harbor, the Second Provincial Congress of South Carolina convened. Its sessions spanned from November 1, 1775, to March 26, 1776. In addition to his Continental Association duties, Henry Felder was elected to the Second Provincial Congress from St. Matthews Parish, replacing Colonel William Thomson, who was commanding the 3rd South Carolina Regiment of rangers.

In short order, the Second Provincial Congress created a navy and mapped out the defenses of Charlestown Harbor. In its first acts, the body further blockaded the harbor against the *Tamar*, *Cherokee* and other British ships.[78] The new president of the Congress, William Henry Drayton, took command of men to scuttle four ship hulls in Hog Island Channel.

On November 11, the British ships *Tamar* and *Cherokee* fired on the American schooner *Defence*. Over the course of two days, more than two hundred cannonballs were fired, with no fatalities reported among the wounded. This was the first South Carolina battle in the American Revolution. Such well-observed defiance to the Crown incited patriotic recruits to pour into Charlestown as the Loyalists' anxiety in the city heightened.

As the Second Continental Congress met in Philadelphia, Christopher Gadsden heard of General Clinton's looming threat to the Carolinas and hurried back to Charlestown to defend it. As he did so, he brought with him a copy of Thomas Paine's *Common Sense*. Published on January 10, 1776, its forty-six pages were a public and persuasive case for independence and were widely circulated in the colonies. Today, this publication remains a best-selling title in print. George Washington said that this pamphlet was a powerful motivator for his army; apparently, Christopher Gadsden felt likewise, as his copy of the work was shared among the South Carolina representatives and his Liberty Boys.

Thomas Paine's pamphlet brought a continuation of John Locke's treatises for government with principles of life, liberty and pursuit of happiness that would later be integrated into many important pre–Declaration of Independence documents. Prior to the Declaration of Independence, John Locke's natural rights were included in the Declaration and Resolve of the First Continental Congress (October 14, 1774), Mecklenburg Declaration (May 20, 1775), Orangeburgh Declaration (May 20, 1776) and Virginia Commonwealth Declaration of Rights (June 12, 1776).[79] While the timing of the Mecklenburg document is disputed, the date is prominently displayed on the North Carolina state flag. As the Second Provincial Congress debated the drafting of a South Carolina constitution, Gadsden assisted in hammering out the state's governance. By this time, Christopher Gadsden and William Henry Drayton were openly advocating for independence. In opposition, Henry Laurens and the Rutledge brothers felt that the movement was indecent and treasonable.[80]

As Gadsden had earlier feared, the British were on the move. British Commander in Chief Sir William Howe ordered his second-in-command, General Sir Henry Clinton, to commence his expedition against the South. Considering a headquarters near Cape Fear, General Clinton planned to spur a Loyalist uprising in North Carolina with the subsequent conflict at the Battle of Moore's Creek Bridge. British General Donald MacDonald arrived in New Bern, arousing suspicion and alerting the Patriots. The British faced Colonel James Moore of the 1st North Carolina Regiment and militia units from New Bern and Wilmington. This battle was fought near Wilmington, in present-day Pender County, North Carolina, on February 27, 1776. The victory of North Carolina Revolutionary forces against the British and southern Loyalists probably stunned the British. The event eroded British political support in North Carolina and triggered an increase in patriotic recruitment. This would not be the last time the British underestimated the resolve of the Carolina Patriots. More than 850 Loyalists were captured, wounded or killed. Many of the prisoners were paroled, but the ringleaders were taken to Philadelphia as prisoners. After the smashing loss, General Clinton refocused his Southern Campaign on a new goal: terrify and punish the rebellious Charlestown citizens.

At the conclusion of the Second Provincial Congress, South Carolina approved its first constitution, replaced the British Union Jack with the crescent flag and established South Carolina as a separate colony from the Crown on March 26, 1776. The constitution was a temporary compromise "until an accommodation of the unhappy differences…can be obtained" and consequently was devoid of direct language regarding independence. The state constitution established the state government and appointments and featured strong words against Britain in taking up arms: "[C]olonists were therefore driven to the necessity of taking up arms, to repel force by force, and to defend themselves and their properties against lawless invasions and depredations." After the abandonment of Governor Campbell to Charlestown Harbor and noting the "utmost efforts to destroy lives, liberties and properties of a good people," the provisional constitution established "that this congress being a full and free representation of the people of this colony shall henceforth be deemed and called the General Assembly of South Carolina."[81]

As an interesting anecdote, South Carolina's first constitution of 1776 did include the oath on government appointments concluding with the phrase, "So Help Me God." History has pointed out that this traditional concluding oath phrase is not included in the U.S. Constitution (Article 2, Section 1); however, it has been used in courtrooms and presidential oaths since 1789. While perhaps not the first to provide these words in an American colony's constitution and official oath, South Carolina is one of the earliest, if not the earliest.

Chapter 10

# Gunpowder Manufacturing in the Americas

In 1775, the colonies did not have sufficient gunpowder to conduct a war.[82] There was only one American gunpowder mill, the Frankford Mill in Pennsylvania.[83] Not only that, but the Frankford Mill (and future colonial mills) turned out low-quality powder. Some gunpowder was captured at British forts or from ships on the high seas.[84] Otherwise, South Carolina attempted to make its own. Gunpowder is a mixture of sulfur, charcoal and potassium nitrate that must be combined in specific ratios. While the formula was well established, potassium nitrate (commonly called saltpeter) was not plentiful in the colonies. In colonial times, potassium nitrate was sometimes harvested from chicken manure and urine. Outside of processing manure, the Continental Congress determined two courses of action: first, seek avenues around its Continental Association boycott to import gunpowder from European suppliers, and second, to solicit each colony government to build its own mills and create self-sustaining sources of gunpowder.

Ultimately and fortunately, the American forces received French assistance for the essential gunpowder throughout the war. France secretly provided supplies in 1775; however, it did not provide military assistance until the Treaty of Alliance of 1778. From 1775 through 1777, an estimate of only fifty tons of gunpowder was manufactured in the colonies.

For South Carolina's response to the Continental Congress's call for self-sufficiency, Henry Felder's duties expanded, as he was assigned to a commission to investigate the manufacturing of gunpowder and construction of an ironwork for the cause. Once he determined feasibility, Henry Felder was asked to manufacture gunpowder.[85] From the *Congressional Journal*:

> *Tuesday, March 5, 1776. The Congrefs* [Congress] *met, And the journal of yesterday was read. Ordered, That Col. Powell, the Rev. Mr. Tennent, Mr. Corbet, Col Gervais, Mr. Felder, and Mr Kerfhaw, be a Committee to confider* [confer] *and report the beft* [beneficial] *means of erecting a powder-mill, and of promoting the making of gunpowder in this colony.*
>
> *Thursday, March 7, 1776. Ordered That Captain Hammond, Colonel Thomas, Major Williamson, Mr. Kershaw, Mr. Beard, and Mr Felder be a Committee to consider and report the most proper places for erecting of Ironworks in this colony, and what encouragement from the public, in their opinion, may be most effectual to promote the establishment of such works, and the manufacturing of iron.*
>
> *Friday, March 22, 1776.…Whereas Henry Felder, Esq.; having proposed to manufacture Sulphur* [sulfur] *and nitre into gunpowder; according to his offer it is Resolved That a proper quantity of nitre and sulphur belonging to the public be put into the hands of the said Henry Felder, Esq., to be by him made up into gunpowder and delivered into the public magazine: That Mr. Felder be allowed seven shillings and six-pence currency for each pound of gunpowder by him so made up from such materials, exclusive of the charge of carriage. And that upon his delivering a quantity of gunpowder into the hands of the Public Receiver, he be, from time to time, supplied with an equal quantity of materials, to be in like manner made up into gunpowder.*

The amount of gunpowder produced by Felder (or other South Carolina's mills) is unknown. Whatever the amount, reports compute that nearly 90 percent of all Patriot gunpowder was imported or seized and not produced domestically in the colonies. Regardless, Henry Felder and his fellow Patriots' activities were about to accelerate; the first serious combat, the Battle at Sullivan's Island, was only three months away.

Chapter 11

# First Congressional General Assembly, 1776

With the new South Carolina Constitution, the Provincial Congress evolved into the First Congressional General Assembly, with Henry Felder elected to the State House of Representatives. The First General Assembly conducted two sessions: from March 26 to April 11, 1776, and from September 17 to October 2, 1776. As a member of the House, Henry was appointed foreman to the South Carolina Grand Jury. During the early colonial days, a selected grand jury was independent and adjunct of the state government as an investigative body in the gathering of charges, indictments or law infringement. And in this instance, as charged by South Carolina Chief Justice William Henry Drayton, it served as an independent protective shield against oppressive prosecution by the British Crown, abuse in government and restraint from government authority overreach. Grand juries were not trial juries for determining guilt, as this was conducted by petit juries.

Many South Carolina officials questioned the colony's legitimacy to establish a state constitution. John Rutledge, president of the General Assembly, had doubts about the legality of a wholly separated government from Britain. Much earlier, Rutledge argued to the Continental Congress during the Continental Association for continued allegiance to the British constitution.[86] After the new state constitution was approved, the district grand juries were charged to conduct a judicial review and, in effect, acted as an advocate or endorsing agent to the South Carolina Constitution of 1776 and an indictment of the British government.

While South Carolina's first constitution focused on British abandonment, Henry Felder wrote a declaration of separation from the English king. The declaration was more forceful and written in the spirit of John Locke and Thomas Paine. Comparing favorably to the words Thomas Jefferson would write seven weeks later, Felder penned, "Whilst engaged in an arduous but glorious Struggle for the preservation of those invaluable Rights and Liberties, which, by the Laws of Reason, and of Nature, all men have a right to possess."[87] As Locke and Paine wrote earlier in persuasive and inspirational language, "We, the People" are governed by natural laws that are discoverable by human reason and reasoning. Human beings, because of their natural existence and reason, have these rights granted by God and nature—our unalienable rights and, as indicated in the Continental Congress Declaration of Rights of 1774.[88]

As Henry Felder and his committee delivered, all men have God-given rights to life, liberty and property. The distinguishing aspect is the belief that "natural rights" are not created by a government; instead, the government only exists to ensure that these rights are not infringed. As they are God-given, neither monarch nor collective rights nor mob rule may supersede these individual rights.[89]

On May 20, 1776, Henry authored, signed and delivered, along with his fellow twelve members, the Address and Declaration (also known as the Orangeburgh Declaration) as a ratifying statement supporting the new and separate government from the British government. Henry presented this declaration to the Honorable William Henry Drayton, chief justice of the Colony of South Carolina, and to South Carolina Assembly. It stated in part:

> *Whilst engaged in an arduous but glorious Struggle for the preservation of those invaluable Rights and Liberties, which, by the Laws of Reason, and of Nature, all men have a right to possess, and without the Possession of which Life itself would be a Burthen.... We declare, that as we do most heartily approve of, so we are determined with our Lives and Fortunes to support, maintain and defend it.*[90]

Early Patriots like Henry Felder represented the planters, farmers, districts and settlers of early South Carolina and were direct and committed to the great cause. Compromise was a thing of the past, and their path was clear, unlike that of their fellow Continental Congress delegates, who were far from unanimous in their thinking toward independence at that moment.

Perhaps these early South Carolina Patriots and future militiamen and citizen soldiers felt that they had little to lose—or everything to lose.

Although the first South Carolina Constitution was not a direct statement of independence, the defiance and boldness of the declaration openly placed South Carolina on a course toward separation from the Crown. One month earlier, Chief Justice William Henry Drayton proclaimed to several South Carolina grand juries with the charge, "the law of the land authorizes me to declare…that George the Third, King of Great Britain…has no authority over us, and we owe no obedience to him."[91]

Setting a trail for the other colonies, South Carolina was the second colony to ratify a separate constitution and one of only three colonies with a constitution prior to the Declaration of Independence.[92] Meanwhile, the Continental political delegates debated, and a few remained reluctant in the struggle.

By June 7, Richard Henry Lee of Virginia had proposed a motion for independence of the American colonies that, in turn, ignited a hot debate that raged for several days. A vote around June 29 indicated a severe split, with only seven colonies in favor of liberty. Edward and John Rutledge remained against, with the younger Edward stating that the time was not "ripe" for independence and that he "effectually opposed" such a resolution.[93] However, on July 2, four days after South Carolina's successful defense against the British on Sullivan's Island, an event likely unknown to the Continental Congress delegates in Philadelphia, the South Carolina delegation finally supported the resolution for independence.

And two months after Felder's committee declaration, the Declaration of Independence was nearly unanimously approved on July 4 but not signed until August 2, 1776. The lone exception came from New York delegates, who abstained.

Chapter 12

# Fort Sullivan and the Battle at the Breach, June 1776

While the debate continued in Philadelphia, Christopher Gadsden and John Rutledge returned from Philadelphia's Continental Congress with warnings of a British movement to the south. The General Assembly and Charlestown quickly strengthened their defenses and recognized Sullivan's Island as a key defense against approaching ships navigating the large sandbars and entrance into Charlestown Harbor. Earlier, Fort Johnson had been seized in September 1775, with the fort protecting the southern region of the harbor while additional ship hulls were sunk to barricade the harbor.

Colonel William Moultrie was given the task of preparing and constructing a large fort on Sullivan's Island. By May 1776, the fortifications were well underway as Charlestown learned that the British fleet was off the coast of Cape Fear. From the Continental forces, General George Washington dispatched Continental army Major General Charles Lee of Virginia with two thousand Continental regulars to aid in the defense of Charlestown. After Britain's stinging loss at Moore's Creek in North Carolina, General Henry Clinton and Admiral Peter Parker deliberated their next moves. While unsure of invading Charlestown, General Clinton was determined to make the city "an object of importance to his Majesty's Service" and, by June 1, 1776, had sailed more than forty vessels in sight of Charlestown. In addition to the ships, General Clinton's fleet now included more than three thousand British regular troops, battle frigates and a bomb vessel named the *Thunderbomb* with heavy mortars.

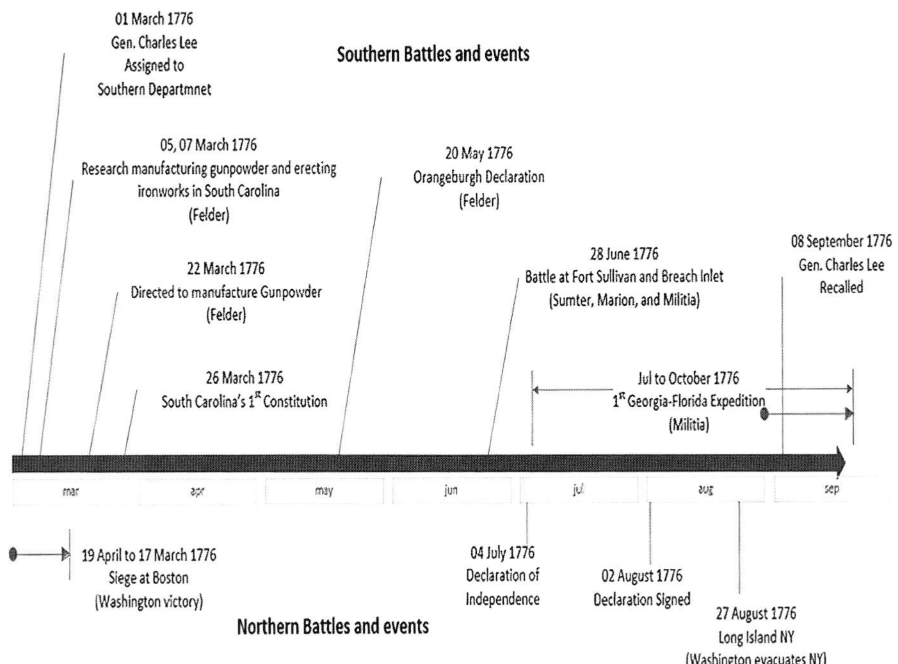


Timeline 1. March 1776–September 1776.

Large man-of-war ships *Bristol* and *Experiment* held more than fifty guns each; *Soleby*, *D'Active*, *Actaeon* and *Syren* each had twenty-eight cannons; *Friendship* had twenty-six cannons; and the *Sphynx* was equipped with twenty cannons. A massive and awe-striking armada of nearly three hundred cannons and mortars was aimed directly at Charlestown. The citizenry had likely never seen such a display, and the Patriots mobilized in defense of the largest southern port.

With his arrival, General Charles Lee took command of South Carolina's Charlestown operations, numbering around 6,000 regular troops, militiamen and town volunteers. Colonel Moultrie continued to prepare Fort Sullivan. Fort Sullivan's fortifications included twenty-foot-high double walls of palmetto logs defended initially by twenty cannons and 435 American soldiers.

While General Lee referred to the fort of sand and logs as a potential "slaughter pen," Colonel Moultrie was confident that his men could hold it. General Lee provided a few additional defenses for Colonel Moultrie, while Lee concentrated the bulk of the defenses closer to Charlestown. By the time of the battle, Fort Sullivan was alleged to be equipped with thirty-one cannons and as many as 650 defenders of regulars, militiamen and slaves. General Lee had such little faith in Fort Sullivan that he withdrew half the garrison and gunpowder prior to the British attack, thereby denying further damage to the British fleet.[94]

With the Moultrie regiment entrenched in the unfinished Fort Sullivan, Colonel William Thomson's 3rd Regiment of three hundred rangers and additional militiamen, including his Orangeburgh District Militia commanded by Militia Colonel Christopher Rowe. The militia riflemen dug in at the northern end of Sullivan's Island at the mile-long gap between Sullivan's Island and Long Island (present-day Isle of Palms). Colonel Thomson had also "acquired two light cannons" to support his rangers' position, an eighteen-pounder and a six-pound field piece. General Lee dispatched South Carolina Regiment Colonel Thomas Sumter's riflemen to assist Colonel Thomson's rangers with caps embroider with "Liberty or Death."

General Clinton initially planned a coordinated land and sea attack, with Clinton landing a large force of British regulars on Long Island that would march to flank the unfinished Fort Sullivan. Admiral Parker's intention was to shell the fort. As anticipated, on June 9, the British landed five hundred

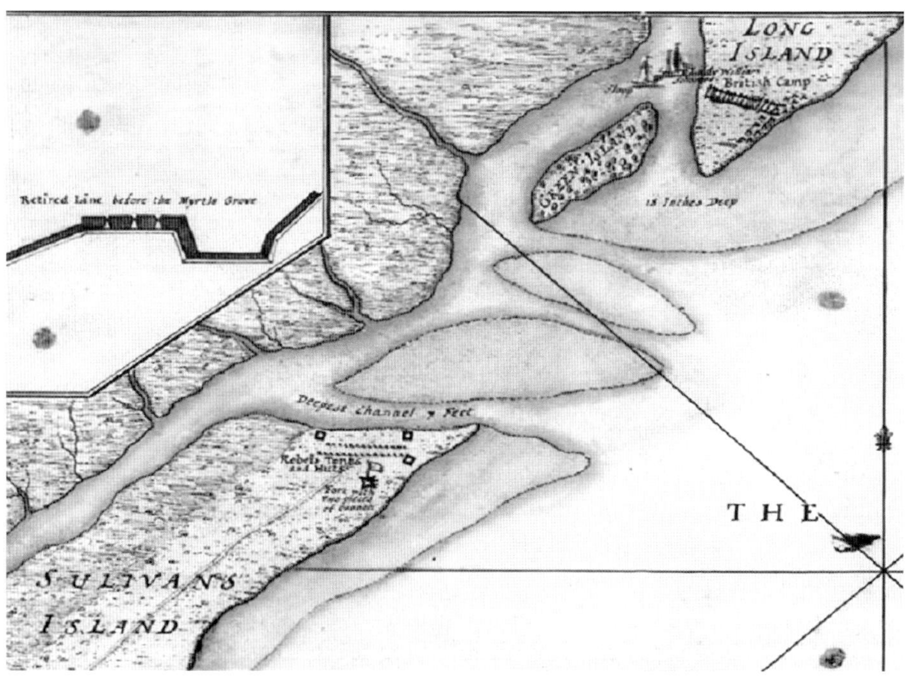


Map of engagement at the Breach Inlet, 1776. *Courtesy of South Carolina Archives.*

Thomson Park at the Breach Inlet. *Photograph by the author at Breach Inlet, Sullivan's Island, South Carolina.*

soldiers on Long Island. By June 18, Clinton had scouted his path to Sullivan's Island and soon realized that the Breach Inlet between the islands was too deep, at least five feet. He ordered every possible boat and raft to be made ready to forge the inlet.

Clinton's landing force was reinforced with Major General Charles Cornwallis's brigade, bringing his invading force to between two thousand and three thousand men. Between June 18 and June 28, the British forces conducted a few skirmishes to probe Colonel Thomson's positions. Ten days of skirmishes did not change the situation for General Clinton, as the British plotted optimal timing of the low tides and weather.

On the morning of June 28, 1776, General Clinton launched fifteen armed flatboats across the inlet. This first attempt and every additional attempt to cross the Breach Inlet were summarily blocked by rifles and cannon grapeshot at every turn. By nightfall, Clinton had called off any further attacks. A British officer later wrote that the "deliberate, murderous, and accurate fire provided no opportunity to advance."

At ten minutes before eleven o'clock the same morning, with rising tide and calm breeze, Admiral Peter Parker launched his attack of nine men-of-war, including *Thunderbomb*. Unfortunately for Parker, the *Syren*, *Sphynx* and *Actaeon* immediately grounded when attempting to flank the fort. The fort fired on the grounded ships and heavily damaged the *Experiment* and *Bristol*. Casualties mounted on the *D'Active* and *Soleby* as well. When the tide refloated the *Syren* and *Sphynx*, the ships moved out, leaving the *Actaeon* to be scuttled and burned. As Parker called off the initial attack, resourceful Patriots boarded the abandoned and burning *Actaeon* and turned the British ship's guns to fire on the *Bristol* as it retreated.

In the late evening, the British called off all operations against the beleaguered fort. All told, the British lost one ship, the *Actaeon*, and suffered significant damage to the *Bristol*. In both engagements, the British lost nearly 200 dead and 220 wounded. Royal Governor Lord William Campbell, the last acting royal governor of South Carolina, was among the wounded on the *Bristol*. Campbell never fully recovered and died two years later at the age of forty-eight.

The American fort counted twenty-five wounded and twelve dead, with only one casualty at the Breach. During the battle, the island suffered incredible carnage—trees and huts lay in ruins—but Moultrie's fort stood. After the fleet retreated off the coast, General Lee sent fruit and vegetables to Admiral Parker as the British licked their wounds off the coast. Clinton returned the favor, sending cheese and casks of port. By late July, the British fleet had left Charlestown waters.

Within days after the conflict, Charlestown residents learned of the signing of the Declaration of Independence. On August 5, 1776, the Declaration of Independence was publicly proclaimed in Charlestown on Broad Street at the Old Exchange Building. Spirits rang high. While Christopher Gadsden and William Henry Drayton continued to embrace these events to forge an independence, John Rutledge, Charles Pinckney and Henry Laurens continued to believe that their dreams were premature.

On the heels of the battle and new Continental Declaration of Independence, the General Assembly reconvened in September 1776 to draft a second state constitution. Although Gadsden and Drayton worked feverishly to create a new and more deliberate independent government, delays and the sectional divide between Charlestown and the backcountry plagued passage until March 1778.

The new language was hailed by some as too conservative and others as not bold enough; John Rutledge rejected its directness toward independence and resigned on March 5, 1778, in protest of the new constitution. The oath of office was changed to declare "South Carolina to be as free, sovereign, and independent State, and that the people thereof owe no allegiance or obedience to George the Third, King of Great Britain, and I do renounce, refuse, and abjure any allegiance or obedience to him....So help me God." The South Carolina Constitution of 1778 provided several changes in "the country of State of South Carolina." These included voting requirements, limited power of the executive government and the establishment of Christian Protestantism as the religion of South Carolina. The state constitution restated several rights that were contained in the Continental Congress Declaration and Resolves (October 1774) and future U.S. Constitutional amendments (1789).

Scholars have been critical on the voting restrictions and established religion elements. However, the new constitution met the two urgent priorities confronting the young colony: first, it provided a response to the Declaration of Independence to further ratify South Carolina as a free and independent state, and second, it established the restraints and balance of a smaller and representative government.

The representatives recognized that never again shall the free people be burdened nor ruled by a dictatorial or elitist government. For the backcountry, their representation remained marginalized. While four-fifths of the South Carolina white population was in the backcountry, their delegates were less than one-third of the assembly, with several of the backcountry representatives living in Charlestown.

## Chapter 13

# Second General Assembly, 1776–1778

The Second South Carolina General Assembly was conducted over several sessions from December 1776 to October 1778. Still perceived as too fiery, Christopher Gadsden narrowly failed to receive a majority of votes to become the new South Carolina president (later retitled as governor) and was instead elected lieutenant governor. As a compromise, Rawlins Lowndes was chosen president of South Carolina. Despite a difficult beginning as an orphan at fifteen when his father committed suicide in a debtor's prison, Rawlins Lowndes rose to prominence. He was appointed as provost marshal at twenty-one and collected fees for seizing property on debts and in turn selling the seized property at auctions. With piracy fears in 1745 and after a hurricane of 1752 that plunged Charlestown into economic crisis, Lowndes promptly became a rich man with his little venture at the wharf. As president, Lowndes was immediately controversial and remained so after his term, as he strongly opposed independence and much later as a representative opposed acceptance of the U.S. Constitution in 1788. President Lowndes presided over three important changes to the South Carolina Constitution: changing the senior executive title from president to governor, creating a Senate by popular election and dis-establishing the Church of England as the religion in South Carolina. Another important event of this assembly was ratification. On February 5, 1778, South Carolina was the second colony to ratify the Articles of Confederation, the first Continental constitution, which came into force after the last state, Maryland, ratified the document on March 1, 1781.

Henry Felder continued to serve the Orangeburgh and St. Matthews communities as their representative. On January 16, 1777, Henry was appointed enquirer and tax collector, a position he was reappointed to in 1779. He was renamed as member of the grand jury on November 5, 1777, and was appointed commissioner of elections for Orange Parish on October 28, 1778.

He was known as a persuasive legislator, and one contemporary fellow representative suggested that whenever Henry brought up a legislative bill, it would pass and become law before he sat down. Records indicate that Henry remained a member of the grand jury until 1779, while sons Henry Jr., Jacob, John, Frederick, and Samuel would also be appointed petit jurors. A petit jury listened to evidence in civil and criminal trials and subsequently rendered a verdict. A grand jury does not determine a verdict, instead only deciding if enough evidence exists that formal charges should be rendered or, as appointed by chief justice, investigate issues of state.

In March 1778, the General Assembly passed the Act of Abjuration and Allegiance requiring all residents of the state to renounce the Crown. The oath was to be administered to all males sixteen years of age or older. Refusal meant forfeiting the right to vote, hold office, serve on juries, acquire property or practice a profession. The new South Carolina president, Lowndes, delayed the date for individuals to swear an oath against the Crown. Lowndes's act brought an immediate call for his removal, as well as threats of violence against him. A supporter of the oath, Christopher Gadsden, interceded and quelled most of the opposition.

Henry Felder's grand jury filed a grievance petition in 1778 demanding "the want of a public general test by which the foes may be distinguished from the friends of the American causes" and recommending that "the adjuration oath be made general [to the general public]." Afterward, the oath was administered to royal appointment holders one by one. Those who refused were given sixty days to remove themselves from the colony. The new Congress offered to pay their passage to the Caribbean or Great Britain.

A few Loyalists, especially medical professionals, avoided the oath by obtaining a sponsor who certified that their presence was in the "true interest of Carolina." For example, Henry Laurens vouched for Dr. Alexander Garden.[95] Dr. Garden, born in Scotland, was internationally known in botanical and zoological research and for his actions during smallpox outbreaks. During the smallpox crisis, Dr. Garden inoculated thousands of residents in Charlestown during the 1760s. The gardenia flower was named in his honor by the Royal Society of England. During the war, Garden was forced to leave the colonies after he wrote several congratulatory letters to Lord Cornwallis. Others fled as local magistrates maintained a roll of the signers and the non-signers.

Many Loyalists escaped to several specific regions, including Camden, Ninety Six and Florida. Camden and Ninety Six became central locations for Loyalists and were fortified as British garrisons. As for Florida, British General Clinton used eastern Florida as a region to recruit and form the Loyalist South Carolina Royalist Regiment. The South Carolina Royalists supported the British capture of Savannah in December 1778 and fought in many South Carolina engagements until the end of the war.

The Second General Assembly reorganized the South Carolina militia and Continental troops. After the last Second Assembly meetings closed in October 1778 and before the next assembly met in August 1779, the Revolution's landscape had changed significantly. The fall of Savannah and the direct threat to Charlestown forced Henry Felder and many Patriots into another full-time role: as soldiers.

## Chapter 14

# From Legislation to Full-Time Militia

While achieving several legislative accomplishments, few prominent South Carolinians were able to balance their political and militia activities. While a war was not yet anticipated, events continued to heighten the likelihood.

As a recap, the series of events was a gradual and increasing call to arms as many South Carolinians transitioned from farmers, tradesmen and professions to Patriots and militiamen. With the Continental Association, Henry Felder was appointed to enforce the boycott in February 1775. In the same month, the Orangeburgh District Militia was formed. The Battle of Concord and Lexington occurred shortly thereafter in April, with South Carolina responding by forming three state regiments in June. Throughout the remainder of 1775, the militia augmented the South Carolina 3rd Regiment of Rangers under Colonel Thomson and engaged in military campaigns to intercept Loyalist supplies, quell discourse among the Indians or perform escorts across the state. Areas most involved were Fort Charlotte, Sullivan's Island, around Congaree, Mine Creek, Ninety Six and Cane Break. The first dramatic battle was the Battle of the Breach in June 1776. The Battle at Sullivan's Island and the Breach was a reminder that the struggle would continue.

On February 13, 1777, Felder, assisted by the local militia, was commissioned to "clear the fork of the Edisto River" to make navigable and address any Loyalists raiding supply wagons and conducting mischief. For this effort, his commission was paid "a sum of Two thousand pounds of paper money belonging to the state." There is little doubt that many small engagements took place and that British Loyalists knew of Henry Felder's activities. Henry's contributions in gunpowder, supplies and participation in the conflict were enough to draw the ire of many British Loyalists in the area.

On September 3, 1778, Loyalists looted and torched Captain Henry Felder's home in St. Matthews Parish for the first time. In the *South Carolina Gazette* issues of October 7 and October 14, 1778, Henry Felder made this announcement:

> *Whereas, the subscriber's house was plundered and burned and all his papers were either burned or destroyed: To prevent fraudulent demands that may hereafter be made on him, he gives this public notice that those persons who have any lawful demands on him either in books of account, bond, note of hand, or otherwise, or desire to make demand on or before the first of January next ensuing, and receive payment; all persons indebted to him are likewise entreated to make payment as far as may be consistent with their knowledge. (signed) Henry Felder.*

The commission's payment of £2,000 of paper money was lost in the fire.

As early as 1775 and into 1779, Captain Henry Felder and as many as four of Felder's eldest sons served in the Orangeburgh militia and likely augmented Colonel Thomson's rangers at various times: Henry Felder Jr., John Felder, Frederick Felder and Samuel Felder.[96]

Henry Felder Jr. served as officer and captain in the Orangeburgh militia at different periods from the beginning of the war until the surrender of Charlestown before joining Colonel Myddleton's mounted infantry.[97] John Felder was an officer of the Orangeburgh militia before assisting Colonel William Washington's cavalry. Frederick Felder served during several periods prior to 1780, including in March 1779 and fifty days between September and November at the Siege of Savannah and likely at the Briars Creek, Coosawhatchie and Stono Ferry skirmishes.[98] Samuel Felder served in the Orangeburgh militia in 1779 and petitioned for loss of a horse around the engagement at Briars Creek in March 1779.[99]

Chapter 15

# The Sieges

## *Savannah and Charlestown, December 1778–May 1780*

The original strategy of the British was to crush George Washington and his Patriots in the northern colonies and blockade the southern ports. With the alliance between the French and the colonies in 1778, the British now faced a two-front war. This complication forced Britain toward more emphasis on encouraging an American Loyalist–American Patriot civil war within the colonies. The British felt that the South was the region most likely to enflame, and consequently, the British interest turned to Georgia and the Carolinas. More than two hundred known battles and skirmishes followed in South Carolina.

British forces dispatched Lieutenant Colonel Archibald Campbell and his troops from New York in November 1778 to capture Savannah. Reinforced by Brigadier General Augustine Prevost, who marched north from Saint Augustine, Campbell made landfall outside of Savannah on December 23 and successfully captured the city six days later.

After the fall of Savannah, the French temporarily paused in their support, and General Washington and the British were stalemated around New York and the Hudson Valley. At this moment, British Secretary of State Lord George Germain and North America Commander-in-Chief Sir Henry Clinton devised the British "Southern Strategy" to encourage and enable the Loyalist-Patriot civil war. Since much of South Carolina was abandoned by Continental troops and because Charlestown was desired as a wealthy port, it was time to encourage southern Loyalists against American Patriots.

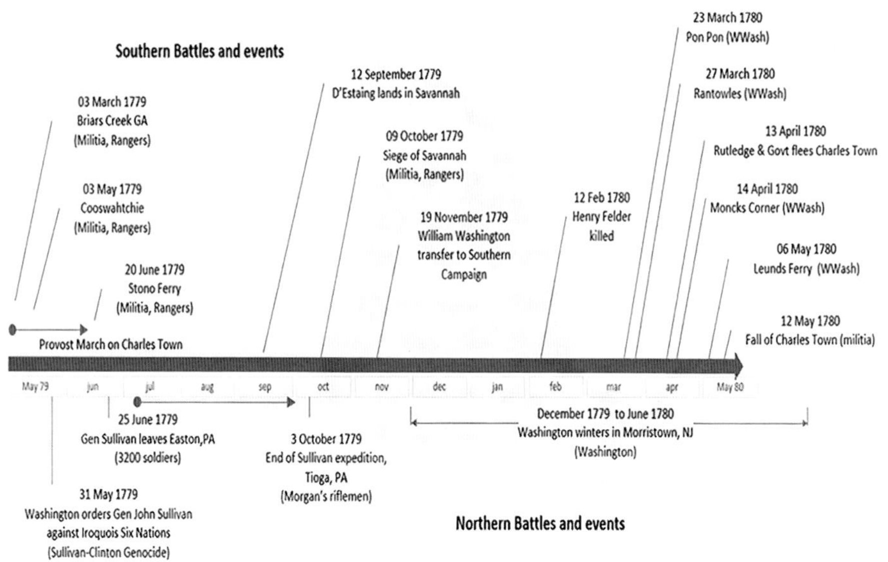


Timeline 2. March 1779–May 1780.

On December 19, 1778, Continental Patriot General Benjamin Lincoln was appointed commanding general of the Southern Department, headquartered in Charlestown. General Lincoln found field artillery rare, with only six artillery pieces in Charlestown, and none of these was operational. He started combining regulars and militia to increase strength to protect the southern ports; however, Savannah fell to British troops on December 29, 1778. John Rutledge, elected South Carolina governor in January 1779, returned to office and would remain the governor until January 1782. By April 20, 1779, Governor Rutledge and General Lincoln had planned a combined regular and militia force to retake Savannah. Marching toward Savannah, General Lincoln left Charlestown mostly unprotected except for Colonel William Moultrie and several units of militia. Within a week, Lincoln had been advised that the British were preparing a march from Savannah to Charlestown; however, Lincoln was not persuaded that Prevost's march was a serious threat.

British troops under General Augustine Prevost sidestepped General Lincoln's troops (as Lincoln was traveling much farther north, more than 150 miles above Savannah) as Prevost moved toward Charlestown. Colonel Moultrie threw his thousand militia men against Prevost, only slowing the much superior British force in a series of minor battles and skirmishes. Prevost continued to march. On May 11, Governor Rutledge requested terms with General Prevost to spare Charlestown if it declared its neutrality for the remainder of the war. This parlay was not popular. Christopher Gadsden and William Moultrie were furious with the governor's offer.[100] General Prevost reminded Rutledge that Britain had not come as legislation emissaries but in a military capacity. His business was with Colonel Moultrie and the army. Prevost was very clear that there would be no conditions. As a godsend, General Lincoln performed a hasty return march with enough men to persuade General Prevost to re-cross the Ashley and Wappoo Creek, resulting in several skirmishes and the British retreat to Beaufort. Believing that Charlestown was now safe, General Lincoln resumed his march toward Savannah.

General Lincoln's Siege of Savannah was to be a synchronized French-American attempt to retake the town between September 16 and October 18, 1779. French Admiral Count D'Estaing would attack from the sea, and General Lincoln and Colonel Francis Marion would charge by land. The strategy required the French, once landed, to charge the Savannah Spring Hill fortification (earthworks and sharp-pointed abatis) from the northeast and the Americans to charge the same fortification from the west—an open terrain march of five hundred yards.

The Americans' front-line assault was planned with the 2nd Regiment of South Carolina, led by Lieutenant Colonel John Laurens and the South Carolina militiamen. Unfortunately, D'Estaing landed early on September 12 without a land force and requested British General Prevost to surrender. Prevost refused, and while awaiting General Lincoln to get into position, the British refortified the city.

On October 9, General Lincoln attacked Savannah with disastrous results: hundreds were killed and wounded, including Sergeant William Jasper, the hero of Fort Sullivan, who had climbed the fort walls to retrieve the South Carolina battle flag. The Siege of Savannah was one of the bloodiest battles of the war, with 1,000 American troops killed, wounded or captured. While the full Orangeburgh District Militia likely did not participate, Henry Felder's son Frederick Felder, under Commander Colonel Charles Heatley, participated in the siege.[101] Once defeated, General Lincoln limped back to Charlestown, and elements of the militiamen returned to their districts, where their homelands were now threatened by the British and emboldened Loyalists. Their retreat to South Carolina was soon followed by the more than 3,500 British troops now turning their attention toward Charlestown.

Sadly, French Admiral Charles Henri Hector D'Estaing returned to France and, later in life, fell out of favor with the French government when he defended French Queen Marie Antoinette. He was guillotined on April 28, 1794. Humorously, before D'Estaing was executed, he suggested, "After my head falls off, send it to the British, they will pay a good deal for it."

Within four months, British General Henry Clinton began his third attempt to take Charlestown. On February 11, 1780, the British landed near Johns Island and within forty-five days had crossed the Ashley River and were knocking on the door of Charlestown. With General Lincoln's return to the Charlestown garrison, his command consisted of around three thousand regular American regiment troops, several South Carolina militias including Orangeburgh District Militia, armed African Americans and French and Spanish troops. Initially, the Orangeburgh militia was assigned to defend Lempriere's Point at the mouth of the Wando River. Located in current Mount Pleasant, the Lempriere battery was between the Wando River and Lempriere Creek (later renamed Shem Creek) and was the last line of communications to Charlestown to fall to the British on April 19.

As the Siege of Charlestown began in early April 1780, and with George Washington's insistence, Governor Rutledge fled the city with his council. For most of the remaining war, the seat of South Carolina government would be mobile. Christopher Gadsden and Charles Cotesworth Pinckney vowed to defend Charlestown to the end. However, after continuous mortar and cannon fire, Charlestown and more than five thousand Patriots surrendered on May 12, 1780.

While it was a stunning blow for the southern Revolutionary cause, the siege lasted long enough for some of the militia to escape, and the remaining militiamen were pardoned and allowed to return to their homes. More than 207 Charlestown citizens met British General Clinton and congratulated him on the campaign to liberate Charlestown; 1,600 citizens came forward to pledge an oath of allegiance to the Crown. Humiliating for Christopher Gadsden and William Moultrie, many prominent Charlestown government members declared themselves by oath or written pledge as "true and faithful subjects to His Majesty the King of Great Britain." These now-indecisive men included Henry Middleton, Charles Pinckney, Rawlins Lowndes, Daniel Huger and an aide to Governor John Rutledge, as well as many others.[102]

Proud Patriots refused to make the oath and were held in closed quarters as prisoners or exiled to St. Augustine, Florida. The fierce Patriot Christopher Gadsden was singled out for a windowless confinement cell at Fort Castillo de Marcos in Florida for forty-two weeks.

After the port fell, British General Clinton requested to resign and return to England, but the Crown refused his request. By June, Clinton had returned to New York. Before he sailed to New York, Clinton performed two controversial actions. First, he ordered the release of all Patriot persons from their paroles, except for the Charlestown garrison, under the condition that they declared allegiance by June 20—otherwise they would be considered enemies of the Crown. Contemporaries felt that this allowed South Carolinians with conflicted loyalties, or who were untrustworthy, to sign on as Loyalist militiamen. This eroded trust between the devoted Loyalists and the newly pledged Loyalists with questionable allegiances. Second, Clinton appointed Major Patrick Ferguson as inspector of the militia.[103] Ferguson was a controversial figure to his fellow officers. He ordered all young men to serve as Loyalist militiamen for six months. Refusal to join would mean becoming a prisoner of war. Major Ferguson and Lieutenant Colonel Nisbet Balfour would soon march through Moncks Corner, Orangeburgh and Ninety Six, rounding up new recruits and forced recruits along the way.

For the Continental Congress, the fall of Charlestown sparked desperation. Rumors spread, if not altogether true, that Congressional representatives were discussing abandoning Georgia and South Carolina to the British in exchange for their freedom and peace.[104] Several conspiracies have been floated, including one of General Philip John Schuyler working in secret with General Washington on the possible exchange. Learned historians acknowledged that a few minority circles discussed this settlement as an avenue to resolve the conflict. However, the exchange was most likely never a serious debate for either General Washington or the Continental Congress.

Between the fall of Savannah (December 1778) and the fall of Charlestown (May 1780), several Felder sons were involved with the militia: Henry Felder Jr., John Felder, Frederick Felder and Samuel Felder. Reviewing their petitions, as well as other militia petitions that referenced the Felders, their officers or detachments indicate several engagements. Frederick's petition references the campaigns between Charlestown and Savannah and the Siege of Savannah (March–November 1779). Samuel's tenure parallels Frederick's service days, and it seems possible that the brothers traveled and served together. As the Orangeburgh militia was assigned to Charlestown during the siege and surrender, one or more of these brothers might have witnessed the fall of Charlestown.

After Charlestown, the militia services splintered to support state militia or nearby district operations. In times ahead, the Felder sons fought with the Orangeburgh District Militia, Upper Craven militia or Berkeley militias under General Thomas Sumter's or General Francis Marion's brigades. Henry Jr. served under Charles Starke Myddleton's 2$^{nd}$ Regiment of dragoons, and Henry's third son, John, served for a time with Lieutenant Colonel William Washington's cavalry. According to Henry Felder Jr.'s petition, John was "commanding a volunteer company of militia in 1781 sent by Colonel [William] Washington on a special & dangerous services"[105] when he was captured with his stepmother's brother, Adam Snell. With the British encamped near McCord's Ferry on the banks of the Congaree River, John and Snell attempted to escape. Snell escaped through the woods, but John jumped into the alligator-infested river and swam across with tied hands while the British guards shot at him. Upon reaching the opposite bank, he was killed by a British guard.

## Chapter 16

# Henry Felder's Death, February 1780

In early February, Captain Henry Felder received word from his old friend and comrade Samuel Rowe that the Loyalists were going to make another attack on Felder's residence. Surrounded by Loyalists, Henry barricaded himself, his sons and an overseer named Fry in his home to rebuff the attack. In the character of an unorganized mob attack, the Loyalists attempted to overwhelm Felder's small garrison home with a larger body of men.

With his wife and servants loading their weapons, Felder's family beat back the attack by the king's men. The Loyalists finally stopped their attack and slipped away from Felder's home, but not before Felder's band had killed or wounded as many as twenty men. Whether the Loyalists' movement was an actual retreat or simply a ploy to draw Felder out of the house was unknown, but Henry sent his sons to circle around the retreating Loyalists for an ambush.

Tragically, the Loyalists turned back before reaching the planned ambush location and resumed their attack on Felder's house, setting fire to hay under Felder's shed. With the shed in proximity, Felder's house was also engulfed in flames. The ploy was obvious: set fire to the house to chase the defenders out and follow swiftly with the sword.

Escaping from the flames, the Switzer Patriot dressed in his wife's clothes fled the house, thinking that the Loyalists would not fire on a woman. He was wrong. As Henry attempted to scale a rail fence, he was cut down by the Loyalist bullets. It is said that his boots may have given his disguise away. Henry's German-Swiss perseverance would not fail him even close to death.

He continued to make his way, limping a few hundred yards before falling. A nearby freeman servant came to his assistance and carried Captain Felder to a safe place, denying his bitter enemies the pleasure of capturing or parading Felder's dead body.[106]

A few days after the skirmish, Felder died of his wounds. By some accounts, Henry died on February 12, 1780. Hans Heinrich "Henry" Felder's last fight was relayed through posterity by his surviving family members and the servant, Fry, who came to his assistance after he was shot.[107] There is disagreement on the date of Henry's death, as other accounts have him participating in the capture of Orangeburgh in May 1781.

From Alexander Salley, another alleged skirmish involving Henry Sr., a Felder ancestor in 1850, a 3rd Cavalry colonel Paul S. Felder, reminisced about a man he knew named Rice who fought alongside Captain Henry Felder. Mr. Rice told a story about Captain Henry leading a small detachment that "whipped" a Loyalist Tory company at Holman's Bridge on the South Edisto River in the Orangeburgh District. Investigation could not reveal additional information; however, the Orangeburgh District Militia, led by Colonel Jacob Rumph, was attacked on February 23, 1781, near Four Mile Creek, and the whipping may have been an encounter around the same time. Many other skirmishes between Loyalists and Patriot militias occurred in and around Orangeburgh throughout the war. The fellow Rice may have been referring to the location of the clash instead of a particular old Holman Bridge, as the bridge at the crossing was not built until 1801. At the time of the Revolution, the crossing was called Tyler's Ferry. Rice may have been referring to Captain Henry Felder Sr. or his son, Henry Felder Jr.

Alexander Salley's turn-of-the-century history of Orangeburgh mentions two latter additional notes that may be potential discrepancies: Henry Felder's reappointment by Governor Rutledge as delegate on September 27, 1781, and several accounts of Henry's direct guidance of Thomas Sumter's approach and capture of Orangeburgh in May 1781. The son Henry Felder Jr.'s petition for payment to the state legislation in 1784 stated his father's death as 1780; however, Henry Jr.'s memory could have been inaccurate. Conflicting accounts are understandable given the identical father/son given names, their same rank and position in the militia and their continuous dangerous activities throughout 1780 and 1781.

At the time of Henry's death, darkness and clouds of desperation had settled across South Carolina. In late May 1780, after the fall of Charlestown, Lieutenant Colonel Banastre Tarleton engaged a body of Virginia Patriots

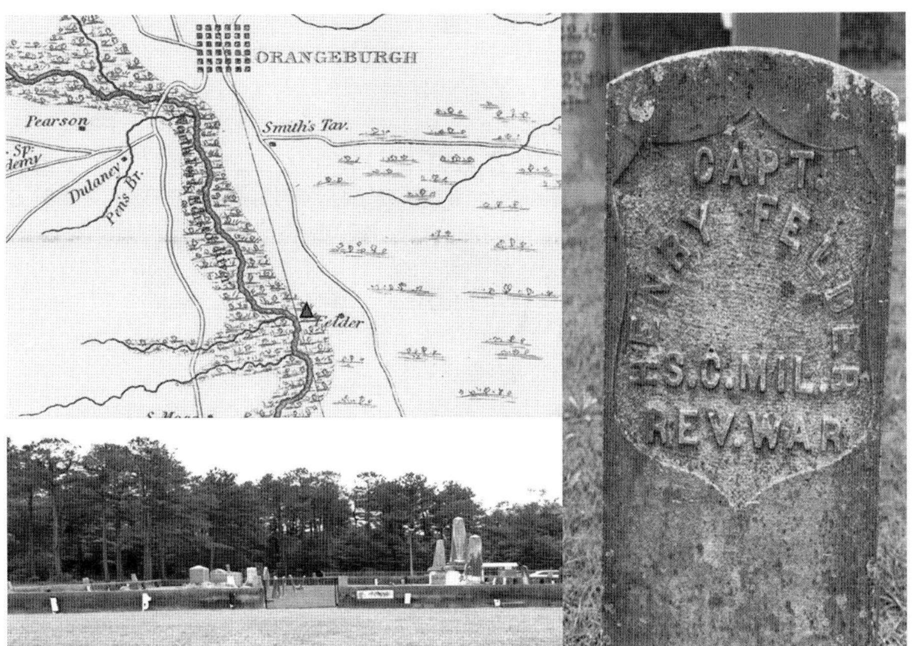


Felder Family Cemetery, south of Orangeburg, South Carolina. *Photographs by the author in Orangeburg, South Carolina*; Orangeburg map, from the *Robert Mills Atlas*, 1825. *Courtesy of South Carolina Archives.*

near Lancaster, South Carolina. Colonel Abraham Buford's Virginia unit had marched toward Charlestown to help defend the city but was too late and "about-faced" a return march north toward Virginia. When Tarleton's cavalry caught them, his army routed the Patriots and refused quarter (a request of mercy or terms of surrender); many surrendering Patriots were massacred at the Battle of Waxhaws. The British murdered 113 American militiamen that day. This spawned the battle cry "Tarleton's Quarters!" which southern Patriots used, especially at the American victory at the Battle of Kings Mountain in October, when the Patriots showed little mercy toward the Loyalists.

From May to June, British Lieutenant Colonel Nisbet Balfour and Major Patrick Ferguson led a campaign through Moncks Corner, Orangeburgh and Ninety Six, recruiting and reestablishing a Loyalist militia by intimidation. In Orangeburgh, Ferguson, with John Fisher, established twelve Orangeburgh Loyalist companies with the aid, maybe under force, of former South Carolina Patriot representatives John Salley and Samuel Rowe as commanders.

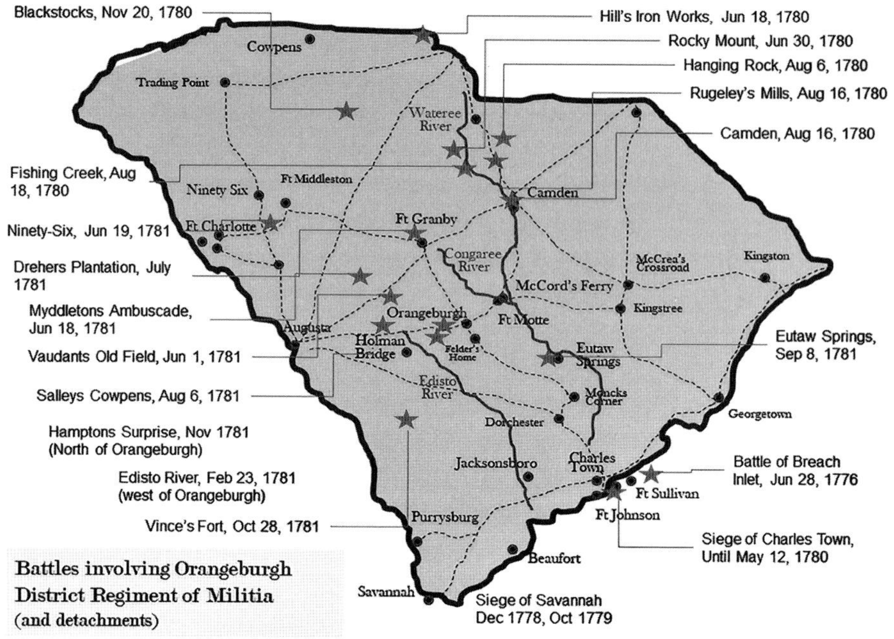


Orangeburgh militia engagements. *Map diagram generated by author from several primary sources.*

British allegiance was mostly coerced, and any resistance was most difficult given the gloomy dilemma. Therefore, Patriots like the Felders were under constant threat. It's important to add that these British allegiances were loose and that Loyalist recruits were proven to be weak. The Loyalist companies deteriorated, as British Major Ferguson drilled these recruits continuously and marched remnants to aid the British garrison in Ninety Six. Loyalist Commander Samuel Rowe may have been the same Samuel Rowe who was the son of Orangeburgh District Militia commander Christopher Rowe and who had secretly warned Henry Felder of an impending and fatal attack.

## Chapter 17

# The Orangeburgh Militia, South Carolina Militia and Continental Army

As American and British tensions increased, followed by conflict, the evolution of the colonial militias continued, with some colony militias formally augmenting the Continental forces outside their own state, while others were more fluid within the state or provided for local needs.

As related earlier, the South Carolinian interior districts formed the militia early, with the Orangeburgh District Militia established in February 1775. This was followed by the South Carolina Provincial Congress's establishment of the first South Carolina militia regiments in June. In March 1776, Continental General Charles Lee took command of the southern Continental army and supervised the fortification and defense of Charlestown prior to the battle at Fort Sullivan. The state militia defended the fort, and elements of both state and district militia fought at the Breach Inlet on Sullivan's Island. General Lee had most of his Continental force positioned near Haddrell's Point as reserves.

After the battle, the Continental Congress and state congresses reorganized the militia in an attempt to create a more stable and steady leadership over the state militias. Some officers with doubtful allegiance were dropped, while other officers were promoted. Ranking officers were selected by the South Carolina General Assembly, typically men with military experience from the Cherokee War and the French and Indian War. Local militias elected their captains and lieutenants.

At this point, the Continental army, state militia and local militias were largely tactically deployed, and often operated separately from the Continental army in the Carolinas, as seen in the Battle of Moore Creek and at Fort Sullivan, where the militias specifically fought and were led by their militia leaders without incident. In time, the Patriots would need to function as a combined force or within a synchronized order of battle. Although separately deployed with their leaders, the militia were complementary force, as demonstrated best at the Battle of Cowpens. This augmentation and strategy evolved slowly due to conflicted leadership and trust that was neither spontaneously accepted nor embraced by the militia.

More unfortunately, the Continental Congress–appointed generals and leaders were hesitant to recognize the state militia's importance in knowing the terrain, the depth of trust or mistrust to overcome, the fragility of patriotic allegiances and the best military tactics for employing the militia's unique capabilities. As William Gilmore Simms suggested:

> *Still, it may be permitted us to wish, henceforward, that the commanders of our troops may be always found among our own people. There might have been found many, at this very point, who, probably, would have been much more fortunate than* [Benjamin] *Lincoln, having a better knowledge of the temper, character, and interest of those whom they would lead, and a proper knowledge of the soil, the situation, and circumstances of the country which they undertook to defend.*[108]

Many historians offer flamboyant debates and argue the usefulness or importance of the militia during the Revolutionary War. They point to the militia's lack of training and discipline or sometimes lack of commitment as militia members; by law, the South Carolina militia could serve only for a finite number of days (usually two to five months) and were required to return to their homes and farms to tend to much-needed crops and supplies to sustain both the colonies and the armies. Few historians may point to frustrations written by well-known, heroic military officers. In *The Day It Rained Militia* (within the epilogue), author Michael Scoggins pointed out that the many battles won by the Carolina backcountry were "extraordinary," in contrast to other historians who "downplayed and even maligned" the performances or stated usefulness of the militia. These historians' opinions deserve further examination rather than oft-repeated subjective criticisms.

In the last quarter of 1776, George Washington was discouraged by the way militiamen tended to run away in the northern conflicts, and he reported to Congress, "If I were called upon to declare whether the militia had been most serviceable or hurtful upon the whole, I should subscribe to the latter."[109] To John Hancock, Washington indicated that dependence on the militia was assuredly "resting upon a broke staff." Washington quotes are often presented as proof of the militia's failures. In a letter to his nephew Lund Washington, General Washington said that he was disturbed by the militia's conduct and discipline, further noting that the troops were not "worth the bread they eat."[110] Washington's most damning statements regarding militia occurred when he unsuccessfully defended New York but brilliantly evacuated more than nine thousand troops and militia. The context of this event and the militia is more noteworthy than condemning.

Unfortunately for Washington, timing was an issue. The militia enlistment period ended in the previous month, August, and many desired to return and defend their homes; others preferred the leadership of General Charles Lee.[111] More simply as volunteers, they preferred the defense of their homes over Washington's leadership. Their actions were hardly dishonorable.

In the Southern Campaign, a few examples may seem to support Washington's observation that the militia was not entirely reliable. However, the majority of the southern militia actions dispute Washington's conclusions. Nevertheless, the southern militia's reliability had less to do with courage and more to do with weapons, tactics and most likely trust in their commanders.

Regarding the weapons, in the beginning, most of the militiamen brought their own weapons and ammunition. From the earliest engaged backcountry militiamen, their weapons were predominately the American long rifle, or Pennsylvania rifle. The long rifle has spiral grooves or rifling. For an experienced marksman, their reasonable accuracy was more than two hundred yards, and reloading could be done once or at most twice a minute. The long rifle was extremely effective in forest skirmishes or at a distance. The militia soldier carried a tomahawk or small axe, powder horn, water canteen, knife, mallet and charger to load ball and powder as well as a haversack. Unfortunately, without the fittings for a bayonet, the militia's weapon was fatally ineffective in mass confrontations and frontal assaults.

In comparison, the Brown Bess muskets used by the king's men and colonial recruits fired a buck-and-ball. The sightless musket has an accuracy of hitting a man-sized target from one hundred yards. As for advantages, it could be reloaded within twenty seconds and required less experience to reload, and the weapon allowed an affixed bayonet for close encounters.

The rifle and muskets had many variations, with mounted cavalry using the shorter rifle. Muskets were manufactured at several locations, including the Americas, France and England, each manufacturing with variations in caliber, length and weight. The following table shows the standard specifications and characteristics:

Table 1. Comparison of Long Rifle to Continental Musket (Specifications)

| | **long rifle** | **Continental Brown Bess musket** |
|---|---|---|
| **length** | 54 to 70 inches | 58 inches |
| **weight** | 7 to 10 pounds | 10½ pounds |
| **standard caliber** | .45, rifled (.40 to 60) | .75 smooth bore (.60 to .75) |
| **bullet** | .445 wrapped lead ball | .69 buck and ball |
| **gunpowder** | 70 grains of fine grounded powder | 110 grains of coarse powder |
| **other** | sighted, no bayonet | not sighted with bayonet |
| **acquisition** | Self-provided, experienced | Provisioned |

*Generated by author.*

The long rifle used an individual-made, cloth-wrapped lead ball that was kept within the holes of a small wooden slate or loading block carried by a cord around the rifleman's neck. The wooden slate carried six to eight shots. Because of necessary tightness, the wrapped ball was forced by mallet into the rifle bore after gunpowder was ramrodded through the rifle's muzzle. In contrast, the Brown Bess muskets were loaded with a mostly provisioned lead ball packaged in an oblong wrapper containing gunpowder. Since ammunition tightness was less required, this prepackaged shot was much easier to load and ramrod by less experienced troops.

Some militia troops fled frontal attacks in battle likely because their weapons were without bayonets and because they had limited ammunition. In other cases, the militia were woefully inexperienced with either rifle or musket. A commander's deployment of militia in open terrain attacks against fortified placements and protracted battles left the militias wary of Continental leadership. Once the rifleman fired, twice if lucky, they were left with only their hatchet to defend themselves against bayonets.

In the traditional order of battle, the opposing armies formed platoon lines for volley fire. Platoons of twenty or more, in two lines, would provide a volley fire at one hundred yards, and then the front line kneeled for the platoon immediately behind them to fire in sequence as the other line reloaded. This was the warfare maneuver known in England and France and seen in other European wars. While the long rifle visually resembles a Brown Bess musket, these instruments of war were as tactically different as a field cannon compared to a mortar. Prior to the Revolutionary War, field generals' understanding and their deployment of experienced riflemen in the order of battle plan was immature and based on their prior experiences and training. With the majority of recruits having muskets, the leaders held fast to use of musket lines.

The military and Congressional leaders disagreed about tactics and whether the long rifle was suitable or effective in war. In June 1775, the Continental Congress authorized a company of riflemen, the 1st Pennsylvania Line under command of Pennsylvania Colonel William Thompson. Other rifle regiments would soon follow across the colonies. John Adams said encouragingly, "These are said to be all expert riflemen and by means of excellence of their firelocks, as well as their skill in the use of them, to send sure destruction at great distances."[112]

TABLE 2. COMPARISON OF THE TACTICS OF THE LONG RIFLE AND THE CONTINENTAL MUSKET

| | **long rifle** | **Continental Brown Bess musket** |
|---|---|---|
| **reload** | three times in two minutes | two to three times a minute |
| **employment** | individually | volley of twenty men in platoon |
| **accuracy 50 yards*** | 100 percent within 3-inch target | 80 percent or more within 10-inch target |
| **accuracy 100 yards** | 100 percent within 1 foot of target | veer (drop) as much as 18 inches to 3 feet of target |
| **accuracy 200+ yards** | accuracy within man-size target | little chance to hit man-size target |
| **comparative quote** | John Adams encouraged, "These are said to be all expert riflemen and by means of excellence of their firelocks, as well as their skill in the use of them, to send sure destruction at great distances." | British soldier quote, "Firing at a man beyond a hundred and fifty yards, you might just as well fire at the moon and have same hope of hitting your target."* |
| *Notes*: From several contemporary field tests using weapons manufactured using exact specifications. Expected accuracy in actual battle would be a function of the shooter's skill and nerves, the quality of the gunpowder and the bracing of the weapon. The British soldier quote is from Colonel George Hanger, commander in Banastre Tarleton's Legion, letter to Lord Castlereagh, 1808. | | |

*Generated by author.*

In South Carolina, the 6th South Carolina, 2nd Rifle Regiment, was authorized on February 28, 1776, initially under the command of Major William Henderson and then Lieutenant Colonel Thomas Sumter until Sumter resigned in September 1778. South Carolina and North Carolina riflemen were successfully deployed at the onset during the Battle of Cowpens in January 1781. The employment of these weapons dictated their most efficient usage.

Expertise with a long rifle was a matter of practice, as southern farmers, mountain men and hunters were skillful shooters, having spent time defending their families, providing meat for the table and serving in the Indian Wars. New recruited troops would be highly inefficient with rifles, which were an expensive and rare alternative to the musket. Without question, in several specific battles, Revolutionary leaders like Daniel Morgan and Thomas Sumter used rifle forces in very opportune moments, changing the outcome of these battles.

The tactics and successful employment of riflemen depended on favorable terrain, timing and the disposition of the friendly forces to the enemy. Having riflemen on an open battlefield was foolish. The rifleman's advantage depended on distance and terrain, such as firing from around trees and structures or from hillsides. Given the ability to brace the rifle against a boulder or tree, a marksman could be dangerous at three hundred yards.

Muskets were more suitable on the battlefield in numbers within platoons, given their speed of reloading and firing. The result of many fired muskets was like a shotgun scatter, offsetting the problem of the musket's lack of accuracy.

In the Northern Campaign, several engagements explicitly deployed marksmen. At the Battle of Saratoga (October 1777), Daniel Morgan used five hundred hand-picked backwoods riflemen in tandem with a light infantry. At one point, a rifleman, at an alleged distance of three hundred yards, killed British General Simon Fraser as he attempted to rally his troops at Bemis Heights and thus shattered Fraser regiment's morale. The event turned into a major Patriot victory. Morgan's riflemen continued to provide valuable service throughout the New York campaign.

In the Southern Campaign, then Colonel Thomas Sumter's 2nd Regiment of riflemen and later General Sumter's army heavily recruited Catawba warriors and backwoodsmen as experienced riflemen. His sharpshooters were very effective in several battles and skirmishes. At the battle at the Breach Inlet (June 1776), South Carolina state and district militia poured devastating rifle fire against the British attempting to cross the inlet.[113]

In the crucial battle at Blackstock's Farm (November 1780), General Thomas Sumter placed his South Carolina Hampton's Regiment of Light Dragoons riflemen in several buildings on the Blackstock plantation. While Tarleton's initial frontal attack was successful against Georgians, a third of the British 63rd Regiment infantry and at least three of their commanding regiment officers were felled by the Hampton's and South Carolina Patriot riflemen. This was the first defeat of the nemesis Tarleton. At Cowpens (January 1781), the loss of Tarleton's officers to rifles was devastating to his ability to reorganize his troops against General Daniel Morgan's army. While other examples exist, the examples at the Breach, Blackstocks and Cowpens represent three significant southern Patriot victories utilizing riflemen and their deployment expertly.

As the war continued, some militia volunteers lacked firing weapons, and General Thomas Sumter recruited blacksmiths to fashion swords and weapons to arm his soldiers. Lord Cornwallis could not deny the success of General Sumter's Patriots and conceded that the militia were a worthy enemy: "I will not say much praise of the militia of the Southern colonies, but the list of British officers and soldiers killed or wounded by them since last June proves but too fatally, they are not wholly contemptable."[114]

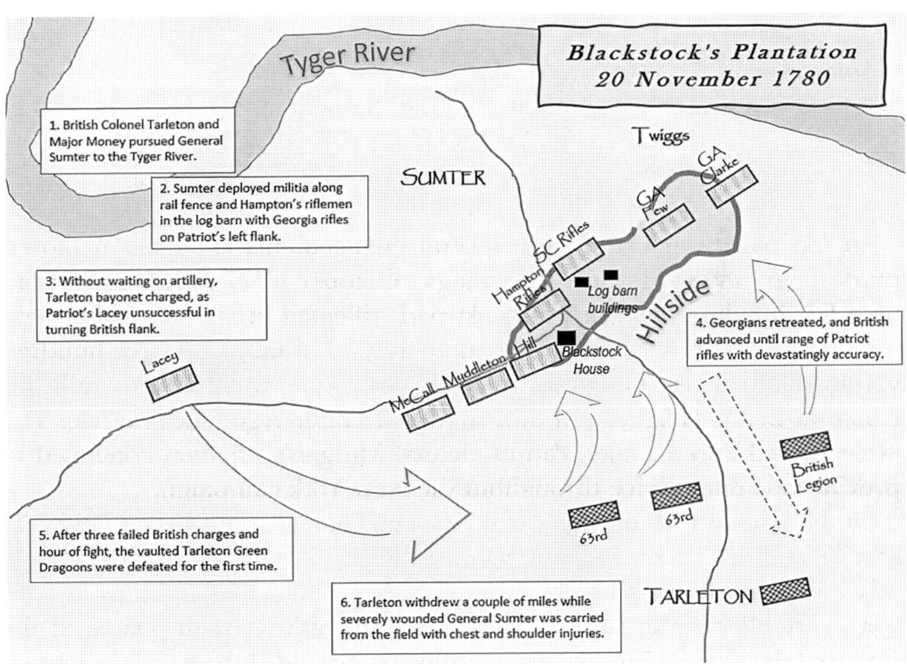


Blackstock's Plantation, November 20, 1780. *Generated by author.*

Criticisms of the militia's effectiveness seem somewhat misplaced as a generalization throughout the colonies and numerous engagements over the more than seven years of war. The condemnation of the militias seems further out of place when the context of the events is shown. Such comparison is as specious as claiming George Washington lacked leadership based on his military losses or his reluctance to leave the Hudson Valley to face the British at Yorktown. General Washington's leadership and courage in the New York campaign and at Trenton are undeniable.

The weapons and tactics were not the only source of discontent in the militia. As stated earlier, some militias traveled across the colonies, and many northern colonial militias fought in the Carolinas. Most of South Carolina militias remained within the state or at the Georgia border, as the Loyalists posed constant threats throughout the war. Prior to the fall of Savannah and Charlestown, state and district militias aided General Charles Lee's expedition travel into Georgia and Florida.

In mid-1777 and again in mid-1778, General Robert Howe's Georgia and Florida expeditions moved militias from their South Carolina homes. And after the fall of Savannah in December 1779, General Howe saw the militiamen dwindle from his Continental ranks as Loyalists threatened the soldiers' home districts.

During this time, squabbles between the Continental leaders, state government leaders and militia leaders were a source of several southern duels. Most notably, Gwinnett Buttons, a signer of the Declaration of Independence, was killed in a Georgia duel against an opposing militia leader. Another famous duel was fought between General Robert Howe and Christopher Gadsden. This friction between Continental, state leaders and field officers did not engender a lot of trust within the militia volunteers toward the Congressional officers.

In the northern colonies, field grade officers and colonels were not solely appointed based on prominence, but rather on military experience, and many were middle class. However, in South Carolina, the elite-controlled legislature promoted twelve field officers as colonels or generals. Ten appointments were legislative members, and the other two were young members of prosperous families. Young militia volunteers would not instantly rally to serve leaders they did not know, and recruitment into the regular ranks struggled and never reached the levels desired by the Continental Congress. Conversely, the militia leaders had less trouble recruiting, as the locals trusted their leadership. However, at times, both Continental and militia recruitments were a source of concern.

As time passed, the Continental line generals and staff demanded shaving, haircuts and other formalities that frustrated regular enlisted privates and junior officers. Punishments, such as lashings, and insubordination were frequent. While Continental leaders were displeased with militia appearances, the militia remained less formal, and most militia served their full enlistment period of thirty to ninety days or as much as six months, then returned home and then reenlisted.[115] Beyond the disgruntlement over shaving, haircuts, discipline and line officers, the regular Continental generals in the Southern Campaign displayed clear military cohesion issues rather than morale and leadership.

In South Carolina, the Continental leadership was dubious. General Charles Lee commanded the southern Continental troops from March to September 1776. General Lee was somewhat dismayed with William Moultrie's preparations at Fort Sullivan and deployed his troops at defenses outside Fort Sullivan and the Breach and as reserves to the actual battle.

After being recalled by George Washington, General Lee was captured in New Jersey by a future pest for South Carolina, Lieutenant Colonel Banastre Tarleton. Later in the war, General Lee disobeyed General Washington's order at the Battle of Monmouth and was court-martialed for it. Afterward and interestingly, after stating disparaging remarks about General Washington, he was wounded in a duel with Lieutenant Colonel John Laurens and released from duty on January 10, 1780.

General James Moore replaced Lee in 1776. However, he fell ill and died within a year of his appointment. Moore distinguished himself in the campaign that led to the Patriots' victory at the Battle of Moore Creek. He is remembered for lobbying for funds and clothing for his soldiers.

General Robert Howe commanded from April 1777 to September 1778. Howe distinguished himself by arguing with state government officials in Georgia and South Carolina and ordering the militias under his command. Unfortunately, Howe and subsequent commanders seemed to forget that state militias are under the complete authority of the state governor and required cooperation with the state congresses. However, instead of seeking resolution with the state officials, he sought and found favor through the Continental Congress and bypassed the South Carolina Congress. With initial agreement with Governor Rutledge, General Howe led unsuccessful expeditions into Georgia and Florida, further straining relations between Continental command and state militia command.

The discontent grew so bad that General Howe challenged retired brigadier general and state representative Christopher Gadsden to a duel.

On August 17, 1778, General Howe fired on the fifty-four-year-old Gadsden from eight paces; however, the bullet whistled by Gadsden's ear. Gadsden deliberately fired into the air and challenged Howe to fire again. General Howe wisely refused.

As an interesting coincidence, Major John Andre, a British officer and the conspiracy partner of Benedict Arnold, published a poem about the Gadsden-Howe duel, "Affair of Honor," the same month. Within two years, Howe would preside over the court-martial of Benedict Arnold and the execution of John Andre. A short time after the duel, Howe was relieved of command, but he remained with the southern command. On December 29, Howe was outflanked at the fall of Savannah, where he lost five hundred Patriots killed or captured. He was investigated for court-martial and acquitted of treason in 1781.

General Benjamin Lincoln replaced General Howe and served as commander from September 1778 until June 1780. Nearly immediately, General Lincoln claimed that the militias were undisciplined, as they refused orders from Continental army officers and, instead, followed direction from state militia regiment commanders. In time, more cooperation led to a plan devised by General Lincoln and Governor Rutledge. Subsequently, General Lincoln initiated the plan to reclaim Savannah, using an extreme northern route of more than 150 miles above Savannah and down the Savannah River, and left Charlestown nearly defenseless.

At this same time, Lincoln declared the militia no longer under the Continental army, placing most of the militias under Colonel William Moultrie, with remaining militia units marching with Lincoln's into the Georgia campaign to retake Savannah. Upon learning of the Lincoln maneuver, British General Augustine Prevost bypassed Lincoln, crossing the Savannah River and pushing directly toward Charlestown. Defense and stalling tactics led by Colonel William Moultrie and Lieutenant Colonel John Laurens and their militia slowed the advancing British until General Lincoln's return to thwart the threat.

General Lincoln renewed his plan but failed during the Siege of Savannah in October 1779, one of the bloodiest battles in the war. In one of General Lincoln's tactics, he used militia to attack across open and fortified terrain. After defeat, General Lincoln returned to South Carolina and was captured in the surrender of Charlestown in May 1780. That loss of more than five thousand troops was one of the worse Patriot disasters of the war.

As an anecdote, General Lincoln was returned to the Continental army under George Washington after a prisoner exchange. Much later, on

October 19, 1781, General Lincoln accepted the British sword of surrender, with Lieutenant Colonel John Laurens, at the Siege of Yorktown. This was a fitting gesture for South Carolina to accept and avenge the fall of Charlestown. In another moment of justice, during a prisoner exchange, South Carolinian Henry Laurens was returned from incarceration at the Tower of London in exchange for the defeated General Cornwallis.

General Horatio Gates commanded from June 1780 until October 1780. Gates was a cunning general, envious of George Washington, and allegedly plotted the day when he would be the supreme general over the Continental army. After the Continental army surrendered in Charlestown, General Gates was eager to confront the British in Camden. The Battle of Camden was a major, tragic blunder due to the aforementioned dismissing an accompanying cavalry and refusing militia support to guide his movements to Camden. After the rout, General Gates fled to North Carolina without much of his army and failed to directly message Colonels Sumter or Marion, making them vulnerable after the defeat.

After General Gates, General Nathanael Greene was the next commander of the Southern Department, leading until the end of the Revolutionary War.

Chapter 18

# Henry Felder's Legacy

## *The Militia as the Lone Resistance, May 1780–August 1780*

With the loss of Charlestown, South Carolina was largely deserted by the Continental army and the Continental Congress from May 12 until newly assigned commander General Horatio Gates crossed the North Carolina–South Carolina border on August 3, 1780. For three months, with few exceptions, backcountry men like Felder, his sons and the South Carolina militia were the lone resistance. Two weeks after Charlestown, Virginia Continentals under Abraham Buford were massacred by Lieutenant Colonel Tarleton at the Battle of Waxhaws, only strengthening the backcountry's determination.

In June, British General Clinton wrote to the British secretary, "I will venture to assert that there are few men in South Carolina that are not prisoners or in arms with us." During these three darkest months in South Carolina, the district militias largely combined with the emergent state militias of Sumter's South Carolina 1st Brigade of Militia, Marion's South Carolina 2nd Brigade of Militia and, in early January 1781, Andrew Pickens's South Carolina 3rd Brigade of Militia.

Colonel Danger Thomson's 3rd Regiment was dis-established after the Charlestown siege, and his Orangeburgh District Militia members served with General Sumter or with other district militias and detachments under one of the three brigades.

Henry Felder Jr. remained a volunteer with the Orangeburgh militia. Serving prior to the fall of Charlestown, John, Frederick and Samuel Felder may have also remained; however, direct service references at this specific time were not found.

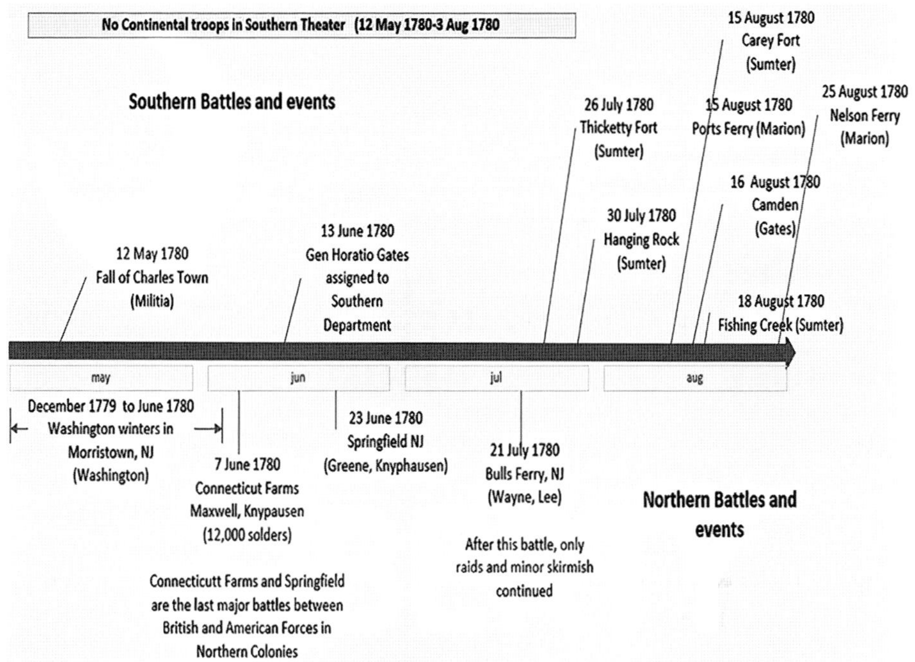


Timeline 3. May 1780–August 1780. *Generated by author.*

Long before the Charlestown surrender, Colonel Thomas Sumter had effectively retired from active service, resigning as commander of the South Carolina Regiment of the Continental Line in September 1778 due to recurring malaria illness and quarrels with General Howe. But the British knew Colonel Sumter as a continual influential leader in the resistance. Two weeks after the fall of Charlestown in May 1780, Colonel Banastre Tarleton dispatched Captain Charles Campbell to capture Sumter at his summer home in Stateburg (near present-day town of Sumter). Finding Sumter not at home, the British harassed his wife and plundered and burned his home.

This ignited a smoldering ember, as Sumter quickly aggregated the remaining militiamen in the region, including the available Orangeburgh District Militia. Sumter's army and several northern South Carolina militias were involved in several minor engagements, pestering Loyalists prior to the Continental army's and General Gates's return to South Carolina: Beckham's Old Field, Stallions Plantation, Williamson's Plantation (also known as Huck's Defeat), Cedar Springs, Thicketty Fort, Rocky Mount and Hanging Rock. While they were not major battles, Colonel Sumter was able to delay British reinforcements as well as capture vital muskets, supplies and wagons.

Just prior to the fall of Charlestown, Colonel Francis Marion had departed the city to mend the broken ankle he had received when he had left a "celebration party" by jumping out of a second-story window. Marion fortunately was spared capture after the Siege of Charlestown. Subsequently, Colonel Marion rebuilt his guerrilla army, initially numbering between twenty and seventy trusted Patriots, and then tripled his strength in a short few months.

While Colonel Sumter and Colonel Marion continued to recruit men and bedevil the British movements, General Horatio Gates was appointed commanding general of the Southern Department. General Gates arrived in Hillsborough, North Carolina, on July 25. Eagerly desiring a major successful confrontation against the British in Camden, he started his march from Hillsborough to Camden two days later.

General Gates was advised to march via a friendlier route nearer the Mecklenburg District, but he refused. He also refused the services of Colonel William Washington's and Colonel Anthony Walton White's cavalries for reconnaissance, rendering General Gates virtually blind in scavenging for supplies and avoiding Loyalists. General Gates espoused a general hesitation in making use of these knowledgeable cavalries and militias.

However, to suppress the British reinforcements while en route to Camden, General Gates directed Colonel Sumter to capture supplies and instructed Colonel Marion to destroy ferries and boats that would aid the British in retreat and hinder reinforcements.

Colonel Sumter's Brigade successfully captured thirty-six wagons of supplies and more than 100 British prisoners in engagements around Wateree River at Carey Fort and Congaree River ferries, west of Camden. Meanwhile, east of Camden, Colonel Marion and his 250 militiamen routed parties of Loyalists around Port Ferry in Williamsburg County. General Gates's army crossed the border into South Carolina on August 3, 1780, ending three months' absence of Continental forces in South Carolina.

On August 16, 1780, General Gates and his army of 1,500 Continental regulars and over 2,000 non–South Carolina militia engaged British General Lord Cornwallis army of 2,000 British and Loyalists. After a brief exchange of artillery, General Gates ordered a frontal assault of the left flank. The Patriots' left flank was composed of inexperienced Virginia militia and faced the British vanguard right flank of the seasoned 22$^{nd}$ and 23$^{rd}$ British Regiments and the 33$^{rd}$ British Infantry Regiment.

The results were disastrous. The Virginians were repelled, along with the reinforcement of the equally inexperienced North Carolina and

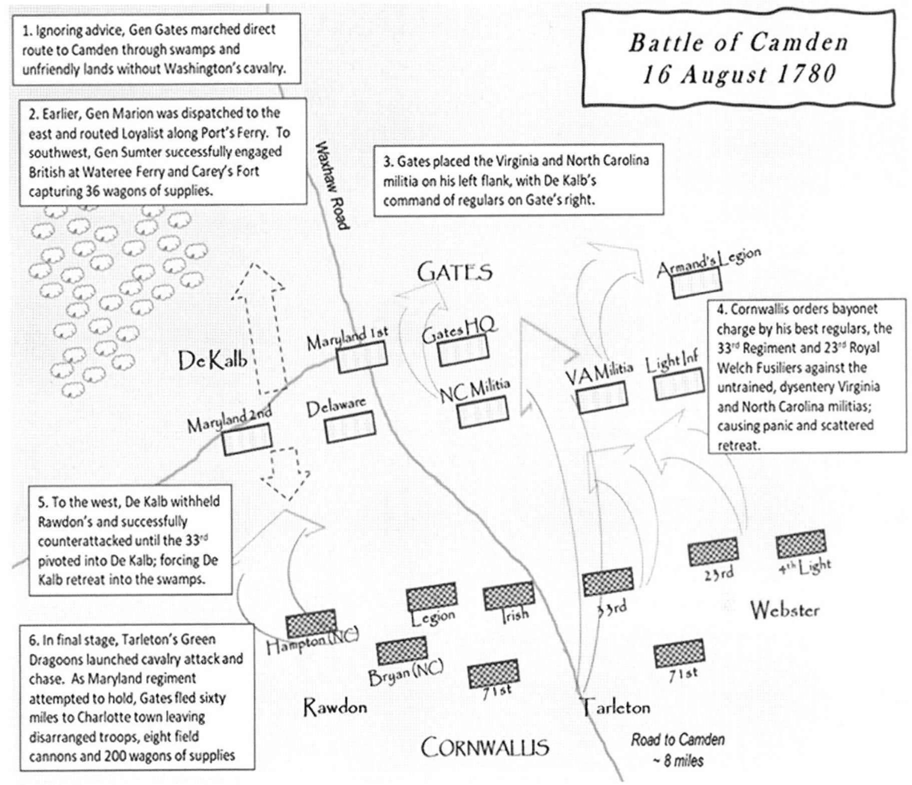


Battle of Camden, August 16, 1780. *Generated by author.*

Maryland militias. The defeat was complete. Nearly one thousand Patriots were killed, wounded or captured; eight cannons were seized; and nearly all supplies were lost. General Cornwallis lost around three hundred killed or wounded.

The Battle of Camden was a major blunder for several reasons. First, the Camden region was a haven for Loyalists, and therefore, the Patriots were unable to find adequate supplies, food, shelter or support in gathering reconnaissance on the enemy. Second, the massing and frontal assaults with inexperienced militia against large, proven British veteran regiments was disastrous. Lastly, due to poor rations of spoiled beef and cornbread, many of the soldiers were sick with diarrhea and vomiting at the time of the battle. Virginia militia General Edward Stevens complained to Gates before the battle, and Gates provided only promises. Gates's army had attempted to forage for food without success while also marching from North Carolina in the heat.[116]

After the battle, Gates retreated overnight to Hillsborough, North Carolina. As Gates complained afterward about the militia, Alexander Hamilton was quoted as saying, "But was there ever an instance of a general running away as Gates has done from his whole army? And was there ever so precipitous a flight? One hundred and eighty miles in three days and a half. It does admirable credit to the activity of a man at this time of life."[117] Within two months of the battle, General Gates was relieved of his command to rejoin Washington's staff in New York.

After General Gates's Camden defeat, Colonel Marion with the Williamsburg militia conducted a series of guerrilla attacks in the Santee and Pee Dee swamps. At Nelson's Ferry, Marion's men intercepted twenty-two British and Tories escorting prisoners from Camden and freed the Patriot prisoners. To Colonel Marion's dismay, some prisoners desired to honor their surrender terms and did not follow Marion. Colonel Marion dutifully reported his actions to General Gates, and in turn, Gates, needing some good news, reported the "successes" to the Continental Congress. Soon, colonial newspapers honored the exploits of "Francis Marien" (misspelled in the papers), and the beginning of a legend was forged.[118]

Colonel Sumter and the Orangeburgh militia were less fortunate. As American and French troops under French Lieutenant Colonel Armand fled from the defeat, Lieutenant Colonel Banastre Tarleton pursued the Patriots for twenty miles north of Camden to Rugeley's Mill. Once the Americans were thoroughly scattered, Tarleton's green dragoons continued farther northwest and caught Colonel Sumter at Fishing Creek, above Great Falls. Colonel Sumter had reorganized his militia and earlier captured horde of forty wagons of greatly needed supplies across the Wateree River, while General Gates escaped that night to Hillsborough.

Taken totally by surprise, Colonel Sumter barely escaped, leaving his saddle and boots behind. According to several sources, remnants of the Orangeburgh militia were present at both retreats. The greater story is that within a week, Colonel Sumter reorganized and recruited one thousand soldiers.[119] By September, Sumter had reestablished his army near Clem's Creek, a tributary of Sugar Creek fifteen miles outside Charlotte. And on October 6, Sumter was promoted to brigadier general of the militia.

Meanwhile, in the northern colonies in June, Washington's army was coming out of winter quarters at Morristown, New Jersey, an encampment much harsher than Valley Forge, Pennsylvania. German

General Wilhelm von Knyphausen moved six thousand troops toward Morristown to attack Washington's army; however, they were fronted by more than twelve thousand militia troops led by General William Maxwell at Connecticut Farms.

The battle further delayed General Knyphausen's objective to fight General Washington. Two weeks later, General Knyphausen attacked Nathanael Greene at Springfield, New Jersey. The strategic goal was to lure Washington's army to reinforce General Greene. General Knyphausen was unable to execute the crossing of the Rahway River, and British General Edward Mathews was foiled by New Jersey militias as he attempted to capture the high ground at Heights of Springfield. New Jersey militiamen's sniper fire from the woods provided protection against the superior numbers of British. And one month later in Bulls Ferry, New Jersey, General Anthony Wayne fought Loyalist Thomas Ward. Two of three New Jersey engagements may be labeled tactical British victories; however, strategically, they were losses and a major turning point in northern British operations. The British were frustrated that they could not directly engage Washington or maneuver without heavy Patriot militia involvement. After the battle in Springfield, General Washington praised the militia: "They flew to arms universally and acted with a spirit equal to anything I have seen in the course of the war."[120]

## Chapter 19

# The Militia Resistance Continues, August 1780–April 1781

After General Gates's defeat at Camden, once again, South Carolina's militia were the colony's only defense, with the noteworthy exception of Lieutenant Colonel Henry Lee's and Lieutenant Colonel William Washington's mounted troops, as well as the brief appearance of Daniel Morgan at Cowpens. Colonels Sumter and Marion re-constituted their militia and were chased again by Lieutenant Colonel Tarleton. As South Carolina brigades reorganized, the battle at Kings Mountain provided needed encouragement to the desperate southern defense.

After the forced recruitment throughout the Orangeburgh and Ninety Six Districts, British Major Patrick Ferguson moved north to Gilbert Town, North Carolina, and overplayed his hand. Major Ferguson's challenge to the mountain Patriots to "cease their actions against the Crown" was quickly met on October 7, 1780. The major battle at Kings Mountain was a Patriot-Loyalist contest, with Major Ferguson the only Brit participating. The mountain militia across the northern Carolinas and beyond surrounded the Loyalists and eventually overwhelmed them. During the course of the fight, Major Ferguson was shot and fell from his horse. With his horse spooked and Major Ferguson caught in the saddle, the horse dragged the dying major into the American militia lines. With the American militia seeking revenge for Tarleton's massacre of Patriots at the Waxhaws, they stripped and urinated on Ferguson's body before burying it in a shallow grave. A marker was erected over Ferguson's grave in Kings Mountain National Military Park.

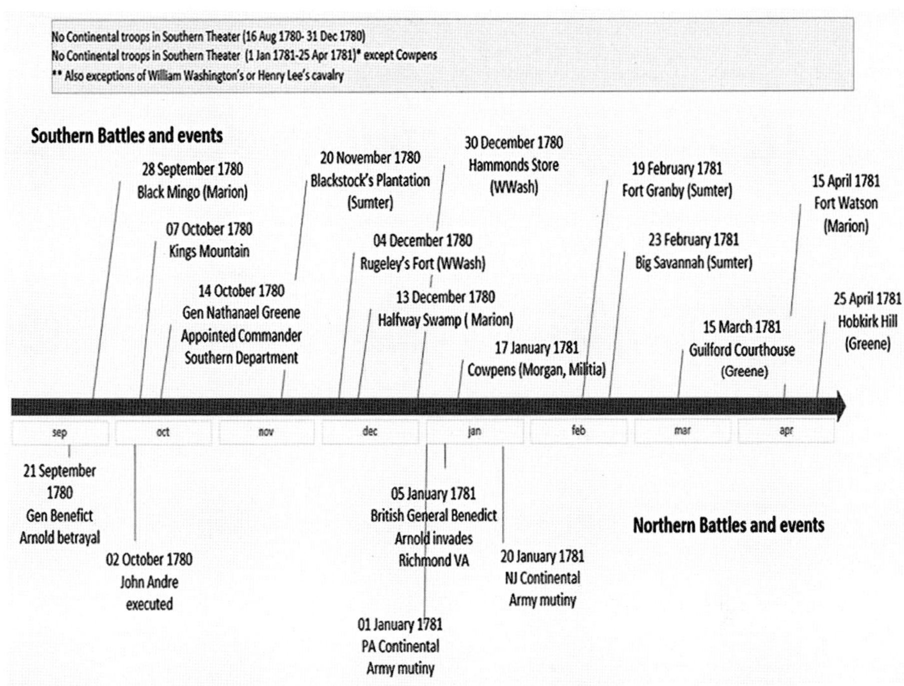


Timeline 4. September 1780–April 1781. *Generated by author.*

By December and early January, Revolutionary War petitions confirmed that nearly every Felder son was in militia service in this difficult time. Henry Jr. continued with the Orangeburgh District Militia, which likely operated with General Sumter or an independent detachment with Colonel Jacob Rumph in several ambushes around Four Mile Creek at the Fork of the Edisto River. John Felder served Colonel Washington's cavalry. Jacob and Samuel Felder are referenced operating as officers in the Upper Craven District, commanded by Colonel Jacob Baxter within Francis Marion's brigade and participating in skirmishes at Halfway Swamp, Georgetown, Wyboo Swamp, Wadboo Bridge and Parker's Ferry. Abraham Felder served as a private (and later lieutenant) under Captain William Dukes and Colonel Richard Richardson Jr. of the Berkeley District Militia. Under Marion's brigade, the Berkeley District Militia engagements included Georgetown, Wyboo Swamp, Sampit Bridge and Fort Watson. Due to his earlier service, Frederick Felder and possibly Henry's younger son Peter operated with the Orangeburgh District Militia and within Sumter's brigade. From the records, the Felder sons' term of services varied between four and five months or more and included periodic reoccurrences.

After intercepting the British at Nelson's Ferry, Colonel Marion renewed his credentials at Black Mingo (September 28) and Halfway Swamp (December 13). With Lieutenant Colonel Henry Lee's cavalry, Marion was able to take Fort Watson (April 15, 1781). At Battle of Black Mingo, Colonel Marion returned from Bladen County, North Carolina, and crossed the Pee Dee swamp with fifty militiamen. The Patriots defeated Loyalist Colonel John Coming Ball and captured British supplies and Colonel Ball's horse—a horse that Colonel Marion had taken for himself and renamed "Ball." This was a small and important skirmish halting Britain's steady seizure of the Georgetown District. With his rising success, Francis Marion was rewarded with a promotion to brigadier general on December 30, 1780.

Under the direction of General Nathanael Greene, Colonel William Washington's cavalry was back operating in South Carolina with a battle at Rugeley Fort above Camden (December 4) and Hammonds Store near Clinton (December 30) before supporting General Morgan at the Battle of Cowpens (January 17). At Rugeley Fort, Lieutenant Colonel Washington's cavalry could not dislodge the fortified barn, resorting to a "Quaker cannon" to bluff the British to surrender. The ploy of using old wagon wheels and pine log as a fake cannon was successful, as Loyalist Colonel Rugeley surrendered more than one hundred Loyalist fighters.

In the 1st Brigade, General Sumter rebuilt a formidable militia and confronted Lieutenant Colonel Tarleton at a key battle at Blackstock's Plantation (November 20). Blackstock's plantation is twenty-five miles south of present-day Spartanburg. In this battle, General Sumter earned his nickname "the Gamecock" from Tarleton, who described Sumter as fighting "like a gamecock"; Lord Cornwallis considered Sumter the "great plague." Unfortunately, General Sumter was severely injured in both shoulders as he rallied his troops. He would remain in convalesce until February, when he attempted to take Fort Granby on the Congaree River and another key victory at Big Savannah.

As South Carolina militias were conducting guerrilla raids to take advantage of the strung-out British supply lines, Lieutenant Colonel Tarleton conveyed to Lord Cornwallis his increasing frustrations chasing Marion and, later, Sumter. Tradition has Tarleton reporting on "the difficulties of the country" in catching Marion and allegedly stating, "Come my boys! Let us go back, and we will soon find the Gamecock [Thomas Sumter]. But as for this damned old fox, the Devil himself could not catch him." After not catching Marion after a seven-hour chase, he noted, "Since the fox avoids me, I will seek the Old Cock [Sumter]. He, I know, will fight, and shall pay the penalty for all the vexations I have suffered from his wily rival."[121] Legend or not, Lord Cornwallis was concerned with Sumter's operations in northern South Carolina and ordered Tarleton to switch his chase and pursue Sumter which, led to the confrontation at Blackstock's Plantation along the Tyger River.

Although fruitless in subduing the Patriot adversary's raids and with pressure on supply lines, the British felt that their Southern Campaign for winning the Revolutionary War was still in hand. Continental Generals Robert Howe, Benjamin Lincoln and Horatio Gates had failed to secure any winning strategy or dislodge Lord Cornwallis, Banastre Tarleton and the British army from their garrisons or British armies roaming, almost freely, across South Carolina.

By mid-October, Daniel Morgan had been promoted to brigadier general and joined General Gates in Hillsborough as Nathanael Greene replaced Gates as commanding general of the Southern Department. At this time, the disorganized Continental army and the South Carolina government under Governor Rutledge remained exiled in North Carolina. General Greene's initial strategy after meeting with General Morgan was to divide his troops—one thousand Continental soldiers with Greene and the remaining six hundred regulars to be moved south with General Daniel Morgan. In turn, the British split their army in pursuit, with Cornwallis in North Carolina and Tarleton continuing the chase in South Carolina. Morgan was shortly joined by Colonel Andrew Pickens's militia at the Battle of Cowpens.

As the war continued, Patriot military tactics adapted slowly to confront the better-trained British and mercenary soldiers. A notable example was performed by Daniel Morgan at Cowpens. Daniel Morgan, a cousin of Daniel Boone, learned irregular warfare from his bitter firsthand experiences during the French and Indian War.

On July 9, 1755, a young Daniel Morgan served as a wagon driver with Daniel Boone while accompanying George Washington and the British army. On this day, their envoy was surprised by the French at the Battle of Monongahela.[122] A band of three hundred French soldiers and Indians soundly defeated General Edward Braddock's British regiment of more than two thousand men and ten cannons. The British suffered more than nine hundred men killed or wounded. The tragedy scarred Morgan's mind, and the event shaped his personal hatred against the British military throughout the Revolutionary War.

At Saratoga, and knowing proper use of militia riflemen, Morgan complemented his tactics with an infantry unit. With Major Dearborn's light infantry (with bayonets) on hand to neutralize British counterattack, protecting the vulnerable riflemen without bayonets, Colonel Morgan used his regiment of sharpshooters to subdue British General John Burgoyne's offense at Saratoga. As Morgan maneuvered, a wounded General Benedict Arnold rallied the Continental armies under General Learned and General Poor. As the tide of the battle shifted in favor of the Patriots, militia general Abraham Ten Broeck and local militias swelled the Patriots' ranks to beat the British to a standstill and blocked Burgoyne's retreat, forcing their complete surrender. Of interest, the scheming General Gates removed General Arnold from command and reported very little about Arnold's heroism at the battle to General Washington. This resentment seeded General Arnold's future betrayal at West Point.

At the Battle of Cowpens, General Morgan tactically placed three lines of forces—the Carolina and Georgia militia sharpshooters were in front, Colonel Pickens's South Carolina militia were in the center and the main Continental army was in the rear. As planned, the sharpshooters and militia provided the initial long-range volley into Banastre Tarleton's charge and then fell back to the rear and reassembled. After losing a significant number of officers due to the militia rifles, Tarleton reformed for frontal advance, only to find the third line of Continental regulars charging with fixed bayonets as the reorganized militia attacked Tarleton's left flank. Tarleton's right flank was attacked by Colonel William Washington's cavalry, which earlier was masked behind the rolling hills in reserve. Lord Cornwallis commented after the war that "there could be no more formable antagonist in a charge, at the head of his cavalry, than Colonel William Washington."

In the end, the decisive victory over Tarleton's Green Dragoons was critical to turn the British's Southern Strategy. After the battle, General Morgan immediately turned his troops toward North Carolina to avoid any further confrontation. With the stunning defeat of Tarleton, Lord Cornwallis set his sights on General Greene in North Carolina, abandoning his personal involvement in South Carolina.

After Cowpens, General Greene's strategy of split armies was virtually paused, as the successful Morgan camped his troops in North Carolina. Meanwhile, Greene's American Continental army remained weak and ill-equipped to confront Cornwallis. At this moment, Greene must have understood three major truths. First, direct and large army attacks against fortified positions did not work. Second, the militia had proven that hit-and-run tactics worked well with their knowledge of the terrain's river, swamps and friendly Patriots. And third, admitted reluctantly, the South

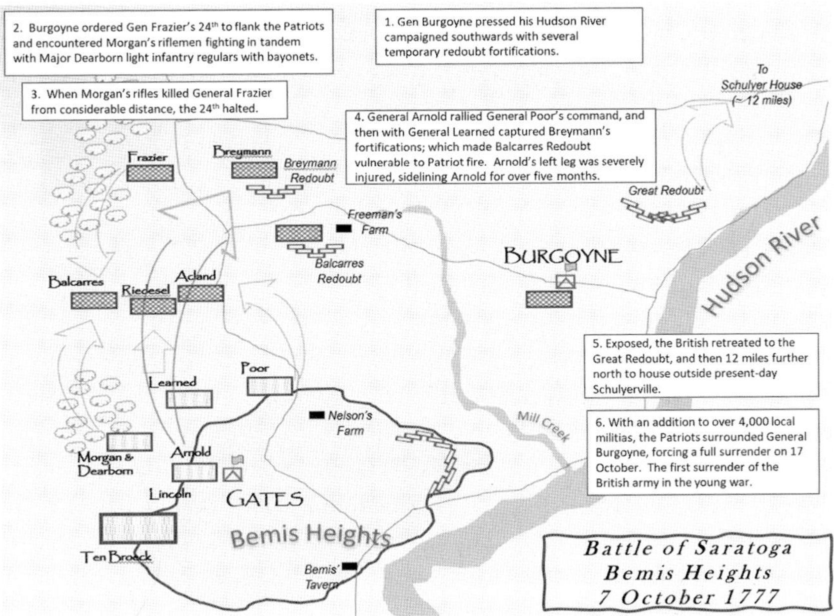


Battle of Saratoga, October 7, 1777. *Generated by author.*

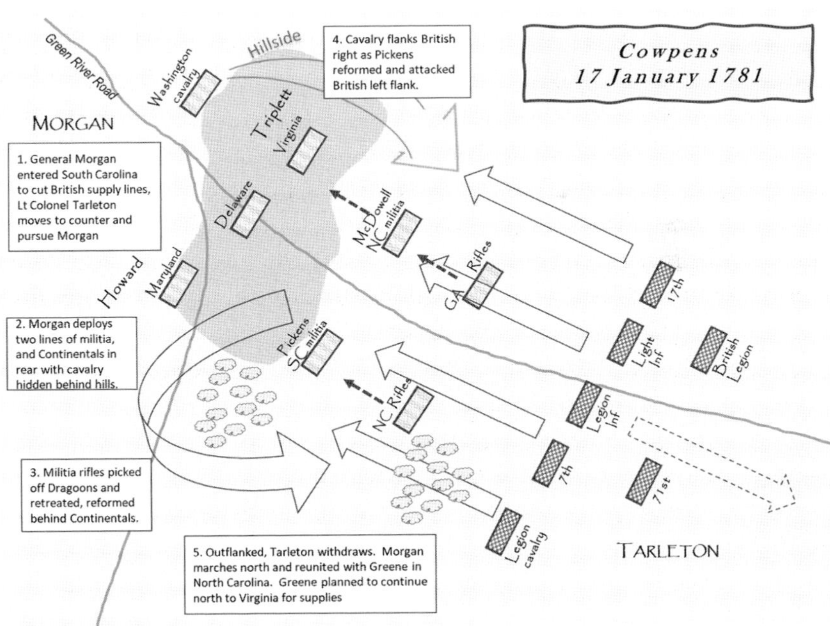


Cowpens, January 17, 1781. *Generated by author.*

Carolinian military leaders were veteran fighters with proven strengths in marshalling militias against the Loyalists and British regulars. Perhaps to assist his communications with the South Carolinians, General Greene appointed South Carolinian Isaac Huger as his second in command, and Huger commanded the Virginia Continental regiments at battles at Guilford Courthouse and Hobkirk's Hill outside Camden.

The earlier strategy of splitting the armies devolved further, replaced simply with the increased militia actions to confound the British. This continued approach follows a concept of a "people's war," written after the Revolutionary War in 1832 by famed military strategist Carl von Clausewitz. In book 6, chapter 26 of *People's War*, Clausewitz explained the importance of moral impulse, material conditions and the smart employment of the militia and other irregular armed civilians against an invading enemy, and he warned that those who ignored this did so at their own peril. This echoes the same sentiment Lord Cornwallis wrote in his chronicles when he said that the militia could not be ignored based on British casualties he suffered.

While the militia was not formally under the Continental army command, General Greene ordered all the state militia to be under the returning General Thomas Sumter's command on February 11, 1781, with specific orders to "destroy all enemies stores and perplex the British in South Carolina." Perhaps in concert to confirm what Greene had earlier ordered, Governor Rutledge reaffirmed General Sumter as full commander of the South Carolina militia on March 15.

At this point, General Sumter and General Marion stepped up raids and intercepts around every British garrison while Greene remained in North Carolina. Unlike his predecessors, General Greene attempted more communication and harmonization between his command and the militia in the Southern Campaign. Finally, the Southern Continental Command learned from experience how essential it was to use the South Carolina militias as well as geography as an advantage.

After the success at Cowpens, General Greene conferred with General Morgan and moved his Continental army of more than one thousand regulars to Guilford Courthouse in the northern part of North Carolina and joined by more than two thousand North Carolina and Virginia militiamen. Greene had dispatched Lieutenant Colonel Lee's cavalry as reconnaissance and met Colonel Tarleton's dragoons. The dragoons fell back toward Lord Cornwallis's camp, which was the prelude to the Battle at Guilford Courthouse.

With superior numbers (two to one), General Greene attempted to use the same three army lines ploy used by Morgan at Cowpens. Greene's first line was the raw North Carolina militia, flanked by artillery, cavalry and sharpshooters with orders to fire two volleys and then retreat. Farther back, the second line were the Virginia militia, flanked with Lieutenant Colonel Lee's cavalry and Virginia riflemen and, as the battle raged, Lieutenant Colonel William Washington's cavalry. At the third line was General Greene and his artillery and remaining Continental line regulars.

The tactical execution at Guilford Courthouse produced a somewhat different outcome. The British fought through each Patriot line of defense, with large casualties on both sides. General Greene's deployment suffered in three significant ways. Unlike Cowpens, the lines were too far apart to support the initial firing of weapons and falling back. Secondly, the militia were less experienced. And third, the terrain was less favorable to protect riflemen or hide the cavalry. At Cowpens, the gentle hills and trees allowed some measure of camouflage of movement, while the terrain at Guilford was less helpful. In the end, Greene was forced from the battlefield, with the British capturing the Patriots' cannons and more than one thousand weapons and ammunitions. The British suffered heavy losses, with five hundred killed or wounded, a quarter of Lord Cornwallis's army. General Greene lost more than three hundred killed or wounded and at least an equal number of unreported militias killed, wounded or missing. In the aftermath, Lord Cornwallis moved east to Hillsborough, on to Wilmington and then northward to Virginia, where destiny awaited his meeting with the French and George Washington at the Battle of Yorktown.

General Greene retreated with most of his army intact and pushed toward Camden and Hobkirk's Hill. With the southern Continental army in North Carolina, General Greene monitored Sumter and Marion's efforts in South Carolina. Marion or Sumter met Loyalists and British at Sampit Bridge (March 28), Waxhaw Church (April 9) and Fort Watson (April 15), while Greene continued to move toward Camden. At Fort Watson, General Marion and Lee's cavalry attacked the British fortified position on the Santee. Without artillery, the Americans employed a thirty-foot tower with militia ranger sharpshooters to great effect. Finally, the British garrison surrendered 120 troops and supplies.

With the British garrison preoccupied at Fort Watson, Lord Francis Rawdon engaged General Greene's army at the Battle of Hobkirk's Hill, the second battle of Camden on April 25. Earlier, General Sumter informed Greene that Rawdon would likely evacuate the fort, but Greene attacked

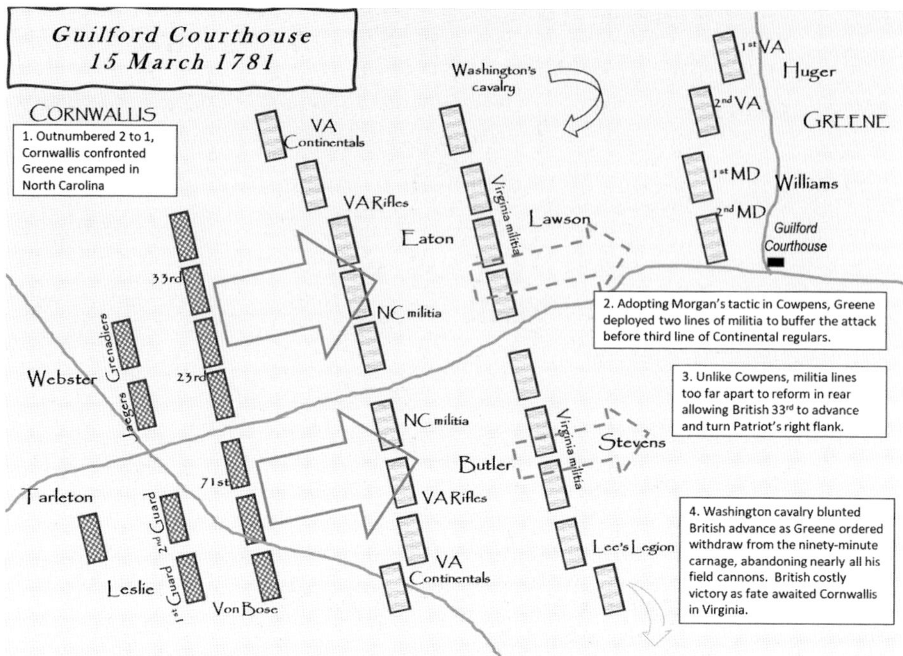


Guilford Courthouse, March 15, 1781. *Generated by author.*

nonetheless. General Greene's army consisted of 1,500 troops against Lord Rawdon's 900. The battle was an exchange of charges and artillery between the belligerents, inflicting large casualties on both armies. The Americans lost 270 killed or wounded, and the British lost 250 killed or wounded.

As Greene's subsequent attempts faltered, he prudently withdrew from the battlefield before losing more men. He considered moving back as far as North Carolina before Marion reported his success in taking Fort Watson and Sumter's timely procurement of a supply of beef for Greene's men. As anticipated, Cornwallis and Rawdon had already decided to leave Camden, and two weeks after the battle, Lord Rawdon evacuated Camden for Moncks Corner.

In the Northern Campaign, General George Washington's army suffered the betrayal of Benedict Arnold (September 21), the trial and execution of co-conspirator Major John Andre (October 2) and mutinies of the New Jersey and Pennsylvania Continental forces. The New Jersey Pompton mutiny was settled when Washington's army intercepted three hundred soldiers heading to the Continental Congress to air their grievances against General Washington. The execution of several ringleaders fully quelled the

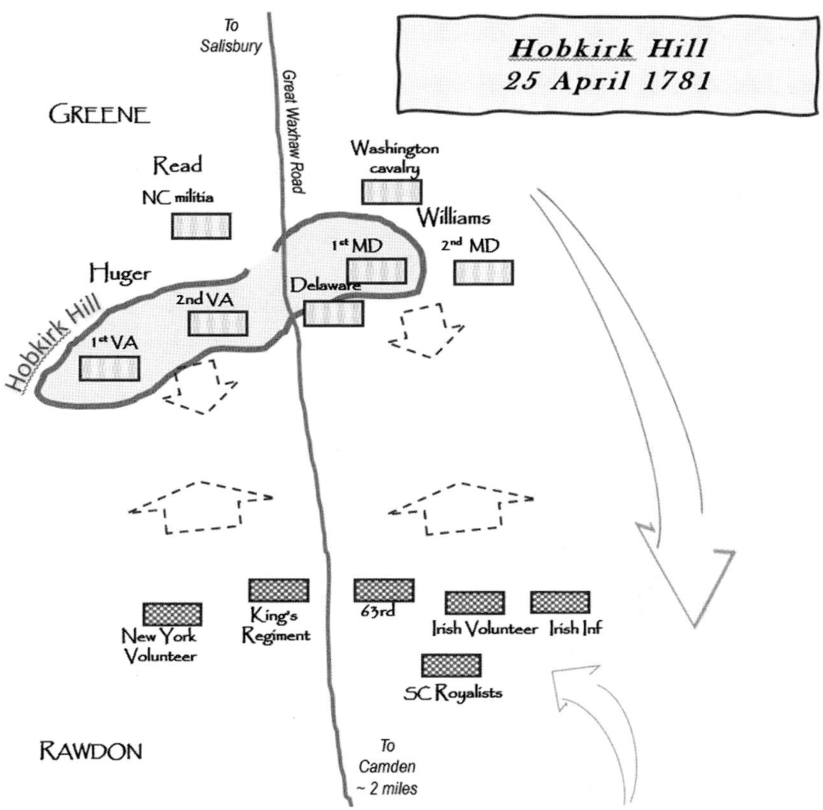


Hobkirk's Hill, April 25, 1781. *Generated by author.*

disagreement. The Pennsylvania Line Continental mutiny occurred due to the deplorable state of supplies with unresolved grievances. While the Pennsylvania soldiers claimed that they would never defect to the British, they would not return to the ranks without remedy. Through negotiations with the Commonwealth of Pennsylvania government, the soldiers returned by the end of January. At the time of the American victory at Cowpens, the new British general Benedict Arnold launched an invasion against the Patriots at Richmond and across central Virginia.

## Chapter 20

# Militia and Continental Army

## *Delicate Balance, April 1781–July 1781*

While General Nathanael Greene retreated from Hobkirk's Hill near Camden, his army did not venture far. Lieutenant Colonel William Washington's cavalry, with Captain Robert Kirkwood, 2nd Infantry Delaware Continental line, previously scouted the Camden region. Lieutenant Colonel Washington found Loyalist Major John Coffin's mounted New York Infantry guarding the battlefield. Coffin and his Loyalists were a known and hated enemy and had earlier torched a Waxhaws settlement above Camden, killing a few of the citizens. Prior to Hobkirk's Hill, General Sumter had set up a chase but was unable to capture Coffin. When Washington spotted Coffin, the cavalry commander devised an ambush to lure Coffin into a fight. The ambush killed half of Coffin's mounted infantry, but once again the illusive Coffin escaped capture.

As the British evacuated Camden two weeks later on May 10, General Greene set as his next battle objective the British garrison at Ninety Six. He requested General Sumter to operate south of Ninety Six and engage any supplies and reinforcements that may move north to support the British position. At this time, General Sumter established several new state regiments to increase his reconnaissance and response in mid-South Carolina, including the 2nd Regiment of State Dragoons under Colonel Charles Starke Myddleton. To protect Sumter's eastern flank, General Greene ordered Marion to move closer to Camden and support any needed operations executed by Sumter.

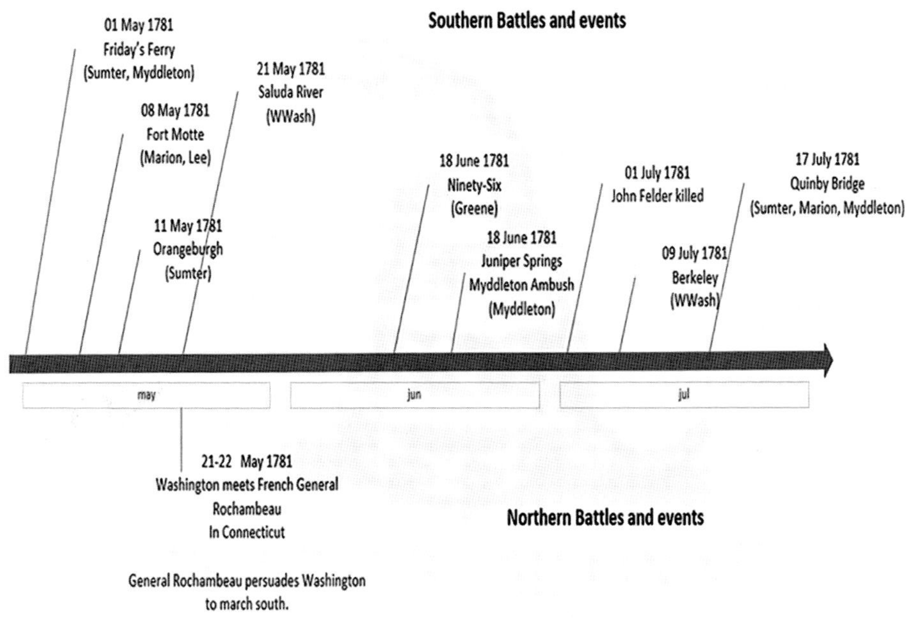


Timeline 5. May 1781–July 1781. *Generated by author.*

The Felder sons remained with their earlier detachments within state militias until their terms of service were met. For example, Frederick Felder served 194 days in 1781 and another 68 days in mid-1782, and similarly, Samuel served 150 days as lieutenant in 1780 and 1781. Henry Jr. joined the newly established Colonel Myddleton's dragoons until January 1782. John Felder was killed near McCord's Ferry around July 1781. As he swam the river and tried to escape, it was reported that he was shot in the back.

During these critical months in 1781, General Greene maintained communications with General Sumter and General Marion whenever possible. During this time, there was a delicate balance and at times disputes between these commanders. From Greene, the Continental general continuously requested forage, supplies and cavalry horses from Sumter. From Sumter, the militia general provided Greene constant yet unheeded advice on opportunities and intelligence while unsuccessfully petitioning Greene for a cannon. General Marion largely ignored Greene's request for horses and supplies, as well as Greene's suggested movements by Marion to support Greene's operations around Ninety Six. Marion's own objective was to protect and retake his own regions west of the Congaree and around Georgetown. The fourth hero in the area, Lieutenant Colonel Henry Lee,

Congaree River, near the location of McCord's Ferry. *Photographs by the author near Fort Motte, South Carolina.*

operated with Marion in most engagements and maintained his own back-channel information to his commanding general, Greene. While their letters were mostly cordial, they were each evasive at times regarding availability of cannons, ability to provide foraged supplies, difficulty in recruitment or commitment to requested movements and the ability to produce good cavalry horses taken from the Loyalist or British soldiers.

Without the cannons at Fort Granby on the Congaree River near present-day Columbia, Sumter was unable to secure this desired prize and consequently dispatched his new mounted regiments to squeeze the supply lines. On May 1, Colonel Wade Hampton with the 1st and 2nd Regiments of state dragoons dislodged a Loyalist and British regiment at Friday's Ferry, a supply route to Fort Granby. As a member of the 2nd Regiment, Henry Felder Jr. likely participated in this engagement.

After Fort Granby, General Sumter moved south, approaching Orangeburgh on May 10, 1781. According to tradition, Sumter was guided by Henry Felder (or his son Henry Felder Jr.) and Henry's cannons. On May 11, 1781, Loyalist Colonel John Fisher with seventy Loyalist militia and twenty-eight British regular troops barricaded themselves in a large brick structure that also served as the Orangeburgh jail to defend against Sumter's assault. According to Thomas Young, a private under Colonel Thomas Brandon of the 2nd Spartan Regiment, the artillery blasted a few breaches into the jail walls and opened the fortifications for the predictable American charge. Realizing the precarious situation, Loyalist Colonel Fisher surrendered quickly. Unlike the earlier failed siege at Fort Granby, General Sumter was aided by a cannon—one he had requested throughout 1780 and 1781 without any aid from Greene.

Whether the cannon was Felder's or miraculously appeared from General Greene is an interesting debate, but it is known that General Sumter did not receive a field piece from General Greene, if at all, until sometime after May 6.[123] Earlier at Colonel Lee's request, Greene dispatched Captain Finley and a cannon, but they got hopelessly lost in the Congaree basin and returned to Greene. At other times, General Greene had lost his cannons at the Battles of Guilford Courthouse and Hobkirk's Hill, so he had no cannons to share with either Sumter or Lee. In early May before the Orangeburgh battle, Sumter and Greene exchanged several letters discussing ammunition, supplies and a possible field piece that Greene indicated he could not deliver but perhaps Sumter could retrieve.

Tradition held that Henry Felder had as many as three to four cannons, most likely taken from Fort Charlotte at the beginning of the war or captured during the war. Movement and ammunition for these six-pounder cannons would have been difficult for Henry Felder and the South Carolina militias during the earliest turmoil, and Loyalist patrols would certainly have captured any cannons when the Orangeburg region was mostly held by the British Loyalists after Charlestown fell. Earlier in the war, at the Battle of the Breach, Orangeburgh District and 3rd Regiment of Rangers commander Colonel William Thomson used an eighteen-pounder and six-pounder cannons with riflemen to subdue the enemy. And during more rapid land maneuvers and engagements, three-pounder galloper cannons or smaller swivel guns were used. Even Lieutenant Colonel Tarleton often engaged before his artillery was in place.

Neither General Sumter nor General Marion maneuvered with agility while carrying cannons or field pieces, if any, nor did they await General Greene's dispatch of reserved artillery regiments. Marion captured Fort Watson without artillery, since Greene's artillery unit got lost in the Congaree swamps.[124] At the Siege of Orangeburgh, one or more cannons were present.[125] At Fort Motte, Marion and Lee were without artillery at the beginning of the siege. However, a reference lists Captain Finley's Virginia Artillery as a late arrival with one six-pounder. At least one memoir written after the conflict disputes that these were Captain Finley's cannons. Nevertheless, the cannon deployed at Fort Motte was critical, as was the cannon used down the road in Orangeburg in the same week.

Regardless of their participation, two of Henry Felder's cannons are proudly displayed in the Orangeburg town square. Tradition provides that Henry Felder's cannons were marked with his interlocking initials or name.[126]

Fortunate with a cannon at Orangeburgh, General Sumter and the Patriots were able to secure a well-stocked garrison in one of the least bloody battles of the war, with no known casualties. After dispatching the supplies and sending the prisoners to General Greene, Sumter's plan was to move toward Fort Motte and McCord's Ferry.

As Sumter was in Orangeburgh, the team of General Marion and Lieutenant Colonel Lee had earlier turned toward Fort Motte, an important garrison and supply route. In early 1781, the British relocated their headquarter garrison from Colonel William Thomson's Belleville plantation to Mount Joseph and proceeded to fortify the home with deep, encircling trenches; it was fittingly referred to as "Fort Motte." Mount Joseph, Rebecca Motte's plantation home, was situated in the Orangeburgh District, near the junction of the Wateree and Congaree Rivers, overlooking McCord's Ferry. McCord's Ferry was a strategic location providing north and south routes through South Carolina's large river and swamp basin. This location is along the Highway 601 Bridge over the Congaree and adjacent swamp. Many ambushes occurred near McCord's Ferry. In one instance, Loyalist Captain John Crawford attacked Captain Moses Liddell's supply wagons to divert supplies intended for General Andrew Pickens on December 7, 1781. The Loyalists killed several Patriots and took prisoners, whom Crawford turned over to the Cherokee tribes. The Cherokees promptly tortured and killed several of the prisoners, including General Pickens's brother John.

On May 8, Marion and Lee surrounded these fortifications. The Siege of Fort Motte followed. Marion and Lee rejected the notion of a frontal attack, deciding instead to burn the house. On May 12, Marion and Lee acquired two cannons, enabling them to initiate their plan.[127] Using the cannons, Marion's forces were able to subdue the British efforts to douse the flames. Subsequently, the British surrendered their troops of 140 men, and the Americans secured a vital supply convoy at this strategic crossroad. While difficult to confirm, the opportune acquisition of cannons was important. As earlier referenced, the cannons at Fort Motte were likely the Continental artillery commanded by Captain Finley, although the letter exchanges between Greene, Marion, Lee and Sumter and historical references are ambiguous if not inconsistent. The importance was a matter of timing, as Fort Motte surrendered just before the British were able to reinforce. After the surrender, Rebecca Motte hosted a dinner with both Patriot and British officers, including General Marion and Lieutenant Colonel Lee. Tragically, during the dinner party, some of Lee's men hanged a few Tory Loyalists in the nearby field.[128] With two victories in Orangeburgh and Fort Motte, the delicate balance remained, although it soon further fractured. Immediately after the fall of Fort Motte, Lieutenant Colonel Lee with *his* cannons marched to Fort Granby and forced its surrender on May 15. Unbelievably, Lee allowed the Loyalists to march out with 340 officers, their two pieces of artillery, supplies and ammunitions. The supplies were mostly stolen materials previously taken from the local Patriot communities. And the same local Patriots watched as their possessions and much-needed supplies were marched away with the British with Colonel Lee's blessing.

The quick and sequential engagements at Fort Watson, Orangeburgh, Fort Motte and Fort Granby were significant but not without controversy.

Fort Motte marker. *Photographs by the author near Fort Motte, South Carolina.*

Allowing the British to escape with their supplies angered militia Patriots around Fort Granby, as the Patriots dependent on capturing these vital and stolen goods from the British. General Sumter sympathized with the nearby South Carolina Patriots, and in his mind, it was a needless concession by the Virginian Lieutenant Colonel Lee. As a result, Sumter offered his resignation, although Greene refused it.[129]

Earlier during the siege at Fort Motte, Francis Marion had offered his resignation to Greene as well, and he had also been refused. Marion's resignation was largely due to his frustration with General Greene that led to morale issues within Marion's militia, plus Greene's continuous bickering requests for Marion to supply the Continental army with captured cavalry horses.[130] Marion was also displeased with Lieutenant Colonel Lee's backchannel communications about captured horses with Greene, as well as ambiguities in Greene's orders. Marion was also having trouble keeping his militia together, often grumbling about deserting troops when their conscript was complete. After complaining to Greene on several occasions, the conflicted General Greene placated the dishearten Marion by writing that the militia did not thirst for liberty enough: "I am sorry the militias are deserting you because there is not greater support [from Greene]....If they were influenced by proper principles, and were impressed with a love of liberty, and a dread of slavery, they would not shrink at difficulties."[131] As both a Quaker and a Continental general, Greene's character is clear in this dismissive exchange.

Marion was not happy with General Sumter either. Marion wrongly accused Sumter of transgressions made by Captain William Clay Snipes. Apparently, Captain Snipes had been using Sumter's name to recruit militia, as Snipes disregarded and ignored requests from Marion's officers.[132] Marion also accused Sumter of excessive plundering (historians cite this plundering as Sumter's Law). Inappropriately, this claim is an overstatement and embellishment of what was occurring in some form or the other within every militia's poorly equipped, paid and supplied armies, including Marion's militia as well as within British and Loyalists ranks. Open for debate or criticism, a thorough reading of General Sumter's letters to both Greene and Marion often provided warning and concerns of Tories and others stripping the land.[133]

The triangle of miscommunications between Greene, Sumter and Marion would continue to plague these leaders; however, Greene's true feelings and lack of expectations from Sumter and Marion armies were shared with General Washington.[134] In the following weeks, on May 22, General Greene reentered South Carolina and laid siege to Ninety Six. While planning the siege and as previously requested, General Greene desired Sumter and Pickens to intercept all British provisioning, and Marion was ordered to proceed toward Ninety Six. Greene recognized the militia's successful harassment of the British garrisons, stringing out the British supply line and diverting resources; however, Greene and the militia leaders continued their awkward letter campaign.

The strained pattern of letters continued and involved desired movements, tactics, supplies, weapons and most often cavalry horses. Greene openly asked Sumter about the dependence on the militia fighting with regular troops. To this Sumter was mindful of the previous tragedy of Continental generals misusing militia in open frontal assaults when he said, "They would not behave well as they have never been accustomed to oppose the enemy openly," and he continued to support the preference of state troops and mounted and equipped troops as light dragoons.[135] Second, Greene depended on the militia for supplies for the larger Continental army. Sumter's April and May letters demonstrated the act and willingness to provide scarce corn, supplies and horses, when possible, to General Greene, with a continuous request from Sumter to Greene asking to spare him gunpowder.[136] While Greene did receive cattle and corn on infrequent occasion from Sumter, Greene seldom reciprocated with weapons or gunpowder. On the subject of fine horses, Sumter assured Greene that he would request Pickens and Marion to aid in supplying horses but informed Greene that a request to Marion might be futile. As shown later in the war, Greene was desperate to increase his mounted infantry even at the expense of depleting the state militia of their cavalry. Beyond the requested supplies and bickering, more importantly, Sumter and Marion were providing Greene precious time and opportunity to reestablish the Continental troops by their perseverance in harassing the British supply lines.

While Sumter fought along the Congaree River, Andrew Pickens's militia troops were patrolling around Augusta, Georgia. Greene's strategy was to lay siege to Ninety Six while the militias were to the west and south of Ninety Six, with Marion protecting Sumter's right flank. But Marion was preoccupied—he left the middle of the state and alternatively headed toward Georgetown. When Greene became aware of the movement, he immediately messaged Marion, stating that Marion could continue toward Georgetown only if two conditions were met: first, that Marion could confirm that Lord Rawdon was not moving to intercept Greene at Ninety Six, and second, that Marion could ensure that Sumter's operations were not exposed to the British. This was followed with Sumter's message to Marion to support Sumter's movement to counter Lord Rawdon's northern advance above Orangeburgh. Indeed, Lord Rawdon's regiments were moving toward Ninety Six. Marion ignored both orders; later, he claimed that the messages were ambiguous. This poor communication created an additional crack in strained alliances and likely exposed Sumter's Myddleton Dragoons to the later ambush.

Similar to Hobkirk's Hill a month earlier, General Greene conducted his siege of the Ninety Six Star Fort, inflicted as much pain as his army could muster and then withdrew in disappointment. In the Battle of Hobkirk's Hill, the British did not surrender Camden, but they abandoned the city one month afterward, as Sumter earlier predicted. Ninety Six did not surrender but would be deserted and burned several weeks after Greene's siege. By mid-July, many Loyalists had followed the British army from Ninety Six to Orangeburgh and eventually retreated to Charlestown.

Meanwhile, General Sumter intercepted Lord Rawdon's British units heading toward Ninety Six. Henry Felder's sons fought in several of these regiments to divert British reinforcements. On June 1, at Vaudant's Old Field, Sumter sent Lieutenant Colonel Richard Hampton, commanding the Orangeburgh District Militia, and Colonel Charles Myddleton, commanding the 2nd Regiment of dragoons, to attack British reinforcements heading north toward Ninety Six. About fifty Loyalists (Royalists) were beaten, and the Loyalist Commander Henry Livingstone was killed. The skirmish took place north of present-day Pelion. Colonel Myddleton's dragoons had been successful harassing Lord Rawdon's rear units foraging the area, slowing their advance to Ninety Six.

Unfortunately, his dragoon regiment, likely including Henry Felder Jr., was ambushed at Juniper Springs (near present day Gilbert) on June 18, 1781. Under bivouac one morning, Myddleton's dragoons were surprised by a better-armed British mounted infantry. Myddleton's cavalry, without swords or weapons for close combat, were defeated with thirty-four Patriots lost, killed, wounded or captured.

After the severe loss at Juniper Springs, Sumter reported that he would not be able to join Greene at Ninety Six. A week later, on June 25, Greene wrote a long letter to Marion on his disappointment that the militia did not heed his need in Ninety Six, and he reminded Marion about supporting Sumter. At this, Marion struck camp and returned to Moncks Corner and Orangeburgh; however, Marion felt that Sumter was a "grand schemer." This friction provided the disastrous fallout waiting down the road between these two great South Carolinian leaders.

After the Siege of Ninety Six failed, British troops stationed at Moncks Corner started to fall back toward Charlestown. Between July 8 and July 12, Greene had all his generals together to engage Lord Rawdon at Turkey Hill (near Orangeburgh); however, the British held a favorable position, and Greene hesitated.

The following week, with orders from Governor Rutledge and General Greene to harass the British whenever possible, General Sumter led General Marion, Colonel Wade Hampton, Colonel Myddleton, Lieutenant Colonel Lee and approximately 550 troops against the British regiment of 600 untested infantry outside Moncks Corner. Given the presence of Colonel Myddleton's mounted militia, Henry Felder Jr. and brother Frederick may have witnessed the following events.

On July 15, Sumter reaffirmed to Greene that his army would "throw every impediment in their [the British] way should they attempt to retreat." As the fleeing British crossed Quinby Bridge on the morning of July 17, British soldiers attempted to loosen the planks and deny the charging Continental cavalry pursuit. After a precarious battle over the bridge, with the British continuing to remove planks as Americans attempted to repair them, the British retreated to Shubrick's Plantation. Unfortunately for the Patriots, Marion and Lee's dragoons had left the artillery behind in their haste during their rapid pursuit. With mostly riflemen and cavalry and few bayonets, Lee and Marion decided not to attack and instead held their positions to await artillery from General Sumter. The pause allowed the British to fortify their positioning among the plantation cabins and house. As ordered earlier by Governor Rutledge and Greene to engage and cut off the British, the moment Sumter arrived, the Patriots attacked. Marion opposed the plan, however, and attacked the right flank as Lee held in reserve and did not engage. In the center, Sumter attacked. His initial attacks were successful. But when ammunition was running low, the British planned a counterattack and overran Sumter's left flank. At this point, Marion ordered his men to engage to aid the weakened flank, and the British were thwarted. Although the Patriots were half the force of the British, the Patriots lost about 30 to 40 killed or wounded overall, while the British lost more than 150 killed, wounded or captured. In the darkness that evening and without informing Sumter, an angry Marion and Lee left, marching their men home.[137] The next day, Sumter was forced to watch the British retreat unmolested. While Marion and Lee objected to continue the earlier attacks and against a superior force, General Sumter's engagement delayed British Lieutenant Colonel Coates from transporting supplies and allowed Patriots to capture loads of ammunition, pay-wagons and large number of supplies designed for Lord Rawdon's regiment.[138]

In the aftermath, Marion and Lee turned against Sumter, alleging that Sumter had needlessly sacrificed men at the Shubrick's engagement, and they refused to fight under Sumter again.[139] In letters between the principals, sharp accusations against Sumter were placed. Historians have been very critical of Sumter, although mostly taken from the principals' perspective rather than the orders General Sumter commanded under and the clear strategic results. In balance, historians Edward McCrady and William Johnson pointed out that while the primary objective to capture the British army was not obtained completely, the benefits at Quinby Bridge and Shubrick's plantation were considerable: the "British interest was materially shaken, their party alarmed and humbled, the spirit of the Whigs [South Carolina militia] raised, and the fact was announced to the world that the country was not conquered."[140] And large stores of supplies and prisoners taken. The paymaster's chest was seized from the British. According to Johnson:

> [P]*erhaps the greatest benefit that resulted from this expedition was the confidence with which it inspired the militia in themselves. The party actually engaged in the attack of British Colonel Coates were almost exclusively South Carolina militia and the bravery they had displayed would have done honour to the veteran troops. It was demonstrated that this species of force wanted nothing but the consistency to enable it to meet the enemy with effects. Their terror of the British bayonet and the British discipline began to diminish whilst the respect of the enemy for their undisciplined valor rose in proportion.*[141]

The South Carolina militia scored a major battle, but the criticism continued. While the losses were sorely felt and were the source for the harsh complaints from Marion and Lee, the killed and wounded of the combatants were comparable to other significant conflicts that drove the British to retreat toward Charlestown. In killed, wounded and prisoner as a ratio of total forces engaged, the Patriots losses (killed, wounded, prisoners) were less than 10 percent, whereas the British suffered more than 20 percent. At Eutaw Springs three months later, the Patriots and British each suffered more than 28 percent in killed, wounded and prisoners. If not for several errors or hesitations, and Lee's Legion not engaging, the battle and losses according to Johnson may have "superseded the necessity of the battle at Eutaw."[142]

After a year of chaos and resentment in command, the conflict finally boiled over. Marion and Sumter were both determined and confident in their own strategies, and likely these characteristics and persistence provided success in dark times while the militia suffered alone in South Carolina against the British.[143] Both operated better independently, easily irritated when others meddled, and each had previously offered their resignations multiple times to General Greene. Most importantly, each had risen to the need despite their differences in early 1780, rallying recruits and inspiring others during desperate times. They represented the unique and inner spirit of the South Carolina militia—striking hard and fast and then retreating to fight another day.

Chapter 21

# From Eutaw Springs to Yorktown, September–November 1781

The years of war had savaged the land, and the British troops found it hard to sustain themselves in South Carolina. By August 1781, Lord Rawdon had withdrawn most of his inland outposts to the safety of Charlestown. In poor health, Rawdon returned to England, leaving Colonel Alexander Stewart in command. Meanwhile, General Greene—with Francis Marion, Henry Lee and William Washington, among others—gave chase to the British retreat, settling outside Moncks Corner, where they established headquarters. The Americans were poorly equipped, underfed and underclothed after several months of fighting and marching. Even with these disadvantages, the Continental detachments and militia continued to pester the British march to Charlestown.

On September 8, British Colonel Stewart led 2,000 well-equipped men out of Charlestown in search of General Greene's forces. The British had dispatched several of their soldiers to a nearby field to dig sweet potatoes to feed the troops. In the early morning, this detachment and Continental scouting parties ran into each other near Eutaw Springs. In the course of the day, the British 2,000 lined up against General Greene's 2,200 in a sequence of attacks, retreats, plunders and counterattacks. Under General Greene's command, Colonel Charles Starke Myddleton's 2nd Regiment of state dragoons, including Henry Felder Jr., patrolled Greene's left flank with Henderson's Brigade and South Carolina militias, with Washington's cavalry against British Major John Majoribanks infantry and grenadiers. Colonel William Washington and Colonel Myddleton were wounded in this engagement while charging through a deep thicket of bushes and trees.

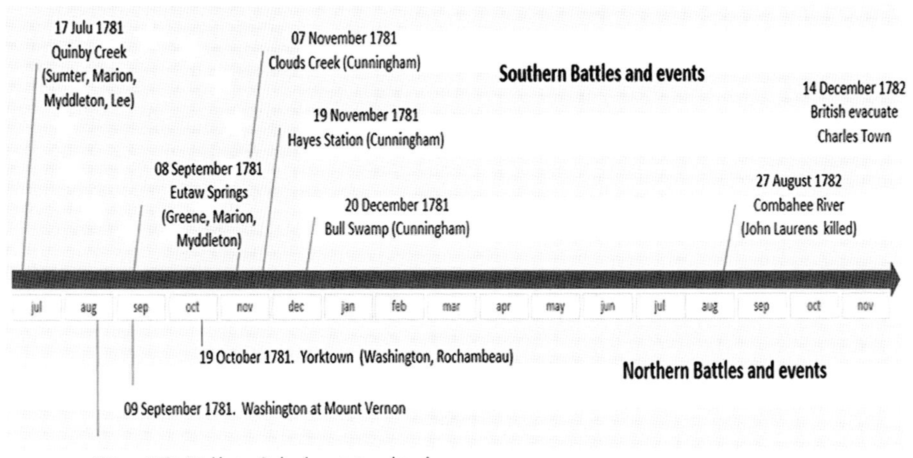


Timeline 6. July 1781–December 1782. *Generated by author.*

In the end, General Greene withdrew seven miles to Burdell's Plantation, leaving Colonel Stewart in control of the battlefield. Both armies were exhausted. The British army would rapidly retreat to Charlestown, leaving the dead unburied and the seriously wounded along the roadside. British had 450 killed and wounded and 430 captured. The American army lost 510 killed, wounded or missing, with 60 captured.

The state song of South Carolina contains the lines "Hold up the glories of thy dead; / Say how thy elder children bled, / And point to Eutaw's battle-bed. / Carolina! Carolina!" referring to this battle. Despite the British tactical victory, they had lost their suppression of General Greene's operations.

As operations continued in South Carolina, the Northern Campaign skirmishes were largely isolated to Virginia. By May 21, 1781, French General Rochambeau had met with General Washington in Connecticut to sway the American army to march south as Lord Cornwallis arrived in Petersburg, Virginia, from the Carolinas. Cornwallis had not received orders to abandon the Carolinas but did so. When Cornwallis arrived in Virginia, he replaced General Benedict Arnold with William Phillips. Arnold and Phillips had been earlier successful raiding Richmond and the surrounding areas.

Washington was still reluctant to leave the New York and the Hudson Valley region, desiring to attack the British in New York. Washington had learned that the British had sent additional troops to reinforce Cornwallis

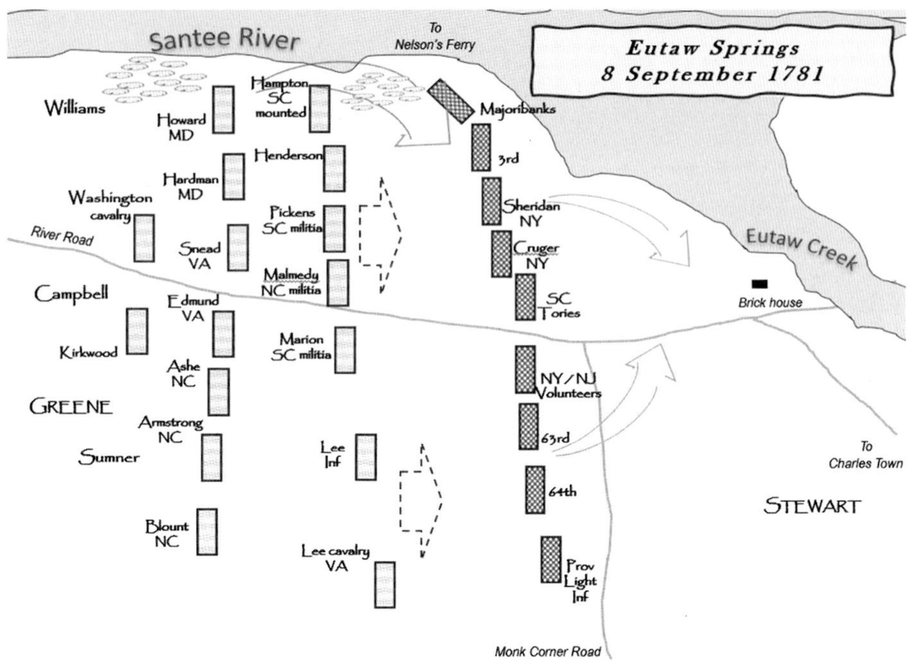


Eutaw Springs, September 8, 1781. *Generated by author.*

in Virginia. Instead of marching on Virginia, as prodded by the French general, Washington reasoned that the British in New York were vulnerable for an attack. Rochambeau disagreed, as he was aware that the French navy would soon rendezvous with the French and American army in Virginia. After Washington received notice that French Admiral Joseph Paul de Grasse was indeed heading for Virginia with 28 warships and 3,200 soldiers, Washington abandoned his plan to take New York and started his march south on August 19 with 3,000 American and 4,000 French troops.

Washington was unsure of his destination and sent fake dispatches to disguise his march south. By this time in Virginia, Cornwallis had given up raiding Patriot supply convoys and chasing the Marquis de Lafayette and withdrew to Williamsburg. On September 5, the French fleet was met by British Admiral Thomas Graves from New York and engaged in a two-hour battle at the Chesapeake that denied Lord Cornwallis reinforcements when Graves returned to New York. Immediately afterward, the French fleet army joined Lafayette, and the empty transports sailed north to pick up Washington's and De Rochambeau's armies. When Washington arrived on September 29, the total command was 7,800 French, 3,100 militia and

8,000 Continental soldiers. The three-week Siege of Yorktown forced the malaria-stricken British and Cornwallis to finally surrender.

One month after Eutaw Springs, on October 19, 1781, General Cornwallis surrendered eight thousand British soldiers in Yorktown. The war moved to the closing chapter. The Felder sons Frederick, Samuel and Jacob Felder continued their terms of service into the conclusion of the conflict in late 1782.

In South Carolina, bloody and minor clashes continued until the British finally evacuated Charlestown in December 1782. From Charlestown in November 1781, Major "Bloody Bill" Cunningham formed an expeditionary force and plundered, ambushed and massacred Americans. From November 13 to November 19, Major Cunningham's troops killed four soldiers at Rowe's Plantation in Orangeburgh, murdered twenty-eight militia at Clouds Creek outside present-day Batesburg and executed eighteen Patriots at Hayes Station in present-day Laurens County.

By December, General Andrew Pickens was on Bloody Bill Cunningham's trail, and he chased Cunningham back to Charlestown. Possibly because of this type of savagery during the war, the British failed to enflame Loyalists against Americans, leading to the overall failure of the British Southern Campaign strategy. In a tragic and last episode of the war, Lieutenant Colonel John Laurens was killed at the minor battle at Combahee River on August 27, 1782. In the same month, the British were ordered to prepare for the evacuation of Charlestown, eventually leaving the port on December 14, 1782. The name of the city would be changed permanently to "Charleston" because it sounded less British.

# Epilogue

The American Revolutionary War campaign in the South succeeded through many individuals rising to the great cause as citizen soldiers, multiple times over six-plus years. Neither success nor independence was secured or guaranteed, but these men volunteered with only the supplies and equipment on their back that they brought to the fight. This meant also that wives, sisters and daughters all had to cope and sacrifice in sundry ways as well.

Consider that many areas in South Carolina changed allegiances several times. Regions were dominated by liberty-minded Patriot militias, then Loyalist militias protected by British troops and then overtaken again by Patriots. Orangeburgh District is a specific example where Loyalists exacted revenge when tides turned and when supported by British detachments in the vicinity. Henry Felder was a casualty of such revenge. On the other hand, his murder may have emboldened Henry's legacy, as his sons fought on. Similar brutality enflamed many backcountry militia to stand and continue their fight against tyranny.

Afterward, the success of Sumter, Marion and Andrew Pickens pestering and capturing vital supply garrisons severely weakened the British army and dispersed the Loyalist militia. By the time General Greene returned to South Carolina, he would lose at Hobkirk's Hill, Ninety Six and Eutaw Springs, but because the militias had sabotaged the British planned reinforcement and supplies, each of these locations would be abandoned shortly after Greene's attack. As an army commander, Nathanael Greene was never victorious in a pitched battle, although his leadership via the delicate balance and communications with the Carolina militia may have been his greatest contribution.

With no grand Patriot victory, how was our Revolutionary War won? As our Continental Congress struggled in early 1776, desiring to protect their rights as Englishmen, these representatives were inevitably forced to speak of liberty and our destiny toward independence, as well as "unalienable Rights… of Life, Liberty and the pursuit of Happiness." Self-interested motivations and collective ideals that lack pureness of the soul will always weaken in the storm. They were all great men, but they had not yet the same mettle and inspirational valor brewing in the citizen soldier. For some, the time was not "ripe," as delegate Edward Rutledge stated in June 1776. But for the backcountry militia, many were first- or second-generation immigrants. Prior to reaching America, they had witnessed or knew the hardships under dictatorships, suppression and tyranny. And in the years before 1776, they had sacrificed, fought and embolden under backcountry leadership against Indians, the Regulator movements, the infancy of judicial and self-government and therefore were able to unite as a colony against the British.

Liberty and freedom's pursuits are individually deliberated and seeded in each citizen soldier's soul. This is America's core and our inner strength. Our American spirit, driven by each individual's thirst for liberty and pursuit of self-reliance, is our core foundation. Deep within the American bosom is a flame—a solid commitment and faith within any individual that can unleash their passions and purpose and rise above any challenge. By their own toil, sweat and sacrifice, they attained achievement and magnificence unimaginable in England, where society, class and vocation were predestined.

While delegates deliberated in Philadelphia, several states and men had already met their magnificent moment, taken up this great cause and willingly died in pursuit of liberty. Without Patriots pressuring their colonial representatives, our destiny as an independent, free country may have been delayed or the opportunity lost altogether.

As far as independence, conclusions are inescapable. The war simply would not have been won without the militia and each volunteer's individual convictions and sacrifice. Like for many South Carolinians, the Carolina militia, Henry Felder and his sons did not seek recognition. They had much earlier adopted this country and were more than willing to give their all for it. As Governor John Rutledge noted:

> *It was then I began to think. It was people, such as these, the ones you never heard of, the names you never know. No statues to honor them, no monuments, but without them where would we be? I could only talk of liberty; they were willing to die for it.*[144]

Appendix I

# Captain Henry Felder and Sons

Table 3. Service Records for Captain Henry Felder and Sons

**Captain Henry Felder**
October 2, 1725
February 12, 1780

Militia
Orangeburgh District
State Representative

**Selected Dates**
1775—Appointed to maintain the Continental Association boycott.
1775—Assisted the establishment of the Orangeburgh District Militia.
November 1775—Elected to South Carolina Provincial Congress.
March 1776—Elected to South Carolina Congressional General Assembly.
May 1776—Grand Jury foreman, "Address and Declaration."
December 1776—Elected to South Carolina 2nd Congressional General Assembly.
1779—Reappointed Grand Jury.
1780—Killed by Loyalists.

**Sources**
Salley, *History of Orangeburg County*, 472, 486+.
O'Neall, *Bench & Bar*, 325, 341, 488–89.
*South Carolina Gazette*, October 7, October 14, 1778.
*South Carolina Congressional Journals and Record*.
Henry Felder (Jr.) petition, AA2336. Petitioner's father's house burned and money stolen in 1778, father killed in 1780.
Captain of Orangeburgh militia. Carolana.com.

---

**Captain Henry Felder Jr.**
September 8, 1748
February 13, 1803

Militia
Orangeburgh District
2nd State Regiment
State Representative

**Selected Dates**
1779–82—Served as captain in the Orangeburgh District Militia.
May 1781–January 1782—Served under Colonel Myddleton's 2nd Regiment of Dragoons.
1782–86—State representative.
1783—Served as commissioner of roads.
1792–93—State representative.

**Sources**
Salley, *History of Orangeburg County*, 472, 486+.
O'Neall, *Bench & Bar*, vol. 2, 341.
*Journals of South Carolina Congress*, biographies.
Henry Felder Jr. petition to South Carolina Congress, *Journals of the House of Representative*, 1783–1784.
Henry Felder petition, AA2336, SC2700. "Beginning to the war until surrender of Charlestown, frequently engaged." May 12, 1781–January 1782, served with Myddleton. 70 head of cattle for Sumter in 1781."
U.S. Roster of Revolutionary Soldiers and Sailors, No409x, Book P. Lost horse on March 1779. Issued May 2, 1785.
U.S. Roster of Revolutionary Soldiers and Sailors, No. 206, Book B. Incident, January 1780. Issued March 1, 1784.
Captain/private various units, Orangeburgh militia, 2nd Regiment. May to January served 2nd Regiment of Dragoons under Colonel Myddleton. AA2336. Carolana.com.

---

**Jacob Felder**
July 22, 1750
May 5, 1790

Militia
Orangeburgh District
Upper Craven District

**Selected Dates**
1780, 1782—Appointed petit juror.
1781–82—Orangeburgh militia.

**Sources**
Salley, *History of Orangeburg County*, 486+.
Camp of General Marion; listed battles at Wadboo, Parkers Ferry and Eutaw Springs. William Abbott petition, S30239.
The officers during that period, as well as he can recollect, were Colonel Baxter (Upper Craven District) and Captains Wats & Felder (no first names given). S. Jeremiah Bunch, C.S., S17867.
William Graves petition, R14570, with Camden District militia (nonspecific).

---

**John Felder**
December 12, 1752
July 1, 1781

Militia
Orangeburgh District
1st/3rd Light Dragoons

**Selected Dates**
1780, 1781—Served as petit juror.
Until 1781—Served in Orangeburgh militia.
1781—Commanded company volunteers with Colonel William Washington's Dragoons.
1781—Killed at McCord's Ferry.

**Sources**
Salley, *History of Orangeburg County*, 486+.
Henry Felder (Jr.) petition, AA2336. Petitioner's brother John served as commanding Volunteer Company of Militia under Colonel William Washington and killed by British.
Felder petition, AA2337. Provided 300 pounds of beef, No. 88, L.Q. Issued May 7, 1785, to Estate of John Felder, for £3 pounds for 300 pounds beef for militia user in 1781. Account audited.
U.S. Roster of Revolutionary Soldiers and Sailors, No. 87, use of pasturage of horses, 1782, issued May 7, 1785.
U.S. Roster of Revolutionary Soldiers and Sailors, No. 88, 300 pounds of beef in 1781, issued May 7, 1785.
Henry Felder Jr. petition to South Carolina Congress, 1783–84.

---

**FREDERICK JOSEPH DANIEL FELDER**
September 1, 1753
June 5, 1813

Militia
Orangeburgh District
3rd Regiment of Rangers

**Selected Dates**
1779, 1780, 1782—Served in Orangeburgh District Militia.
1779—Augment with Colonel Thomson 3rd Regiment of Rangers.
1779—Siege of Savannah.

**Sources**
Salley, *History of Orangeburg County*, 486+.
Revolutionary War petition, C.S., A.A. 2335, S537, S538. No. 1593, No. 1594. Lib Y, issued February 2, 1788, to Frederick Felder for a horse lost in public service from the Comm.
Frederick Felder, lost horse in March 1779. Lost wagon, horses and bay mare, November 15, 1779. Loss of gray horse December 1779. Served as private under Colonel Charles Heatley during Georgia expedition and Siege of Savannah. SC Petition 2335.
Frederick Felder, 50 days from September 12 to November 1779. SC Petition 2335.
Frederick Felder, 194 days in militia 1781. Petition 1785, No. 538. SC Petition 2335.
Frederick Felder, 68 days as private in militia from June to August 1782. SC Petition 2335.
U.S. Roster of Revolutionary Soldiers and Sailors, No. 537, 50 days in militia in 1779, issued June 20, 1785.
U.S. Roster of Revolutionary Soldiers and Sailors, No. 538, served militia 1781 and 1782, issued June 20, 1785.
U.S. Roster of Revolutionary Soldiers and Sailors, No. 1593, lost horse, issued February 2, 1788.
U.S. Roster of Revolutionary Soldiers and Sailors, No. 1594, lost horse, issued February 2, 1788.
Private, wagoner, September to November 1779 (50 days), Siege of Savannah under Healy, June to August 1782 (68 days), AA2335. Carolana.com.

**Samuel Felder**
June 5, 1755
May 5, 1807

Militia
Orangeburgh District
Upper Craven District

**Selected Dates**
1779, 1780, 1782—Served in Orangeburgh District Militia.
1780, 1782—Served as petit juror.
1782—Quartermaster.

**Sources**
Salley, *History of Orangeburg County*, 486+.
Captain under Upper Craven (Colonel Baxter). J.D. Lewis, *The Evolution of Marion's Brigade after the Fall of Charles Town, 1780–1782*.
Revolutionary War petition, C.S., W272; Inman Aaron, R5489.
Served 151 days as lieutenant, 1780–81, thereafter captain, December 1780–May 1781, AA 2338, SC petition and various militia duty/material in 1779 and 1782. Lost one horse, March 1779.
Revolutionary War petition, C.S., S17867, Jeremiah Bunch (not specific).
U.S. Roster of Revolutionary Soldiers and Sailors, No. 65, militia in 1779 and 1782, issued July 7, 1784.
Served in militia 1779 and 1782, AA2338, SC petition.
March 1779 and 34 days as private, June 1 to August 31, 1782, and as quartermaster, AA2338, SC petition, 2701.
Lieutenant, captain of Orangeburgh militia, 151 days. Carolana.com.
Captain, lieutenant 1780–81 (151 days), Orangeburgh militia and Upper Craven County. Carolana.com.

---

**Abraham Felder**
March 28, 1757
September 4, 1832

Militia
Orangeburgh District
Berkeley District

**Selected Dates**
1780, 1782—Served as lieutenant and captain in Orangeburgh District Militia.
1780—Served with Colonel Thomson 3rd Regiment of Rangers.

**Sources**

Salley, *History of Orangeburg County*, 486+.

Revolutionary War petition, C.S., A.A. 2334; W284. No. 284. Lib W, issued August 15, 1785, to Mr. Abraham Felder, for £13 for 186 days' duty in 1780 and 1781 as per account audited.

186 days, December 1, 1780–June 4, 1781, under Captain William Dukes (Berkeley regiment) and Colonel Richard Richardson Jr., AA2334, Petition SC2698.

U.S. Roster of Revolutionary Soldiers and Sailors, No. 284, served 186 days 1789–81, issued August 15, 1785.

Lieutenant, SC 3rd Regiment; private, Berkeley Regiment, 1780–81. At Georgetown no. 6 (January 24, 1781), Fort Watson no. 2 (April 16, 1781), Fort Motte (May 7, 1781) and likely Halfway Swamp.

December 1780–June 1781. 186 days as private under Dukes and Richardson (AA2334). Carolana.com.

Lieutenant, SC 3rd Regiment Rangers. Carolana.com.

---

**ADAM PETER FELDER**

April 2, 1759

May 12, 1824

Militia

Orangeburgh District

**Selected Dates**

1780, 1782—Served in Orangeburgh District Militia.

1809—Left South Carolina for Mississippi.

**Sources**

Salley, *History of Orangeburg County*, 486+.

HENRY FELDER JR. (1748–PRIOR TO 1803)

Henry Felder Jr. was born on September 8, 1748, and baptized on September 25. Henry Jr. received a grant in 1773, a 250-acre tract on Pon Pon (Edisto) River.[145] After the war in 1793, Henry married Maria Catherine Stoudemire (born in 1752), and they had eight children.

He served with his father in the Orangeburgh militia until the fall of Charlestown and then under Colonel Charles Starkey Myddleton's South Carolina 2nd Regiment of state dragoons. In his petition, he dated his

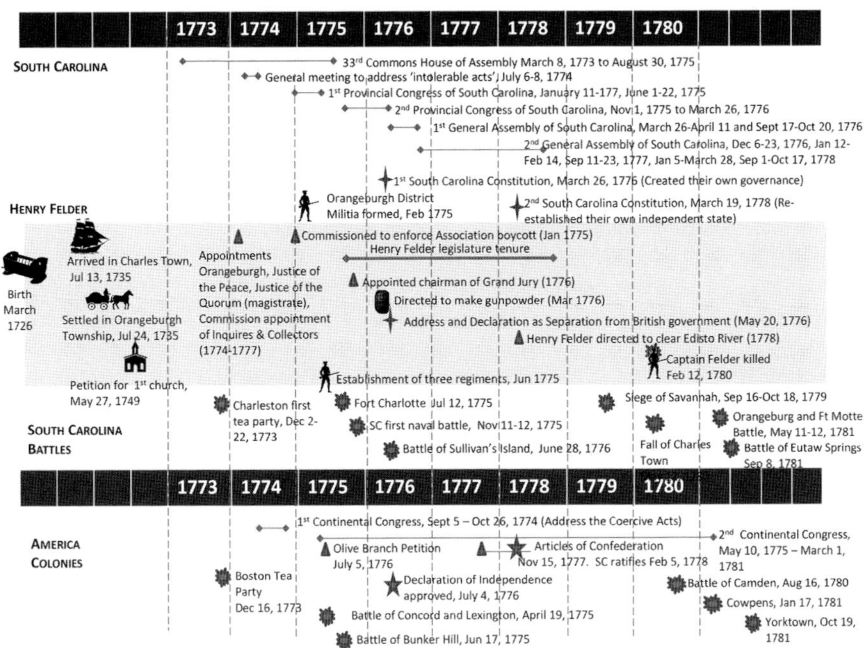


Timeline 7. Henry Felder timeline. *Generated by author.*

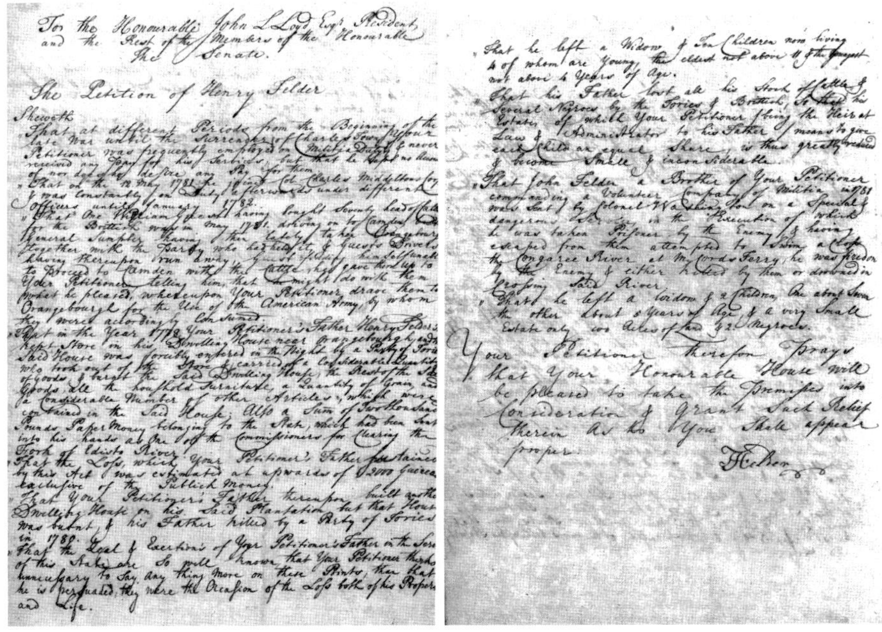

To the Honourable John L Lloyd Esqr. President and the Rest of the Members of the Honourable the Senate.

The Petition of Henry Felder

Sheweth

That at different Periods from the Beginning of the late War until the Surrender of Charles Town your Petitioner was frequently employed in Militia Duty & never received any Pay for his Services, but that he hopes [illegible] for them.

That on the 12 May 1781 he joined Col. Charles Middleton & was Constantly on Duty afterwards under different Officers until January 1782.

That One William [illegible] having bought Seventy head of Cattle for the British was in May 1781 driving on to Camden but General Sumpter having then lately taken Orangeburg together with the Party who had it, & those Drivers having thereupon run away [illegible] to proceed to Camden with the Cattle they gave them up to Your Petitioner telling him that he might do with them what he pleased, whereupon Your Petitioner drove them to Orangeburgh for the Use of the American Army, by whom they were accordingly Consumed.

That in the Year 1778 Your Petitioner's Father Henry Felder kept Store in his Dwelling House near Orangeburgh & said House was forcibly entered in the Night by a Party of Tories who took out of the Store & carried off a Considerable Quantity of Goods & from the said Dwelling House the Rest of the Goods, all the household Furniture, a Quantity of Grain and a Considerable Number of other Articles, which were contained in the said House; Also a Sum of Two thousand Pounds Paper Money belonging to the State, which had been lodged into his hands as One of the Commissioners for Clearing the Fork of Edisto River. That the Loss, which Your Petitioner's Father sustained by this Act was estimated at upwards of 2000 Guineas exclusive of the Publick Money.

That Your Petitioner's Father thereupon built another Dwelling House on his said Plantation but that House was burnt, & his Father killed by a Party of Tories in 1780.

That the Zeal & Exertions of Your Petitioner's Father in the Service of this State are So well known that Your Petitioner thinks it unnecessary to Say any thing more on these Points, than that he is persuaded, they were the Occasion of the Loss both of his Property and Life.

That he left a Widow & Ten Children now living 4 of whom are Young, the eldest not above 11 & the youngest not above 4 Years of Age.

That his Father lost all his Stock of Cattle & Several Negroes by the Tories & British, So that his Estate, of which Your Petitioner (being the Heir at Law & Administrator to his Father) means to give each Child an equal Share, is thus greatly reduced & become Small & inconsiderable.

That John Felder a Brother of Your Petitioner commanding a Volunteer Company of Militia in 1781 was sent by Colonel Washington on a Special & dangerous Service, in the Execution of which he was taken Prisoner by the Enemy, & having escaped from them attempted to Swim across the Congaree River at McCords Ferry, he was pursued by the Enemy & either killed by them or drowned in crossing said River.

That he left a Widow & 2 Children, the one about Seven the other about 5 Years of Age & a very Small Estate [illegible] of two Negroes.

Your Petitioner therefore Prays that Your Honourable House will be pleased to take the Premises into Consideration & Grant Such Relief therein as to You Shall appear proper.

H Felder

Henry Felder Jr.'s petition. *Courtesy of South Carolina Archives.*

service under Colonel Myddleton from May 1781 until January 1782. In 1784, he filed a petition to the South Carolina General Assembly requesting redress for his family's economic losses during the war, specifically for his widowed mother, Catharina Magdelene (Schell) Felder, and his brother John's widow. In his written petition, he specifically stated that he did not request compensation for his family nor for his service to the great cause, but rather desired recompense only for the loss of cattle and property. He also discussed his brother John's service under Colonel Washington and how he was captured in a secret mission and killed trying to escape.

After the war, Henry Jr. served as commissioner of roads for Orange Parish and commissioner to repair the courthouse and jail (1783), clearing the navigable of Edisto River (1784, 1785) and justice of the peace (1785). Like his father serving as representative, Henry Jr. was elected for the 4th, 5th, 6th and 10th House of Representative in the South Carolina General Assembly spanning 1782–86 and 1792–93.[146] He apparently lost a contested election for the 9th General Assembly to Samuel Rowe when Rowe and his appointee were allowed to record the ballots. Records suggest that Henry Jr. owned over 880 acres near Saltketcher River and the south fork of Edisto River—five lots in the township. According to Alexander S. Salley's *History of Orangeburgh*, Henry Felder Jr. died prior to February 1803.

Jacob Felder (1750–1790)

Jacob Felder was born on July 22, 1750. On June 21, 1775, He married Mary Elizabeth Myers (born in 1755), daughter of Daniel Myers and Mary Ann Myers. Jacob and Mary may have had as many as six children. He served in the Orangeburgh militia in 1781–82 and was with Francis Marion's army under Captain John Armstrong and Captain Clark. According to petitions, Jacob served with General Francis Marion brigade, likely with Marion's detachments during battle of Wadboo Bridge (January 1781), Parker's Ferry (August 1781) and Eutaw Springs (September 1781). He was noted outside Marion's camp outside Charlestown (December 1782) while the British evacuated the city. Sources indicate various dates of death—February or May 1790 or as late as May 5, 1807. One questionable reference suggests that his death took place at St. Marks, Craven County, of cabin fever on July 1, 1781, which conflicts with petition suggestions of Revolutionary War events in 1782. At some point, he moved to Sumter District, Clarendon County, South Carolina.

Captain Snipes, Sergeant McDonald, Sergeant Jasper, Reddin McCoy, Mr. Pringle, Rayer Bradley, Nathan Maples, Benjamin Hodge, Francis Richardson was in the horse. Jasper Harroll, James Dickey, Josiah Forner, Henry Hanesworth, Cato Simmons was an officer he thinks aid to the general & Mitchell the other Catan [?] was also there Frederick La Sane & Meshow Captain John Canty, James Gaulden, Josiah Gale, John Maham, Thomas Bradford, Thomas Niell, William Raglin, William Mitchell, John Caudle, William Reese, Randall Singleton, Benjamin Guess, Shadrach Inman, he says were with him in the 1st campaign. Ambrose Gale, John Singleton, Abraham Pool, John Whalen, Adville Atkinson, John Odle, Harris Michael, John Chaney, William P. Brown, Jacob Felder, William McCorico, Abel Baynell, Henry dates, James Bates & John Molett are other who he recollects to have been acquainted with while in service.

I William Abbott do hereby relinquish every claim whatever to a pension or annuity except the present & declare that my name is not on the Pension roll of the Agency of any state.

Witness

S/ G. D. Boyd S/ William Abbott, X his mark

William Abbott's petition (reference Jacob Felder). *Courtesy of South Carolina Archives.*

JOHN FELDER (1751–1781)

John Felder was born on December 12, 1751. He acquired one hundred acres on September 8, 1772, and married Sarah Snell (born on July 16, 1758, daughter of Johannes Adam Schnell) in 1775. They had five children.

John, like his elder brothers, was involved with the early Orangeburgh militia and at some point became a scout or messenger with the state cavalry operating in the area. According to Henry Felder's Jr. petition, John served under Colonel William Washington, Continental Dragoons, in some official capacity as an officer. John was captured during a reconnaissance mission with his cousin Adam Snell. According to Salley's *History of Orangeburg*, John and Adam escaped while the British were having dinner, with Adam running through the woods and John swimming the river with his hands tied. Upon John's reaching the other side, a British guard shot and killed him, allegedly with John's own rifle. This event happened around July 1, 1781, near McCord's Ferry, St. Mark's Parish, Craven County.

At the time of John Felder's death, he may have been intercepting and sending dispatches to Washington concerning several events that occurred in the McCord's Ferry and Orangeburgh region. Lieutenant Colonel William Washington conducted a raid in Berkeley County in mid-July

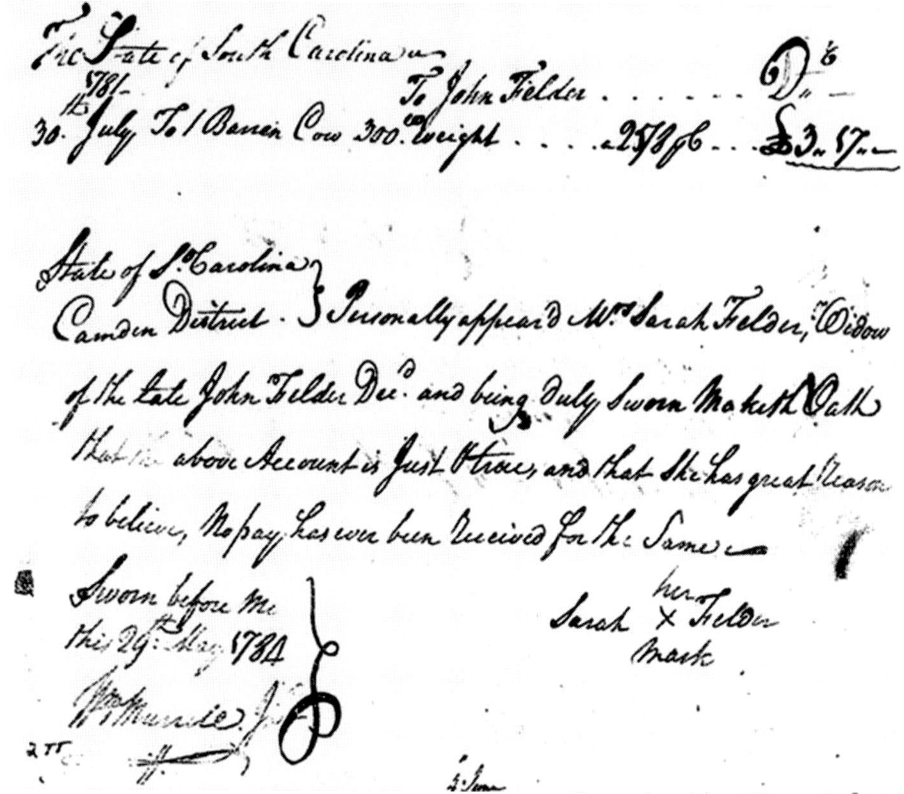

The State of South Carolina
To John Felder ..... Dr
1781
30th July To 1 Barren Cow 300 weight .... 25/8 ... £3..17..

State of So Carolina }
Camden District } Personally appear'd Mrs Sarah Felder, Widow of the late John Felder Decd and being duly Sworn maketh Oath that the above Account is Just & true, and that she has great Reason to believe, No pay has ever been Received for the Same —

Sworn before Me
this 29th May 1784
Wm Murrie J.P.

Sarah her X mark Felder

Sarah Felder's petition on behalf of John Felder. *Courtesy of South Carolina Archives.*

1781. Between July 9 and July 18, a detachment of Colonel Washington's 3rd Continental Dragoons defeated two unnamed companies of British dragoons, killing or capturing more than fifty prisoners. The letters indicate that Colonel Washington was patrolling the roads between McCord's Ferry and Charlestown Road.

In another set of engagements around Orangeburgh, July 25, Colonel Washington set Captain John Watts out with twenty men to harass the British, who were foraging every day in the area. Major John Doyle of the Volunteers of Ireland, with about thirty men, were conducting these British raids until they ran into Captain Watts at sunrise on July 25. In a quick and furious fight, the Patriots gave more than they received from the British. Major Doyle had two men killed and seven men captured, while the Americans suffered one man wounded: Cornet Julius Hite. John Felder's reconnaissance missions may have helped with these intercepts and engagements.

Separately, John Felder's family petitioned for reimbursement for three hundred pounds of beef for the militia in 1781. After John's death, Sarah Snell married John Ragin.

FREDERICK JOSEPH DANIEL FELDER (1753–1813)

Frederick was the fourth son of Henry Felder, born on September 1, 1753. He was baptized on October 21, 1753, in John Giessendanner's church. He married Anna "Catharina" Horger (born on March 25, 1758) on March 23, 1778, during the war. Catharina was the daughter of Henry and Catharina Horger. Frederick and Catharina had as many as six children.

In the South Carolina Archive, exhibits verify several records of Frederick Felder's service: in March 1779; 50 days between September and November 1779 at the Siege of Savannah; 194 days in 1781; and 68 days between June and August 1782. Frederick's service may have been continuous days or within increments because of state law on consecutive day tenures.

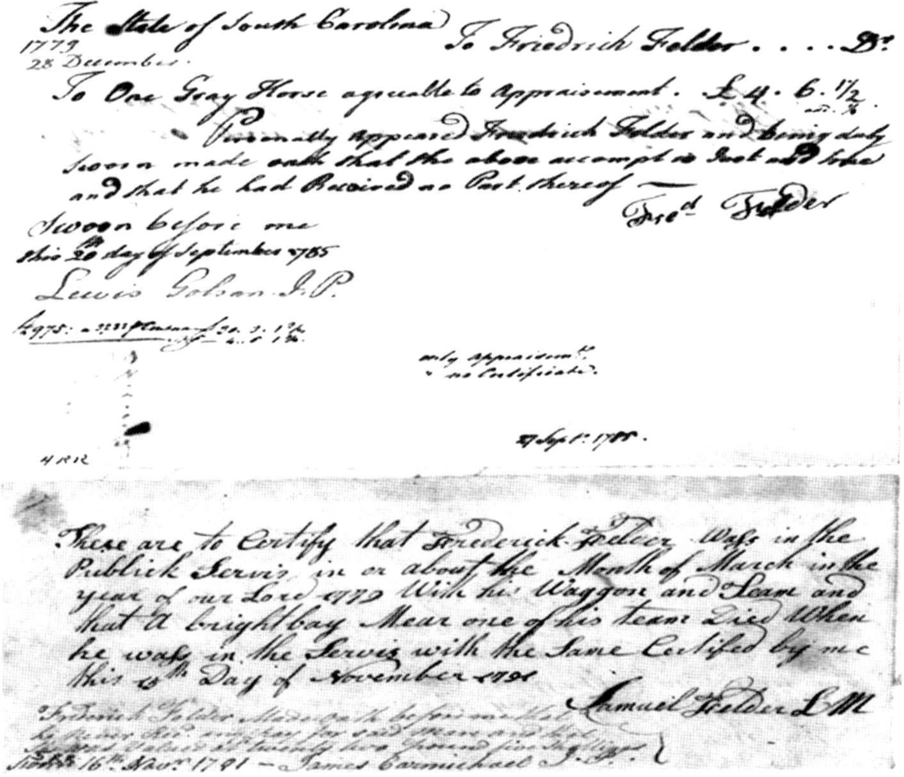

The State of South Carolina To Friedrich Felder . . . Dr

1779 28 December

To One Gray Horse agreeable to Appraisement. £4. 6. 1½

Personally appeared Frederick Felder and being duly sworn made oath that the above account is Just and true and that he had Received no Part thereof — Fred Felder

Sworn before me this 20 day of September 1785

Lewis Golson J.P.

These are to Certify that Frederick Felder Was in the Publick Servis in or about the Month of March in the year of our Lord 1779 With his Waggon and Team and that a bright bay Mear one of his team Died When he was in the Servis with the Same Certified by me this 15th Day of November 1791

Samuel Felder L.M.

Sworn 16th Nov. 1791 — James Carmichael J.P.

Frederick Felder's petition. *Courtesy of South Carolina Archives.*

The information records his petition for a wagon and team of horses serving the "public service" during the war in March 1779. The date corresponds to Colonel Thomson's South Carolina rangers' conflict at Briar Creek, Georgia. The battle was a bloody exchange where the Americans lost 150 or more militiamen, while the British suffered only 5 killed.

Colonel William Moultrie said that this loss allowed the British invasion of South Carolina, headed by General Prevost to continue, yet it slowed the British advancement to Charlestown. The delay allowed General Lincoln to return with enough men to temporarily save Charlestown. Frederick was under Colonel Thomson's rangers during his service in Georgia (Siege of Savannah). He served as a private under Major William Heatley's company in Colonel Charles Heatley's militia in South Carolina. Several documents relate to a gray horse he lost during the Georgia expedition and subsequent bloody siege. In 1781, Frederick continued in the Orangeburgh District Militia, which supported several conflicts, including Orangeburgh, Ninety Six, Eutaw Springs and Myddleton's ambush in Gilbert, South Carolina. Frederick died on June 5, 1813.

Samuel Felder (1755–1807)

Samuel Felder was Henry's fifth son, born on June 5, 1755, in Four Holes, Orangeburgh District. He married Mary Ann Myers, born in 1759 and daughter of Daniel Myers, in 1781. After Mary's death, he remarried Ann Horger in 1796. Ann Horger was the daughter of Jacob and Lovisia Shaumloffel Horger, a possible relative of Anna Catharina, who married Frederick Joseph Felder. Through two marriages, Samuel had around eight children.

Samuel served in the Orangeburgh militia at various times between 1779 and 1782. His petitions were for a loss of a horse in March 1779 and additional service in series of petitions in the South Carolina Archives, SC2338. Samuel served 151 days as a lieutenant and later as a captain between December 1780 and May 1781 under Heatley's company. Samuel is listed with Upper Craven Regiment under Colonel Jacob Baxter from 1782 to 1783. In June 1782, he served 34 days as a quartermaster. After the war, he served as a county judge in 1784. Samuel died on May 5, 1807.

Samuel's son, John Myers Felder (1782–1851) became a South Carolina representative. He was a graduate of Yale and Litchfield Law School, Connecticut, and roommate to close friend John C. Calhoun. John Myers served as major during the War of 1812 and died at Union Point, Georgia.

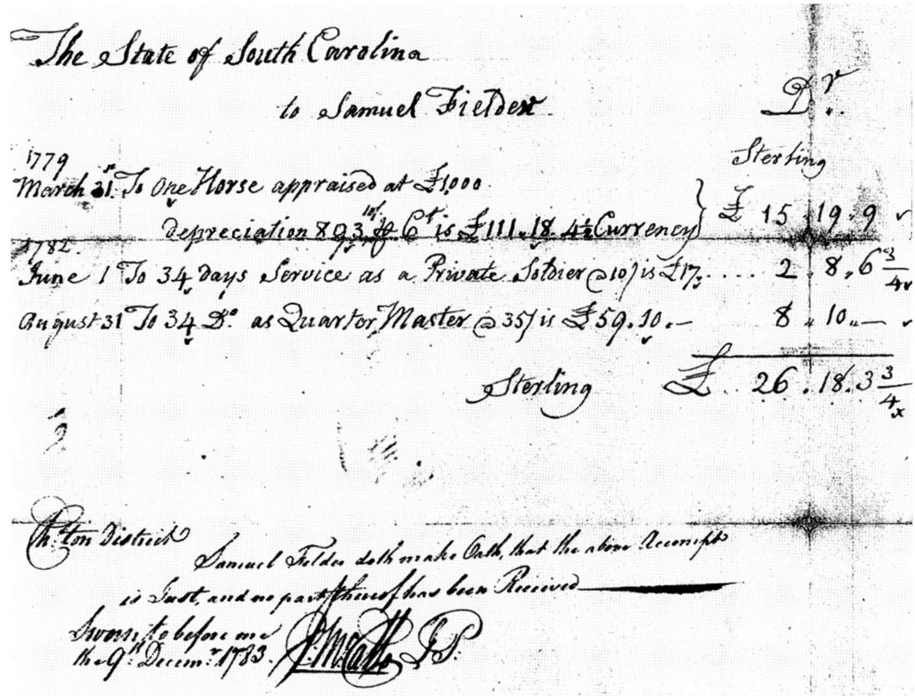

The State of South Carolina
to Samuel Fielder Dr.

Sterling

1779
March 31 To One Horse appraised at £1,000
depreciation [illegible] is £111.18.4½ Currency } £ 15 . 19 . 9

1782
June 1 To 34 days Service as a Private Soldier @ 10/ is £17 . . . . 2 . 8 . 6 3/4
August 31 To 34 Do. as Quarter Master @ 35/ is £59.10.— 8 . 10 . —

Sterling £ . 26 . 18 . 3 3/4

Ch.ton District Samuel Felder doth make Oath, that the above Account is Just, and no part thereof has been Received
Sworn to before me the 9th Decem.r 1783. [illegible] J.P.

Samuel Felder's petition. *Courtesy of South Carolina Archives.*

He is buried at the family's Midway Plantation in the Felder family cemetery. John Myers Felder's portrait hangs in the State Senate Conference Room, third floor, Gressette Building.

ABRAHAM FELDER (1757–1832)

Abraham was born on March 28, 1757, and settled in present-day Elloree, west of Orangeburgh. Abraham married Mary "Polly" Erlanger (May 15, 1757–1793) in 1780, and they had at least seven children. Abraham served 186 days between December 1780 and June 1781 under Captain William Dukes and Colonel Richard Richardson Jr. Another petition indicates that Abraham served in 1780 and 1782 as a lieutenant and captain in the militia. He died in September 1832 in Felderville, South Carolina.

ADAM PETER FELDER (1759–1824)

Adam Peter Felder was born on April 2, 1759, and married Elizabeth Lowe (May 7, 1759–May 12, 1848) in 1780. Elizabeth Lowe was the daughter of John and Nancy Anne Butler Lowe. They had at least eight children. From

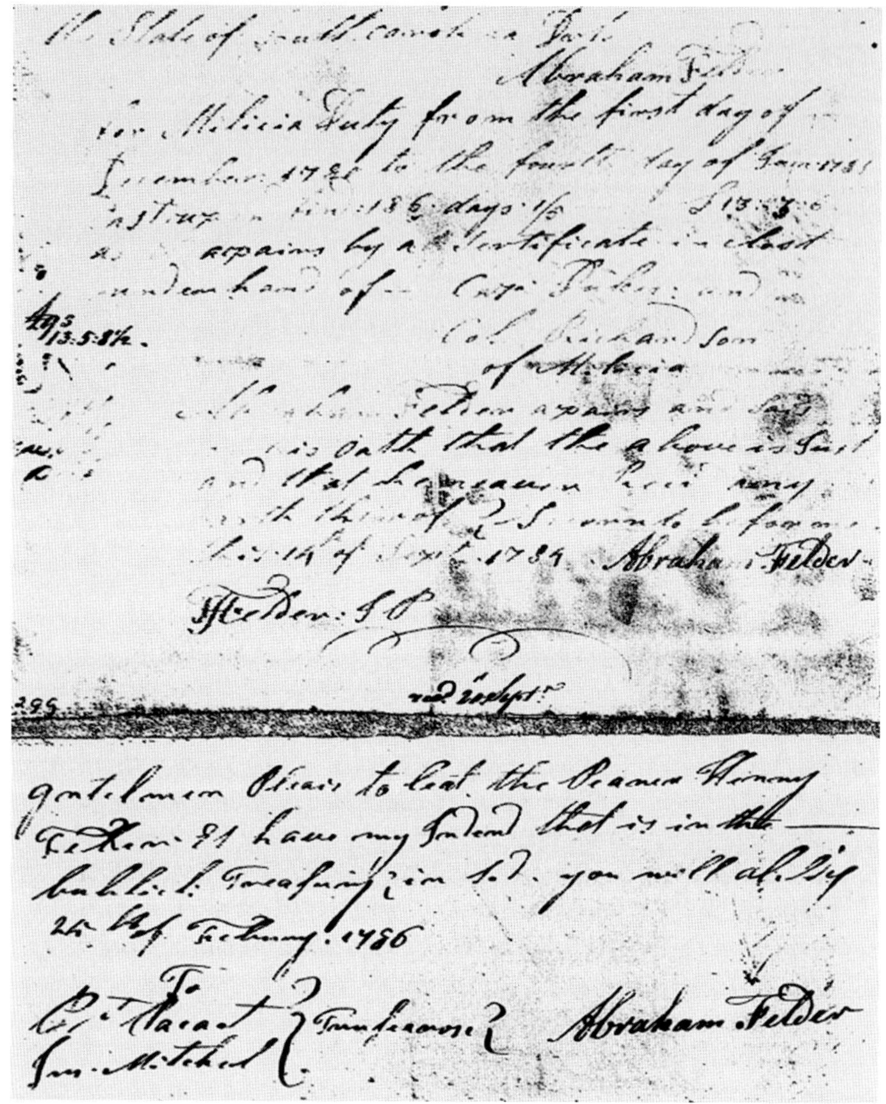
The State of South Carolina Dr. to
Abraham Fel[illegible]
for Militia Duty from the first day of
December 1780 to the fourth day of Jan 1781
[illegible] 186 days [illegible] £13 [illegible]
as appears by a Certificate [illegible]
under hand of Capt. Baker and
Col. Richardson
of Militia
Abraham Felder appears and says
on his Oath that the above is just
and that he [illegible]
[illegible]
[illegible] 14 of Sept. 1784 Abraham Felder

Gentlemen Please to let the Bearer Henry
Felder have my Indent that is in the
publick Treasury [illegible] you will oblige
24 day of February 1786
To [illegible] Abraham Felder

Abraham Felder's petition. *Courtesy of South Carolina Archives.*

Alexander Salley's *History of Orangeburg County* and similar references, Adam served in the Orangeburgh militia in 1780 and 1782. After the war, he left South Carolina and moved to Vaughn Place near Magnolia Pike County, Mississippi, around 1809 and became a minister.

He died around May 12, 1824 (or 1848), in Pike County, Mississippi, and was buried at Isaac Felder Cemetery, Mississippi.

## Appendix II

# Ursula Felder's Will, August 1739

Ursula Felder's will was dated August 30, 1739, and was recorded on November 8, 1739. Her will was written in German, but an English translation was done at the time by Christian Motte:

> *A True and Exact Translation from the German into the English Tongue of the Last Will & Testament of Ursula Felderin late of Orangeburgh Township Widow deced Made the 30th day of August 1739 Translated P Christian Motte—Anno 1739 the 30th August Have I Ursula Felderin upon my Sick Bed, in Consideration of my Dear Child, whose name is John Henry Felderin I have ordered to be wrote that he after my Death all that from me and his deceased Father Shall be left, that shall he as Rightfull Heir as his property take to hand, but as the Child is not Yet in Condition the from his Father and Mother left Effects himself to Manage, So have I (as being yet in good Sense) Mr Henry Wurzer him in his Care delivered with body & Goods, till He Namely John Henry Felder Nineteen or Twenty years of age Shall be, and again promises to be unto him as a Father & to take Care of his Body and Soul So fan- God shall give his Grace & shall mentioned Child pay no Boarding unto Henry Wurzer and Shall the Child be Obedient to him till the said time Now followeth wherein the Left Estate Consists, First Two hundred Acres of Land left by Father and Mother, More One hundred, more fifty acres from Gelser, in Summs the Child be an Heir of all, be it of horses of Cattle or of Debts yet standing Out or House furniture, or whatsoever name it may have Now*

*do I Henry Wurtzer promise to take Care of the Boy and his Estate as if it were my Own, without Pay Ursula Felderin. Test Henry Wurtz, W Goreing, George Giesendanner, Jacob Christaller, Michell Christopher Rowe Recorded this 8th Day of November 1739.*

Appendix III

# Gunpowder Directive, March 1776

*Tuesday, March 5, 1776. The Congrefs* [Congress] *met, And the journal of yesterday was read. Ordered, That Col. Powell, the Rev. Mr. Tennent, Mr. Corbet, Col Gervais, Mr. Felder, and Mr Kerfhaw, be a Committee to confider* [confer] *and report the beft* [beneficial] *means of erecting a powder-mill, and of promoting the making of gunpowder in this colony.*

*Friday, March 22, 1776. . . . Whereas Henry Felder, Esq.; having proposed to manufacture Sulphur* [sulfur] *and nitre into gunpowder; according to his offer it is Resolved That a proper quantity of nitre and sulphur belonging to the public be put into the hands of the said Henry Felder, Esq., to be by him made up into gunpowder and delivered into the public magazine: That Mr. Felder be allowed seven shillings and six-pence currency for each pound of gunpowder by him so made up from such materials, exclusive of the charge of carriage. And that upon his delivering a quantity of gunpowder into the hands of the Public Receiver, he be, from time to time, supplied with an equal quantity of materials, to be in like manner made up into gunpowder.*

Appendix IV

# Declaration of Rights, Nature's Law and Independence

During the continued debates in the Continental Congress and governing bodies within the colonies, the language of "unalienable rights by Nature and Nature's Law" slowly matured within state documents. And similarly, Declaration of Independence sharpened as Britain rebuffed attempts for reconciliation and the colonies' requests for rights as British citizens. Today, many state historians and states claim to have been "the first" to coin the phrase, "Rights granted by God" or the first organized body to "declare full independence."

History overlooks South Carolina. The words of Henry Felder and his grand jury should be acknowledged when placed within these significant events and official government acts and declarations. Following is a timeline, with the written words related to the claims in context.

*Event: December 1773—Charlestown and Boston Tea Parties*

Declaration and Resolve of the First Continental Congress (October 14, 1774)

- "That the inhabitants of the English Colonies in North America, by the *immutable laws of nature*, the principles of the English Constitution, and the several Charters or Compacts, have the *following Rights*:...

  Resolved, N.C.D. 10. It is indispensably necessary to good Government, and rendered essential by the English Constitution, that the constituent branches of the Legislature be independent of each other; that, therefore, the exercise of Legislative power in several Colonies, by a Council appointed, during pleasure, by the Crown, is unconstitutional, dangerous, and destructive to the freedom of American Legislation."

*Event: October 20, 1774—Passage of the Continental Association*

Bush River Declaration, Harford County, Maryland, March 22, 1775

Single statement or declaration, signed by thirty-four county representatives in a tavern. It was not a statement of separation or independence, although it's been claimed to be the first declaration of independence from Britain by a representative body in America. The declaration's last sentence is also claimed to be an inference to Thomas Jefferson's Declaration of Independence.

- "We, the Committee of Harford County, having most Seriously and maturely Considered the Resolves and Association of the Continental Congress, and the Resolves of the Provincial Convention, do most heartily approve of the same, and as we Esteem ourselves in a more particular manner intrusted by our Constituents to see them carried into Execution, we do most solemnly pledge ourselves to each other, and to our country, and engage ourselves by every tie held sacred among mankind, to perform the same at the risque of our lives and fortunes."

*Event: April 19, 1775—Lexington and Concord Battle*

Mecklenburg Declaration (May 20, 1775), published April 30, 1819

- "1. Resolved, That whosoever directly or indirectly abetted, or in any way, form, or manner, countenanced the uncharted and dangerous invasion of our rights, as claimed by Great Britain, is an enemy to this County, to America, and to the *inherent and inalienable rights of man*."...
- 3. Resolved, That we do hereby *declare ourselves a free and independent people*, are, and of right ought to be, a sovereign and self-governing Association, under the control of no power other than that of our God and the General Government of the Congress."

Mecklenburg Resolve (May 31, 1775), published 1847

Statement against laws of Parliament, response to Continental Congress's statement of resolve.

- "[A]ll Laws…derived from the Authority of the King or Parliament, are *annulled and vacated*," and that the Provincial government "under the Great Continental Congress is invested with all legislative and executive Powers…and that no other Legislative or Executive does or can exist, at this time, in any of these Colonies."

New Hampshire Constitution (January 1776)

Written from December 1775 to January 1776.

- "Have taken into our serious consideration the unhappy circumstances, into which this colony is involved by means of many grievous and oppressive acts of the British Parliament, depriving us of *our natural and constitutional rights and privileges*…
- Declaring that we neaver sought to throw off our dependence upon Great Britain, but felt ourselves happy under her protection, while we could enjoy our constitutional rights and privileges. And that we shall rejoice if such a reconciliation between us and our parent State can be effected as shall be approved by the Continental Congress."

South Carolina Constitution (March 1776)

- "South Carolina Constitution: XXVIII. That *the resolutions of the Continental Congress, now of force in this colony*, shall so continue until altered or revoked by them."

Halifax Resolves (April 12, 1776)

Empowered North Carolina delegates to declare independence from Great Britain.

- "Resolved that the delegates for this Colony in the Continental Congress be *impowered to concur with the other delegates of the other Colonies in declaring Independency*, and forming foreign Alliances, resolving to this Colony the Sole, and Exclusive right of forming a Constitution and Laws for this Colony, and of appointing delegates from time to time (under the direction of a general Representation thereof to meet the delegates of the other Colonies for such purposes as shall be hereafter pointed out)."

Orangeburgh Declaration (May 20, 1776)
Posted in the *South Carolina and American General Gazette*, October 17, 1776.

- "Whilst engaged in an arduous but glorious Struggle for the preservation of those *invaluable Rights and Liberties*, which, by the *Laws of Reason, and of Nature, all men have a right to possess*, and without the Possession of which Life itself would be a Burthen;
- A Constitution evidently framed for the Good, Welfare and Happiness of those who are to live under it. We declare, that as we do most heartily approve of, so we are *determined with our Lives and Fortunes to support*, maintain and defend it."

Virginia Commonwealth Declaration of Rights (June 12, 1776)
Written by George Mason between May and June 1776.

- Article 1 states that "*all men are by nature equally free and independent*, and have certain *inherent rights* of which…they cannot deprive or divest their posterity; namely, the enjoyment of life and liberty, with the means of acquiring and possessing property, and pursuing and obtaining happiness and safety,"
- Articles 2 and 3 state the concept that "all power is vested in, and consequently derived from, the people…"[12] and that "whenever any government shall be found inadequate or contrary to these purposes, a majority of the community hath an indubitable, unalienable, and indefeasible right to reform, alter or abolish it, in such manner as shall be judged most conducive to the public weal."
- Section 14: "That the people have a right to uniform government; and, therefore, that no government separate from or independent of the government of Virginia ought to be erected or established within the limits thereof."

Virginia Constitution, June 1776
Included Virginia Commonwealth Declaration of Rights

America Declaration of Independence (July 4, 1776, signed August 1776)

- "The unanimous Declaration of the thirteen united States of America, When in the Course of human events, it becomes necessary for one people to dissolve the political bands which have connected them with another, and to assume among the powers of the earth, the separate and equal station to which the *Laws of Nature and of Nature's God* entitle them, a decent respect to the opinions of mankind requires that they should declare the causes which impel them to the separation.

We hold these truths to be self-evident, that all men are created equal, that they are endowed by their Creator with certain *unalienable Rights*, that among these are Life, Liberty and the pursuit of Happiness. That to secure these rights, Governments are instituted among Men, deriving their just powers from the consent of the governed, That whenever any Form of Government becomes destructive of these ends, it is the *Right of the People* to alter or to abolish it, and to institute new Government, laying its foundation on such principles and organizing its powers in such form, as to them shall seem most likely to effect their Safety and Happiness."

Appendix V

# Address and Declaration, May 1776

Sources: *South Carolina and American General Gazette*, October 17, 1776; A.S. Salley, *History of Orangeburg*.

*For a New Form of Government, and Self-Governing Constitution*

*At a Court of General Sessions of the Peace, Oyer and Terminer, Assize and General Gaol Delivery, begun and holden at Orangeburgh for the District of Orangeburgh, on Monday the 20th, Day of May, 1776. Before the Honorable William Henry Drayton, Esq. Chief Justice of the Colony of South Carolina.*

*The Address and Declaration of the Grand Jury of the said District, to his Honour the Chief Justice.*
*May it please your Honour,*

*Whilst engaged in an arduous but glorious Struggle for the preservation of those invaluable Rights and Liberties, which, by the Laws of Reason, and of Nature, all men have a right to possess, and without the Possession of which Life itself would be a Burthen; it was Matter of no small Grief to us that any Men should be found amongst us ready to add to the Distress of an oppressed and injured People, by endeavoring to introduce Anarchy and Confusion and thereby to light up the Flames of Civil Discord in the Bowels of this once happy Country.—We are fully convinced that those must have been the nefarious intentions, and base Hopes which induced the King's Judges to refuse the Execution of their Offices, and by so doing to put a Stop to the Administration of Justice in the Courts under their Jurisdiction; to the great Danger of the Lives, Liberties, and Properties of the good People of this Colony. But however great our Grief, we cannot say we are surprised at their Conduct—Strangers in this Land, as they are, and, induced by no Ties of Affection to this Country, or its Inhabitants, they acted as may ever be expected from the wretched Hirelings of an arbitrary and despotic Power. We trust they are the last Officers of the Kind this Colony will ever know, and hope it will be an additional Cause, for us hereafter to rejoice that we resisted, that we thereby became sensible of the true Interest of America in this, as well as many other Respects. To the base Conduct of our late Judges, among other Causes, we owe however the excellent Constitution lately established amongst us: A Constitution evidently framed for the Good, Welfare and Happiness of those who are to live under it. We declare, that as we do most heartily approve of, so we are determined with our Lives and Fortunes to support, maintain and defend it. And to that End, we will, to the utmost of our Power, endeavor to make known its Excellency to all around us, to promote and encourage Peace, Harmony and good Will among the People; and whilst we treat with the tender Hand of Pity and Compassion those few, if any, of our Brethren, who, from the Want of Information, or the artful Designs and Intrigues of wicked Men, may be found at present unfriendly to the sacred Cause in which we are now engaged, we will use our utmost Efforts to teach and instruct them what, and how many Grievances we labour under; the dutiful, humble, and we cannot help now thinking too submissive. Petitions and Remonstrances, we have vainly presented for Redress; the appeal made by our oppressors to the Sword, and driven as we are by dire necessity, the becoming and spirited Measures we have pursued and are now pursuing for a vigorous, manly, and virtuous Defence of the Liberties of ourselves and, which are still dearer to us, of our Posterity. Thus acting, we doubt not but that we shall be able to create such an Union among them, as if extended over the whole Colony, will, with the Assistance of that gracious Providence which has hitherto manifested itself in our Favour; the Goodness of our Cause, the Advantage of our Situation, our Use to Arms, and our Equality, if not Superiority in other Respects to those who are, or may be sent against us, insure us, if called to Action, both Victory and Peace.*

*GREAT BRITAIN has forced us into a new Form of Government: she may continue the Sword so long unsheathed that by observing its Superiority over the old, we may be unwilling to part with it. We now have Rulers of our free Choice and Judges of our own Election; a full and equal Representation in the Government; Blessing we hope we should never lose, and which the Wisdom of the Continental Congress will enable us long to keep Possession of. In our present Situation it would be needless for us to present any Grievances to this Court: From the Joy we are in, and the Pleasures we feel in observing the Attention paid to the Interests of the Colony, at the first Session of the Assembly under the present Constitution, by the Law for the once more opening the Courts of Justice amongst us, and, the many other excellent Laws passed in that Session, we can think of none we labour under: Should there be any, we have the greatest Confidence that your Honour would pay proper Attention to them, were they pointed out, and that the Legislature will at all Times be ready to provide adequate Remedies, when they are.*

*Henry Felder, George King Michael Leitner, William Heatly, Garrit Fitzpatrick, Adam Snell, Gaspar Brown, John M Williams, Henry Rickenbacker, Henry Whetstone, Henry Crum, Godfred Drelve, Jonas Beard*

Appendix VI

# Burning of Felder's Store, October 1778

From the *South Carolina and American General Gazette*, October 7 and 14, 1778. Henry Felder made an account:

> *Whereas, the subscriber's house was plundered and burned and all his papers were either burned or destroyed: "To prevent fraudulent demands that may hereafter be made on him, he gives this public notice that those persons who have any lawful demands on him either in books of account, bond, note of hand, or otherwise, or desire to make demand on or before the first of January next ensuing, and receive payment; all persons indebted to him are likewise entreated to make payment as far as may be consistent with their knowledge. Henry Felder."*

## Appendix VII

# Orangeburgh Militia and Rangers

Table 4. Orangeburgh Militia Engagements

| Orangeburgh District Militia. Commissioned around February 1775 under the command of Colonel William Thomson until Thomson was appointed commander of the 3rd Regiment of Rangers. The Orangeburgh militia operated frequently with the 3rd Rangers until the fall of Charlestown in May 1780. Afterward, the militia detachment supported operations around Orangeburgh District with General Thomas Sumter and General Francis Marion. Henry Felder, Henry Felder Jr., Samuel Felder and likely the other Felder sons may have volunteered in some capacity. | |
|---|---|
| June 28, 1776 | Battle at the Breach Inlet |
| March 28–May 12, 1780 | Siege of Charlestown |
| June 18, 1780 | Hill's Iron Works |
| July 30, 1780 | Rocky Mount |
| July 30–August 6, 1780 | Hanging Rock |
| August 16, 1780 | Camden |
| August 16, 1780 | Rugeley's Mills |
| August 18, 1780 | Fishing Creek |
| November 20, 1780 | Blackstock's Plantation |
| February 23, 1781 | Fork of the Edisto River |
| May 21–June 19, 1781 | Siege of Ninety Six |

| | |
|---|---|
| June 1, 1781 | Vaudant's Old Field |
| June 18, 1781 | Myddleton's Ambush at Juniper Springs |
| July 1781 | Dreher Plantation |
| August 6, 1781 | Salley's Cowpens |
| September 8, 1781 | Eutaw Springs |
| October 28, 1781 | Vince Fort |
| November 1781 | Hampton's Surprise |

*Generated by author.*

## TABLE 5. 3RD REGIMENT OF RANGERS ENGAGEMENTS

| SOUTH CAROLINA 3RD REGIMENT OF RANGERS. Established on June 6, 1775. Orangeburgh District Colonel William Thomson was appointed as commanding officer. At the fall of Charlestown, Colonel Thomson was taken prisoner and then paroled to his home at Belleville until the end of the war. Abraham Felder, Frederick Felder and other Felder sons were involved with the 3rd Regiment. | |
|---|---|
| July 12, 1775 | Fort Charlotte |
| September 18, 1775 | Sullivan's Island |
| October 31, 1775 | Congaree River |
| November 3, 1775 | Mine Creek |
| November 19–21, 1775 | Ninety Six |
| December 22, 1775 | Great Cane Brake |
| December 23–30, 1775 | Snow Campaign |
| June 26, 1776 | Cherokee Indian towns |
| June 28, 1776 | Battle at the Breach Inlet |
| July 15, 1776 | Lyndley's Fort |
| August 1, 1776 | Seneca Town |
| August 8–11, 1776 | Cherokee towns |
| August 10, 1776 | Tugaloo River |
| August 12, 1776 | The Ring Fight |
| August 12, 1776 | Tamassee |
| September 1776 | St. Augustine Expedition (FL) |

| | |
|---|---|
| October 14, 1776 | Altamaha River (GA) |
| February 23–March 15, 1777 | Fort McIntosh (GA) |
| December 29, 1778 | Savannah (GA) |
| January 6 to 10, 1779 | Fort Morris (GA) |
| February 3, 1779 | Port Royal Island |
| March 3, 1779 | Briar Creek (GA) |
| April to July 1779 | Prevost's March |
| May 3, 1779 | Coosawhatchie |
| June 20, 1779 | Stono Ferry |
| September 16–October 18, 1779 | Siege of Savannah (GA) |
| March 12, 1780 | Two Sisters Ferry |
| March 28–May 12, 1780 | Siege of Charlestown |

*Generated by author.*

## Table 6. 2nd Regiment of Dragoons Engagements

| South Carolina 2nd Regiment of State Dragoons, 1781–83. Formed in April 1781 under the command of Colonel Charles Starke Myddleton, son-in-law to Colonel William Thomson. Previously Myddleton was a lieutenant colonel in the Orangeburg militia. In April 1781, with authorization from Governor John Rutledge, Brigadier General Thomas Sumter raised five new regiments of South Carolina troops. Two of these regiments were under Colonel Wade Hampton and Colonel Myddleton, which remained effective until the end of the war. Myddelton was wounded at Eutaw Springs. Henry Felder Jr.'s petition verified his service under Colonel Myddleton from May 12, 1781, to the end of January 1782. | |
|---|---|
| May 1, 1781 | Friday's Ferry |
| May 11, 1781 | Orangeburgh |
| June 18, 1781 | Myddleton's ambush at Juniper Springs |
| July 17, 1781 | Quinby Bridge |
| July 17, 1781 | Shubrick Plantation |
| September 8, 1781 | Eutaw Springs |

*Generated by author.*

Appendix VIII

# Henry Felder Jr. Petition for Mother, 1784

*Source*: *Journals of the House of Representatives*, 1783–84, page 484.

*For the Honourable John L, Loyd Esqr President and the Rest of the Members of the Honourable the Senate.*

*The Petition of Henry Felder*
*Shewth*
*That at different Periods from the Beginning of the late War until the Surrender of Charles Town Your Petitioner was frequently employed in Militia Duty & never received any pay for his Services, but that he kept no Account of nor does he desire any Pay for them.*

*That on the 12 May 1781 he joined Col. Charles Middletons* [Myddleton] *Corps and was constantly on Duty afterwards under different Officers until January 1782.*

*That One William Guest having bough Seventy heads of Cattle for the British was in May 1781 driving on to Camden, but General Sumpter* [Sumter] *having then lately taken Orangeburgh together with the Party who had held it & Guests Drivers having thereupon run away, Guest finding himself unable to proceed to Camden with the Cattle, he gave them up to Your Petitioner telling him that he might do with them what he pleased, whereupon Your Petitioner drove them to Orangeburgh for the use of the American Army, by whom they were accordingly consumed.*

*That in the Year 1778 Your Petitioner's Father Henry Felder, Senr. Kept Store in his Dwelling House near Orangeburgh and the Said House was forcibly entered in the Night by a Party of Tories who took out of the Store & carried off a considerable Quantity of Goods, & burnt the Said Dwelling House, the Rest of the Said Goods, all the household furniture, a Quantity of Grain, and a Considerable Number of other Articles, which were contained in the Said House; Also a Sum of Two Thousand Paper Money belonging to the State, which had been Sent into his hands as One of the Commissioners for Clearing the Fork of Edisto River.*

*That the Loss, which Your Petitioner's Father sustained by this Act was estimated at upwards of 2000 guineas exclusive of the Publick* [public] *money.*

*That Your Petitioner's Father thereupon another Dwelling House on his Said Plantation but that House was burnt & his Father killed by a Party of Tories in 1780.*

*That the Zeal of Exertions of Your Petitioner's Father in the Service of this State are So well known that Your Petitioner thinks it unnecessary to Say anything more on these Points, than that he is persuaded they were the Occasion of the loss of his Property and Life.*

*That he left a Widow & Ten Children now living 4 of whom are Young, the eldest not above 11 & the youngest not above 4 Years of Age.*

*That his Father lost all his Stock of Cattle & Several Negroes by the Tories & British, So that his Estates of which Your Petitioner, being the Heir at Law & Administer to his Father, means to give each child an equal Share, is thus greatly reduced & become Small & inconsiderable.*

*That John Felder a Brother of Your Petitioner commanding a Volunteer Company of Militia in 1781 was Sent by Colonel Washington on a Special & dangerous Services in the Execution of which he was taken Prisoner by the Enemy & having escaped from them attempted to Swim across the Congaree River at McCords Ferry, he was fired on by the Enemy & either killed by them or drowned in crossing Said River.*

*That he left a widow & 2 children, One about Seven, the other about 5 years of Age, & a very Small Estate only 100 Acres of land & 2 Negroes.*

*Your Petitioner therefore prays that Your Honorable House will be pleased to take the Premises into Consideration & grant Such Relief therein As to You Shall appear proper.*

*Signed. HFelder*

Appendix IX

# Henry Felder's Cannons

According to Orangeburgh historians, when the British finally abandoned Orangeburgh sometime after July 1781, the British cannons were disabled and piled up near the Edisto River. Sometime afterward, several of the cannons were mounted vertically to form corner posts and hitching posts. However, the Felder cannons were kept on the Felder family homestead since the immediate sons, grandsons and descendants were immensely proud of their contribution to the war. Following was written Kelly H.S. Felder, May 11, 1989.

*The Two Old Guns of Captain Henry Felder*
*The setting was the small village of Orangeburgh, May 11, 1781. Cannons roared as a vital sequence of the American-British Revolution took place within the boundaries of the Orangeburgh District. The two old cannons before you played a vital part in making the Orangeburgh District free of British Tyranny and alive with the American freedom we enjoy today.*

*Under the command of General Sumter, Capt Henry Felder's Militia Company included seven of Capt Felder's sons guided Sumter's troops by way of the Belleville Road down Russell Street and into the Orangeburgh village. Firing cannons along the way, Capt Felder's troops defeated the British Militia and gained control of the Orangeburgh post.*

*These cannons were Capt Henry Felder's pride and joy. For many years there could be seen, plainly cut, on these old guns "HF" on one and "H Felder 1781" on the other.*

Cannons on Orangeburg Town Square. *Photographs by the author in Orangeburg, South Carolina.*

> *Felder was a staunch patriotic man who brought love of liberty from his native Swiss land. He spoke of his father land with pride and was willing to risk all rather than submit to the tyrannies of the British. Nearing the end of the Revolution, Capt Felder was killed by British Tories while defending his home. He is gone but to this day, the freedom he fought and died for in the village of Orangeburgh lives within us all.*

Today, the iron brackets supporting the cannons obscures the "HF" trademarks.[147]

*Notes*: According to a City of Orangeburg pamphlet, Henry Felder had four cannons, with only two provided as exhibit for the town square, as noted in the *Times and Democrat*, September 3, 2014. Additionally, a cannon on the Charleston Battery also bears the initial "HF," although the cannon's history is unknown and is linked to an additional fake cannon, a real British cannon originally on Longitude Lane and a dubious story from 1933.

Appendix X

# Heritage of Surname Felder

Who were these Felders? Although difficult to directly link genealogically (without much more research in France, Germany and Switzerland), the origin of the name Felder is strongly associated with engagement, independence and willingness to fight. The name Felder has ancient Anglo-Saxon and Swiss-German origins, with many variations. Suggested surname origins range from De la Feld, De la Feild, Delafeld, Delfeld, Felde, Feld, Fields and Felder, as well as German variations like Veld, Velde, Velder and De Velde. One of the earliest recorded is the surname De la Feld, connected to the De la Feld counts of Colmar in the sixth century and other counts and knights in the Lorraine region of northwest France into the tenth century.

Born in Colmar, Haut-Rhin Alsace-Lorraine, France, Roger de la Feld (born before 960 and died around 1040) was earliest named line of De la Feld nobles during the Middle Ages. In Alsace, the De la Felds entertained the eleventh-century Pope Leo IX (1002–54) and his court on the way to consecrate the Cathedral of Strasburg, where the first cathedral stone was laid in 1015. References suggest that the De la Feld castle ruins remain somewhere within the hundred miles between Mainz, Germany, and Colmar, France, although the exact location and pictures have not been found. Roger de la Feld's grandson Hubertus de la Feld (1030–92) came to England with William the Conqueror (1028–87) during the Norman conquest of England.[148] As a reward and grant for his service, Hubertus acquired lands during the Norman occupation of England. Records show that Hubertus settled on these conquered lands in the county of

Lancaster, above Manchester, in 1068. As a historical note, the practice was commonplacc for nobles or knights to settle on their conquered land. As example, the Scandinava viking Gaange Rolf, the Duke of Normandy, also known as Rollo, succesfully seiged Paris between 885 and 886 and remained and settled in northern France. William the Conqueror is the direct descendant of Rollo. By tradition, Sir Hubertus settled near the city of Chester for the remainder of his life.

During the Norman regime in London, King John granted Streatham estate in Surrey outside London to a John de la Feld, a possible relative or descendant of Roger de la Feld, in 1109. Another John de la Feld (born in 1224) married Elizabeth Fitzwarine (born in 1228) within the barony of Fitzwarine.[149] As another linkage, a Robert de Felde is listed in the registry of the Knights Templars in the County of Gloucestershire, England, in 1185. In financial records called Pipe Rolls, a Hugo de la Felde lived in the county of Bedfordshire, England, in 1188. Richard de la Felde is mentioned during the reign of King John, the builder of churches (1199–1216). Many of these names are traceable to Sir Hubertus but not officially due to lack of records. One branch relates Sarah de la Feld as the blood line of Princess Elizabeth Plantagenet (Elizabeth of Rhuddlan), daughter of King Edward I.

Through the next century, English records indicate many land deeds to Da la Feld, Felde, Feidler, Fielde, Fields, De la Felden and Le Felder.[150] As the Anglo and France conflicts continued in these centuries, many French prefixes, like the "de la," were dropped from the England surnames to create an Anglo-Saxon native tongue. The surnames De la Feld and Felde refer to a person who works in pastures, open terrain, and clears the land and fields. Two additional surname variants list a William de la Felden in 1286 and Geoffrey le Felder in the county of Sussex in 1327. By the 1400s and into the 1500s, many baptisms and christenings are recorded in the Surrey and Sussex region of England with similar surnames.

As the families of Hubertus de la Feld immigrated into England from northern France, the Counts of de la Feld held considerable lands in northwestern France, Lorraine region, with alliances, through marriage, with the Earls of Flanders and the House of Habsburg (Hapsburg). Built in 1020, the Habsburg Castle near Zurich was the original seat of power for the Habsburg empire. From the twelfth to fourteenth centuries, French and Holy Roman Empire pressures, Catholic and Protestant tensions and other instabilities had many people immigrating from the Lorraine region. The immigration included two prominent areas. First, the region bordering Lorriane included the modern-day Neuchatel into western Switzerland and northward into southern Germany. West of Neuchatel are the lands of Uri, Schwyz and Unterwalden, the original Swiss Confederacy formed in 1291. When eight other "states" were included, this area grew and was known as the Old Swiss Confederacy, which lasted into the fifteenth century. Duke Frederick IV of Austria and the House of Habsberg would eventually lose the Habsburg Castle and Canton of Aargau to the Swiss Confederacy in 1415. Switzerland, smaller than the state of South Carolina, was formally recognized as an independent country from the Holy Roman Empire in 1648. When and why the De la Feld, Felde or Felder families may have immigrated into regions set to become modern-day Switzerland and Germany are likely linked to desires for religious freedoms, tolerance and opportunities.

Consider several conceivable immigration theories. First, the Lorraine counts and De la Feld family were associated by marriage with the House of Habsburg, and possibly the early Felde/Felder family immigrated based on family associations to lands central House of Habsburg outside of modern-day Zurich. A second theory is related to Christianity and the Crusades. Between 1095 and 1191, elements of the initial Christian Crusades were launched from the French regions near Lorraine-Alsace through lands of modern-day Switzerland. Perhaps these lands were alluring and settled by the early Felde/Felder families during their pilgrimages or through the returning crusaders from the Holy Lands. An adjacent theory parallels the rise, fall and persecution of the Knights Templars and Knights Hospitaller.

A predecessor of the Knights Templar, Lorraine nobleman Godfrey of Bouillon led the successful army in the First Crusades, carrying the Cross of Lorraine as his banner and becoming "King of Jerusalem" after defeating the Muslims in 1099. A group of his Frenchmen would band together as the Templars. The Knights Templar trace their origins to shortly after the First Crusade. Around 1119, French nobleman Hugues de Payen and eight knights swore an oath and vowed to protect pilgrims' journeys to the Holy Lands. The original charter grew rapidly throughout western Europe, integrating similar Templar orders in France, England and Scotland. Unfortunately, their financial successes and power brought about the ire of religious and monarch leaders. When King Phillip IV of France imprisoned the Grand Master Jacques De Molay and arrested scores of Knights Templar in 1307, numerous Templar orders dissolved in France and England by 1312. Many Templar and Christian followers feared continued persecution and fled to neighboring regions known for religious tolerances and freedom away from England, France and the Catholic Church. Some fled to Scotland, a region of declared independence from England by Robert the Bruce. Many others crossed the French border into the lands of Schwyz, Uri, Unterwalden and the Habsburg Castle. The House of Habsburg's dominant ethnicity was German. The dissolution of the Knights Templar gave rise to a sister order. The Knights Hospitallers, also known as the Order of Saint John, founded several commanderies in Switzerland. The commandery in Fribourg, Switzerland, was founded before 1229 and belonged under German tongue and priory of Germany.[151]

The pressures of the Holy Roman Catholic Church and German monarchy for religious freedom shadowed the immigration from France into Switzerland and Germany. As these Swiss communities (or cantons) grew, many of the cantons' symbology, crests and flags were mason trowels, or the Malta Cross, and the Cross of Lorraine, very comparable to many Templar symbols. Moreover, Swiss lore includes shadowy knights as protectors of villages, and with Switzerland's long history of financial banking institutions (the Knights Templar financial holdings were vast), early Switzerland and the Knights Templar have many similarities. A debatable direct connection to the theory is more fascinating: the Templar "founding" of Switzerland. Historically, the migration of English and French families into the German-Swiss regions searching for religious freedom tracks with the organized growth in these regions from the thirteenth to sixteenth century. In these centuries, Germany and Switzerland grew from less than 8 million to over 12 million, while areas of England and lower France grew substantially less as a percentage of population and smaller regions declined as much as 20 percent.[152]

The English, German and Swiss linkages of the Felder family require further examination, and if DNA results provide evidence, inferences may suggest plausible migration theories.[153]

As for the early Swiss-German Felders, Petrus im dem Velde lived in Mengen, Germany, in 1216. By the late 1400s and 1500s, several Felders are found in Germany and Switzerland. A Hanns Felder baptism of his daughter Margreth in Basel, Switzerland, is recorded on May 21, 1553. Another Hans Velder (1536–65), married to Catharina Mayer, lived in Holzgerlingen, Wuerttemberg, Germany.

In 1466, a Hans Felder initially from Oettingen (Bavaria) settled in Lucerne, south of Zurich. From 1473 to 1475, the stonemason Hans Felder built the church in St. Wolfgang, Hunenberg, Canton of Zug. And from 1478 to 1483, Hans built the Late Gothic St. Oswald's Church in Zug and provided additional renovations from 1492 to 1494. Hans Felder is known for several churches, buildings and structures around Zug and Zurich.

Possibly a son of the former, another Hans Felder is also known as a builder from 1497 to 1521. Hans Felder (the latter) is known for the construction of Peter Falck's Chapel between 1515 and 1521 within the St. Nicholas Cathedral, Fribourg, Switzerland. Peter Falck was the mayor, diplomat and scholar of Fribourg and hired Felder for the construction. In 1518, Hans provided additional construction plans for the cathedral, and construction continued until 1627. Started years before Felder in 1283, the St. Nicholas Cathedral's Gothic architecture and the large tower were built over several centuries by several architects but never completed. The Fribourg Town Hall was built by Gylian and Hans Felder between 1501 and 1522. The town hall's interiors were patterned on Louis XVI's sixteenth-century Gothic style. Nothing further is known of Hans Felder after he left the city of Fribourg around 1521. Of interest, however, Fribourg is twenty-six miles west from St. Josef Chapel in Schupfheim, built by Peter Felder around 1680.

An hour west of Fribourg, Zug and Zurich is the Krinau and Toggenburg region of Switzerland. This region hosted several wars for independence. In the early 1400s, the Appenzell War was a successful uprising of farmers and craftsmen over the oppressive Holy Roman Empire feudal abbot and

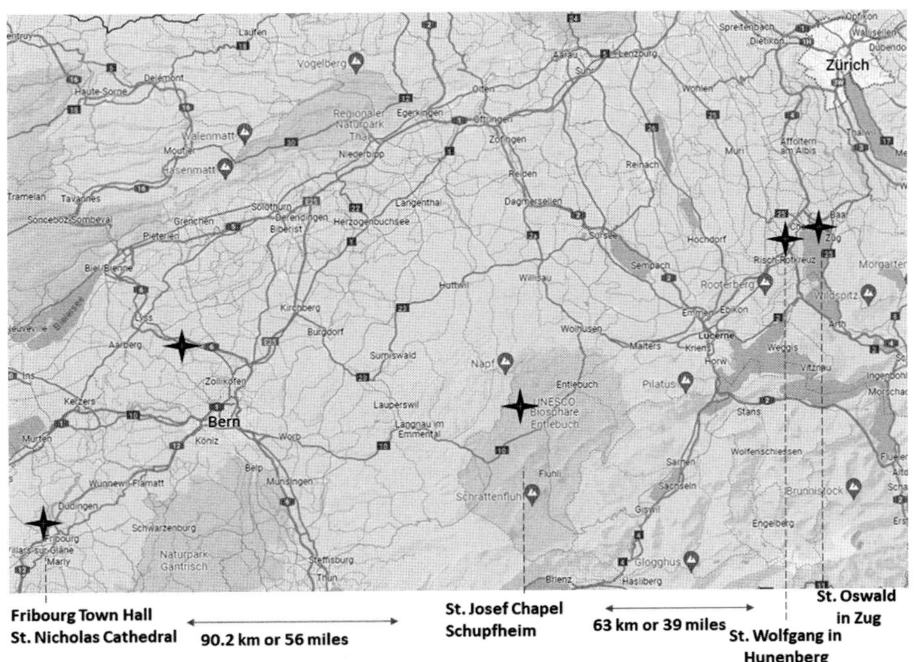


Felder's churches across Switzerland. *Generated by author.*

the House of Habsburg. A few centuries later, the Toggenburg War in 1712 was another civil war between Catholic and Protestant cantons, with the Protestants toppling the balance of political power in the region. Hans Heinrich "Henry" Felder's ancestry is associated with this rebellious region and in the canton of St. Gallen.

Similar surnames to De la Feld, Felde and Fields come from the England and French cousins; the surname Felder is derived from a topographical distinction for someone who lived on land, cleared forest and provided the sweat to convert land into pasture for agricultural cultivation. Most Felder coat-of-arms crests feature prominent timber elements such as trees, branches or logs. Traditional symbology suggests that these represent strength, heroism and victory, as well as faith and heritage. Two Felder crests were found within the Swiss library of cantons. One shows a mason trowel or plow, suggesting the builder and cultivator of the land, with red clovers symbolizing faith, love and hope. This family crest is very similar to the crest found in Schupfheim's St. Josef Church, built by Peter and Heinrich Felder. A second Felder crest features the similar red clover vines with a six-pointed star, traditionally symbolizing a spiritual protectorate. Each crest and interpretation seem befitting of Henry Felder, whose family arrived in the new American colonies when it was still a wild land, an undefined country—land the Felders were willing to tame with sweat and blood, shaping it into a country to fight and die for.[154]

John Henry Felder was born on March 2, 1725, in Ober-Wattwil,[155] present-day Ebnat Kappel, Canton of St. Gallen, Switzerland, and was baptized as Hans Heinrich Felder on March 21, 1726. Henry's parents were the senior Hans Heinrich Felder (1672–1738) and Ursula Zuber (1692–1739). Birth and baptism references indicate that Henry's parents had several children, with only Henry living into adulthood. Henry Felder's father, Hans Heinrich (also has been spelled "Henrich") Felder was a planter and a "Meister Rotgerber," or a master red tanner, in the colonies. A master tanner used oak oil to process cattle hides into strong, durable leather used in boots, shoes and bags. The oak oils provided the red hue.

As referenced earlier, Hans Heinrich Felder has been associated with the St. Josef Chapel (or St. Joseph Church) in Schupfheim, Switzerland, west of Lucerne, in the Entlebach Valley, where a stained-glass window bears the name Heinr Felder. Schupfheim is eighty miles west of Ebnat Kappel. Research reveals that Hans and Heinrich are common Swiss names and that the Felder descendants were prominent in both regions. Fragments of sources convey the story of a Peter Felder, a rich cattleman

Felder crest and coat of arms.

in the region. As the story goes, during a robbery, Peter prayed to God that if his life would be spared, he would build a church. At that very moment, several dogs began to bark, scaring away the highwaymen. To keep his promise, the church was built by Peter Felder sometime around 1680. Church records suggest that Peter Felder had two grandsons or great-grandsons, each named Johann (Hans) Heinrich Felder. Stories indicate that around 1780, the church was expanded by a Heinrich Felder. Henry's father, Hans Heinrich Felder, came to America in 1735. If the dates are accurate, the timeline shows that these were two different Heinrich Felders; however, they may be relatives of the original builder,

St. Josef Chapel, Schupfdeim, Switzerland. *Author photograph.*

Peter Felder. The chapel's stained-glass windows bear each name: Peter Felder and Heinr Felder. The stained glass was replaced, and the original window was refurbished by a Felder descendant in Arizona.

The Felder ancestry is strongly connected to this region in Switzerland. Research indicates that Patriot Henry Felder is a descendant of a Joss Joseph Felder (Job Fälder)[156] (1569–1608/9) and Verena Egg (or Margreth Heydler) from the same region. Unverifiable evidence has identified both spouses.[157]

Joss and Margreth's son Heinrich Felder (1594–1667) married Ursula Mueller. Heinrich and Ursula's son Bernhardt Allen Felder (1627–1702) married Eva Grob. Bernhardt and Eva's son Han Heinrich Felder married Ursula Zuber and would travel to America with his young son, Henry Felder. While these references are sourced, inconsistencies persist, and genealogical work continues.

Appendix XI

# James Addison Felder (1841–1893)

Some may desire to trace their roots to these early South Carolina militia heroes. Some contemporary Felders may trace their Henry Felder ancestral branch to James Addison Felder from the Orangeburg and Fort Motte areas of South Carolina. The following is a short biography of Henry Felder's ancestry.

James Addison Felder was the great-grandson of Frederick Felder, son of James Felder and Rachel Rebecca Felder. Born on October 3, 1841, James Addison Felder was a farmer who lived in several places, including Walnut Grove, Bowman, Four Holes and Fort Motte communities. After the Civil War, he lived in Cow Castle, south of Orangeburg. He had no brothers and one half-sister, Victoria Utsey, who married Henry Cook and lived in Bowman, South Carolina.

When the Civil War broke out, James, in his early twenties, enlisted as a private in the army and served for the entire war. Muster rolls verify his enlistment on December 24, 1861. He was in the cavalry division and rode his own horse. He served in the CSA Cavalry, 5th Regiment, under General Wade Hampton; the 14th Battalion, South Carolina, under Colonel Dunning; and Company B under Captain John C. Edwards. The 14th Battalion served in Georgia, South Carolina and Florida before moving to Virginia in March 1864. The regiment fought in the Battle of the Wilderness and the bloody battle of Cold Harbor. In January 1865, the 5th South Carolina Cavalry was reassigned to General Wheeler's Cavalry

Felder's grave and Mizpah Baptist Church. *Author photograph in Fort Motte, South Carolina.*

for the purpose of engaging General William T. Sherman as the Union marched through South Carolina and into North Carolina. A week after General Robert E. Lee surrendered at Appomattox Courthouse, the 5th South Carolina Cavalry surrendered after the Battle of Bentonville, North Carolina, on April 17, 1865.

When the war ended, with a bullet wound in his leg, he was allowed to return home with his horse. He recovered from the wound but walked with a slight limp for the remainder of his life. James Addison named his first son Hampton Henry Felder in honor of the general he had served under during the war, General Wade Hampton.

In the last years of his life, he lived in Fort Motte in the Peterkin-Wienges community. While there, he, along with Eustan Bryant and Dick Carson, founded Mizpah Baptist Church. Initially, there were no Baptist church buildings in the area, so the Episcopal Church members allowed the Baptists to use their church building for afternoon Sunday school. This church was the St. Matthews Episcopal Church, called the "Red Church" for many years due to the fact that the building was painted brownish-red. James later helped with the construction of the Mizpah Baptist Church building, founded in 1888.

Felder, J. A.
Co. B, 14 Battalion
South Carolina Cavalry.
(Also called 2 Batt'n, 1 Batt'n and 1 Squadron S. C. Cav.)
Subsequently became part of 5 S. C. Cav.
(Confederate.)
Private Private
CARD NUMBERS.
1 49194657
2 4740
3 4810
4 4883
5 4957
Number of medical cards herein 0
Number of personal papers herein 0
Book Mark
See also

(Confederate.)
F | 14 Batt'n Cavalry. | S. C.
J. A. Felder
Pvt. | Capt. J. C. Edwards' Company, 1 Battalion Cavalry, South Carolina Volunteers.*
Age ____ years.
Appears on
Company Muster Roll
of the organization named above,
for Dated Jany 7, 1862.
Joined for duty and enrolled:
When Jany 7, 1862.
Where
By whom
Period 12 Mos.
Valuation of horse, $75 100; equipments, $ 100
Remarks:

*This company subsequently became Company B, 14th Battalion South Carolina Cavalry.
The battalion was organized in December, 1861, and January, 1862, and officially designated by the A. & I. G. O. as the 2d Battalion South Carolina Cavalry, but it was mustered in the field as the 1st Battalion (or Squadron) South Carolina Cavalry. In May, 1862, the official designation was changed to the 14th Battalion South Carolina Cavalry.
By S. O. No. 18, Headquarters Department of South Carolina, Georgia and Florida, dated January 18, 1863, this battalion was consolidated with the 17th Battalion South Carolina Cavalry and two independent companies and formed the 5th Regiment South Carolina Cavalry, this company becoming Company A of that regiment.
Book mark:
J A Boyd
Copyist.
(642)

James Addison Felder's roll. *Courtesy of South Carolina Archives.*

James Addison Felder died on December 20, 1893, and was buried at Mizpah Baptist Churchyard, Fort Motte, South Carolina. The following is his obituary, from the *Times and Democrat*:

> *DEATH OF A GOOD MAN—Mr. Jas. A. Felder, of Fort Motte, died at his home a few weeks ago after a protracted illness, which he bore patiently to the end. He was 53 years of age. He leaves his wife and nine children to mourn his loss. Mr. Felder was a most excellent man and his death is greatly regretted by a host of relatives and friends outside his immediate family. He was a member of the Baptist Church and was a true Christian. He was a gallant Confederate soldier and served his country faithfully to the close of the war.*[158]

## *The 1st Battalion (1st and 2nd) Cavalry, 5th South Carolina Regimental Cavalry*

The 1st Battalion South Carolina Cavalry was established in December 1862, designated 2nd Battalion Squadron South Carolina Cavalry, into Confederate service, commanded by Major Paul Stroman Felder of Orangeburg District until it was redesignated the 14th Battalion, commanded by Major Joseph Morgan.

In January 1863, the battalion was consolidated into the 5th South Carolina Cavalry Regiment under command of Colonels Samuel Wragg Ferguson, Robert J. Jeffords, J.C. Edwards and John Dunovant. Several Felders were listed in this regiment.

It served in South Carolina, Georgia and Florida. In March 1864, it moved to Virginia with 1,200 effectives. Assigned to Butler's Brigade, the regiment fought in the Wilderness Campaign, the battles at Cold Harbor and south of James River.

In January 1865, the 5th South Carolina Cavalry was reassigned to Wheeler's Cavalry Corps, Tennessee, CSA, and returned to South Carolina under General Wade Hampton to slow General William T. Sherman's advancement in the South. The Confederate troops repeatedly skirmished with numerically superior Union forces as they moved through Columbia, South Carolina, and into North Carolina. The final battle of the Carolinas Campaign was at Bentonville, North Carolina, and formal surrender came on April 17, 1865. About 1,750 men served in the 5th South Carolina Cavalry between 1861 and 1865, and 17 percent were killed or wounded.

# CHILDREN OF JAMES ADDISON FELDER

(1) Annie Rachel Felder (June 40, 1868–November 25, 1961). Lived on Sellers Avenue, Orangeburg, Ward 4. Married John Backmon Etheredge around 1889. John Backmon Etheredge (April 27, 1867–January 24, 1917) was the son of Jacob Burdette Etheredge and Elizabeth Catherine Wertz. His occupation was listed as street overseer for the City of Orangeburg; they had three children. Annie and John are buried at Sunnyside Cemetery in Orangeburg, South Carolina.

(2) Mary Elizabeth Felder (August 3, 1869–October 21, 1947). Lived on a farm in Amelia area of Orangeburgh. Married Frederick George Rickenbaker Sr. in 1883. As a farmer, George Rickenbaker (October 18, 1861–May 21, 1941) was the son of Artemus and Carrie Rickenbaker. Mary Elizabeth and George had six children. Mary and Frederick are buried at Congaree Baptist Church Cemetery.

(3) Laura Jane Felder (August 18, 1872–January 19, 1956). Lived in Givhans and Dorchester areas in South Carolina. In 1895, she married Daniel Pinckney Pendarvis (September 25, 1870–March 8, 1934), son of Harmon Pendarvis and Rachel Jane Knight. He is listed as a farmer, and they had five children. Laura Jane and Daniel are buried at Indian Fields Methodist Church Cemetery in Rosinville, South Carolina.

(4) Carey Effie Felder (May 21, 1874–October 5, 1963). Lived in Amelia on McCord Ferry Road, Calhoun County. In 1893, she married John Jacob Arant (1866–1933), son of David D. and Margaret Arant. He was a farmer, and they were buried at Mitzpah Baptist Church in Fort Motte, South Carolina. They had six children.

(5) Ella James Felder (May 14, 1875–August 9, 1894). Ella James died at the age of nineteen and is buried at Mitzpah Baptish Baptist Church, Fort Motte, South Carolina.

(6) Gussie Felder (1876–1878). Gussie Felder died as an infant and is buried at Walnut Baptist Church, Orangeburg, South Carolina.

(7) Hampton Henry "Hamp" Felder (March 4, 1877–October 22, 1956). In the 1900 census, Hampton was living with sister Carey (Felder) and John Arant and then later moved to Jefferson Street, Alachua, Florida. In 1909, Hampton married Annie Elizabeth Griffin (July 20, 1885–June 20, 1958), daughter of Jessie I. Griffin (from South Carolina) and Mary Grissett (from Alabama). Hampton was a farmer in South Carolina, and then he moved to Florida with the timber industry, treating lumber (1940 census). Hampton Felder is buried at Jonesville Cemetery, Newberry, Florida, and his wife, Annie, is buried at Greenwood Cemetery, Orange, Florida. They had four children.

(8) Charles Frederick Felder (April 25, 1882–April 30, 1941). Charles was a merchant and grocer and worked in a sawmill. He lived on Jellers or Sellers Avenue in Orangeburg. Charles married twice, first to Mary Jane Bolen (December 8, 1892–October 11, 1918) on December 27, 1908; she was daughter of Jerome David Bolen and Rena Pauline Stevenson. The second marriage was to Margaret Lenora "Maggie" Zeigler (1884–1942). Charles had four children and is buried at Sunnyside Cemetery in Orangeburg, South Carolina.

(9) Grover Tolson Felder (September 1, 1885–February 24, 1946). Tolson was a grocer and merchant and lived on Doyle Street and Zion State Highway in Orangeburg, as well as possibly in a boardinghouse he may have managed (based on 1920 and 1930 censuses). Later in life, he was a clerk at JW Berry at 18 West Russell Street and worked at an aluminum plant. In 1906, he married Selina Barbara Lucas (October 29, 1886–July 20, 1919), the daughter of John Antley Lucas and Polly Lee Saylor. Grover and Selina are buried at Sunnyside Cemetery, Orangeburg, South Carolina. They had two children: Dr. Lin Shecut Felder and Lottie Tolson Felder O'Cain.

(10) Thomas Clemon Felder (1889–1953). Thomas married Bessie Beulah Evans (1894–1934). He is buried at Elmwood Cemetery, Columbia, South Carolina.

# Notes

## Introduction

1. Phillips, *1775*, vii.
2. "As 1775 ended, the only place the British still controlled was occupied Boston." Phillips, *1775*, viii.

## Chapter 1

3. Address and Declaration, also known as the Orangeburgh Declaration, May 20, 1776. In April 1776, South Carolina Chief Justice William Henry Drayton expounded unto several district grand juries to review the newly formed South Carolina government, as some legislators, like prominent John Rutledge, questioned South Carolina's legality to create a new state constitution.
4. After the Revolutionary War, militia veterans filed petitions for lost property. Individual petitions named events and unit members, providing valuable cross-references to other Patriots.
5. Henry Felder petition, South Carolina Congress, *Congressional Journals*, 1783–84, AA Archives no. 2336, SC 2700, South Carolina Archives.
6. Frederick Felder petitions, AA Archives no. 2335, South Carolina Archives.

7. Lieutenant Colonel William Washington, Continental dragoon commander and George Washington's second cousin, once removed.
8. Aaron Inman petition, R-5489 and William Abbott petition, S30239, Revolutionary War petition archives.
9. William Abbott petition, S30239, Revolutionary War petition archives.
10. Abraham Felder petition, SC Archive no. 2334, AA no. SC2698, W284, South Carolina Archives.

## CHAPTER 2

11. See Sirmans, *Colonial South Carolina.*
12. See Tepper, *New World Immigrants.*
13. Purry, *Description of the Province of South Carolina.*
14. Faust, *Swiss Emigrants in the 18th Century*, 1:6.
15. McCrady, *History of South Carolina Under the Royal Government*, 121.
16. Faust, *Swiss Emigrants in the 18th Century*, 1:8.
17. *South Carolina Gazette*, July 19, 1735.
18. One reference suggests Ann Felder, later married to Jacob Pfund (Pound) in 1760, as the fourth member; however, no reference was found indicating Ann Felder as Heinrich's child or family member.
19. Grant to Hans Heinrich Felder, September 17, 1736.
20. Faust, *Swiss Emigrants in the 18th Century*, 1:69.
21. Avis-Blatt of Zurich, Glarus pastor, letter dated October 15, 1765, Faust, *Swiss Emigrants in the 18th Century*, 2:26. Reference within Orangeburg County Historical Society Archives, Orangeburg, South Carolina.
22. Giessendammer Petition, May 27, 1749.
23. See Salley, *History of Orangeburg County.*
24. Burial location is uncertain, possibly Felder Cemetery, Gulbrandsen Road, Orangeburg, South Carolina.

## CHAPTER 3

25. Phillips, *1775*, xviii. In the Carolinas, the backcountry population outnumbered the coastal areas by two or three to one.
26. Christopher Gadsden's eighteen resolutions to the Stamp Tax Congress, Gladney, *No Taxation without Representation*, 95.
27. Ramsey, *History of South Carolina*, 1:121; Edgar, *South Carolina History*, 213.

28. From 1764 to 1775, Charles Montagu and William Bull exchanged the governorship several times when Montagu was absent.
29. Snowden, *History of South Carolina*, 1:290.
30. McCrady, *History of South Carolina Under the Royal Government*, 642–43, 750.
31. Depending on sources, the Moderator was named differently as Colonel Joseph Coffell, Scophol, Schovel, Scouil or Schofeld. His followers were called Scopholites, Schouilities, Schofilities or otherwise British Tories.
32. Salley, *History of Orangeburg County*, 369.
33. Ramsey, *History of South Carolina*, 121.
34. Snowden, *History of South Carolina*, 1:291.
35. Snowden, *History of South Carolina*, 1:314.
36. *South Carolina Gazette*, January 7, 1775.
37. *Journals of Provincial Congress of South Carolina*, June 8, 1775, 42.

## CHAPTER 4

38. Russell, "Life of Southern Colonies"; Fraser, *Charleston! Charleston!*, 132. College of Charleston was founded in 1770, the oldest college in South Carolina.
39. *Dutch* is the Anglicization of the term *Deutsche*, or German. Early settlers spoke German, maintaining their German heritage.

## CHAPTER 5

40. Simms, *History of South Carolina*, 44.
41. Between 1521 and 1526, Spanish explorer Lucas Vazquez de Ayllon founded the first settlement in the New World in Winyah Bay, near present-day Georgetown. After one month, the explorer abandoned South Carolina and moved his five hundred settlers to below Savannah. Neither settlement was successful, but technically they were the first attempted settlements in the New World. Charles Town was not established until 1670, 150 years later.
42. Gregorie, *Thomas Sumter*, 44.
43. Fort Loudoun is below present-day Knoxville, Tennessee, and about 145 miles from Fort Prince George. Fort Prince George is under present-day Lake Keowee, Pickens County, South Carolina.

44. Salley, *History of Orangeburg County*, 88; Johann Martin Boltzius, 1703–1765, German-born minister known to establish Protestant church in Ebenezer, Georgia.
45. Drayton's journal letters, Report to the South Carolina Council of Safety by William Tennent, St. Matthews Parish, September 10, 1775.
46. Salley, *History of Orangeburg County*, 404.
47. While Sumter established his riflemen, Daniel Morgan's Rifles were a similarly established regiment and formed the Provisional Rifle Corps at General Washington's instruction in June 1777. Morgan's Rifles were prominent at the Battle of Saratoga, October 1777.
48. Bass, *Gamecock*, 34, 55; Gregorie, *Thomas Sumter*, 44, 52, 54, 191.
49. From August 1780 to April 1781, William Washington's cavalry engaged in two skirmishes; however, they left South Carolina with Daniel Morgan after Cowpens, January 1781. Morgan fought at Cowpens and then returned to North Carolina and never returned. Nathanael Greene maneuvered around the South Carolina border with no engagements until Hobkirk's Hill (Camden) in April 1781. Colonel "Light-Horse Harry" Lee's cavalry joined Francis Marion in April 1781.
50. William Washington's cavalry included several Catawba warriors at McBee's plantation on the Pon Pon River, March 23, 1780.

## CHAPTER 6

51. Term limit and elections varied. Assembly members were elected annually between 1745 and 1748 and biannually from 1759 to 1761.
52. Simms, *History of South Carolina*, 71.
53. An original Son of Liberty was Lieutenant John Calvert (1734–1803), my sixth-great-grandfather on my paternal side. These early Patriots met as early as the fall of 1766.
54. Laurens to Leigh, *South Carolina Gazette*, July 2, 1772, and October 22, 1772.
55. Subsequently, on July 6, 1774, Charlestown formed the Committee of 99 and selected delegates to the First Continental Congress and in November, at a general meeting, established South Carolina's First Provincial Congress in 1775.
56. Fraser, *Charleston! Charleston!*, 125. A "necessary house" is an outhouse or a toilet.
57. See Russell, *American Revolution in the Southern Colonies*; Fraser, *Charleston! Charleston!*, 125.

## CHAPTER 7

58. Fraser, *Charleston! Charleston!*, 136–37.
59. William Legge, Earl of Dartmouth, British Secretary of State over the Colonies, letter to Royal Lieutenant Governor Bull, February 5, 1774.
60. Simms, *History of South Carolina*, 115.
61. John Adams diary, September 14, 1774.
62. John Adams diary, September 3, 1774. John Adams wrote about many of the delegates, including the Rutledge brothers, finding Edward high-spirited and good-natured, though conceited and not too deep. The senior Rutledge was "not very promising. There is no keenness in his eyes."
63. John Adams diary, October 11, 1774.
64. Simms, *History of South Carolina*, 121.
65. "Fourth…we will not, directly or indirectly, export any Merchandise, or Commodity whatsoever, to Great Britain, Ireland, or the West Indies, except Rice, to Europe." Continental Association, October 20, 1774.
66. Extract from the *Journals of Provincial Congress of South Carolina*, January 11–17, 1775, 22–23.
67. Phillips, *1775*, 262. South Carolina was the only colony to enforce a colony-wide Patriot organization with appointed leaders' prohibition of British trade.
68. Ryan, *World of Thomas Jeremiah*, 34–37; William Henry Drayton Proceedings, General Committee of South Carolina Report, vol. 2, April 10, 1775, 182, *South Carolina Gazette and Country Journal*, March 28, 1775.
69. Fraser, *Charleston! Charleston!*, 140; Ryan, *World of Thomas Jeremiah*, 34–37.

## CHAPTER 8

70. Extracts from *Journals of Provincial Congress of South Carolina*, November 24, 1775, 150.
71. Simms, *History of South Carolina*, 131.
72. Between August 5 and August 15, 1775. McCrady, *History of South Carolina…1775–1780*, 3:43. Report to the South Carolina Council of Safety by Drayton, King's Creek, near Enoree, August 16, 1775. After leaving Congaree store, Drayton stopped at two taverns in Dutch (Deutsch) Fork area, one of which was McLaurin's in Spring Hill (Drayton memoirs, footnote pages 359+). An existing Spring Hill

tavern, built around 1752, later owned by Thomas Veale and Henry Eleazer, was possibly one of these stops. Also referenced in *The Journal of Alexander Chesney*, edited by E. Afred Jones.

73. Drayton Committee of Safety, letters, *Memories of the Revolutionary War: Drayton Memories by John Drayton*, Chapter IX (1821), 363. See also *The Journal of Alexander Chesney*, edited by E. Alfred Jones.

74. Chappell, *North of the Broad River*, chapter 2; Paul Bartow, Eleazer House National Register Petition, 2017. Eleazer family history was also consulted.

75. Stephen Eleazer petition, SC Archives exhibit, file no. 2191, Claims Growing Out of the American Revolution.

76. A historic marker referencing the tavern is located at Mount Olivet Lutheran Church, Spring Hill, about a half mile from the tavern location. A South Carolina Archives historical paper indicated that it was built prior to 1770. The McLaurin store and the latter Eleazer-Veal tavern were in Spring Hill, hence these may or may not be the same tavern. Records cannot prove or disprove either plausible assumption. Upper Richland County Historical and Architectural Inventory, June 2002; National Register of Historic Places registration form, Paul Bartow, April 2017.

77. Phillips, *1775*, viii, 4, 14–15. Before 1776, according to Phillips, the Patriot militias controlled every major area of the colonies except Boston, and all royal governors had fled or were absent.

## CHAPTER 9

78. The blockage consisted of sinking several ship hulks to limit the British ability to maneuver in the harbor.

79. Historians debate the first representative body to declare independence from British and first representative body to claim "natural rights" by God. The early expression of "rights" were those rights under the British constitution and as British citizens, and such "independence" was carefully worded in the hope of a reconciliation that never came. Such claims as "first" depend on interpretations of the actual declaration or resolution. (Further information in Appendix IV).

80. Fraser, *Charleston! Charleston!*, 148.

81. South Carolina Constitution of 1776.

## CHAPTER 10

82. When Washington took command in June 1775, the gunpowder supply was around eighty thousand pounds and often misfired due to poor quality and lack of potassium nitrite.
83. Dick, "Gunpowder Shortage."
84. Simms, *History of South Carolina*, 126. Captain Lempriere captured a British man-of-war off the coast of St. Augustine with large stores of gunpowder and military arms.
85. Extract from the *Journals of the Provincial Congress of South Carolina*, March 5, 1776, 245.

## CHAPTER 11

86. John Adams's notes from the Continental Congress debate, September 8, 1774.
87. Address and Declaration, also known as the Orangeburgh Declaration, principal Henry Felder, May 20, 1776. *South Carolina and American General Gazette*, October 17, 1776; Salley, *History of Orangeburg County*, 266+.
88. Declaration of Rights and Resolve, October 14, 1774.
89. Our Declaration of Rights is embedded in several American benchmarks, including the Virginia Declaration of Rights (George Mason principal author, June 1776), Pennsylvania Declaration of Rights (Benjamin Franklin, August 1776) and Massachusetts Declaration of Rights (Samuel Adams, June 1780).
90. Address and Declaration, the Orangeburgh Declaration, principal and foreman Henry Felder, May 20, 1776.
91. On April 23, 1776, South Carolina Chief Justice William Henry Drayton expounded to grand juries in Charlestown. District grand juries provided responses. Cheraw provided a statement similar though less verbose: "[F]rom too sad experience are convinced of the wicked schemes of their [Britain] treacherous rulers to fetter them with the chains of servitude, and rob them of every noble and desirable privilege which distinguishes them as freemen; justice, humanity, and the immutable laws of God, justify and support them in revoking those sacred trust…a separation which now proves its own utility, as the only lasting means of future happiness and safety."

92. New Hampshire Constitutional Convention, December 1775; Virginia adopted its constitution in late June 1776.
93. John Adams's notes on the Congressional Congress proceedings.

## Chapter 12

94. Simms, *History of South Carolina*, 147.

## Chapter 13

95. Lambert, *South Carolina Loyalists*, 45.

## Chapter 14

96. Revolutionary War petitions of service cross-reference several fellow soldiers' petitions referencing the Felder sons.
97. Henry Felder petition, AA no. 2336, February 1786, SC 2700, South Carolina Archives.
98. Frederick Felder Revolutionary War petitions, AA no. 2335, including exhibit S537, S538, South Carolina Archives.
99. Samuel Felder petitions AA no. 2338, South Carolina Archives.

## Chapter 15

100. Bass, *Swamp Fox*, 24; McCrady, *History of South Carolina…1775–1780*, 3:366–69.
101. South Carolina Archives. Several notes reference Captain Heatley and Frederick Felder serving at the siege.
102. Fraser, *Charleston! Charleston!*, 163.
103. Lambert, *South Carolina Loyalists*, 69.
104. McCrady, *History of South Carolina…1775–1780*, 3:538–39.
105. Henry Felder Jr. petition to South Carolina Congress, *Journals of the House of Representative*, 1783–84.

## CHAPTER 16

106. The story of Henry Felder is conveyed by several stories, narratives in archives or parts of stories passed by tradition.
107. An additional debate is found in a Loyalist's journal, *Journal of Alexander Chesney*, edited by E. Alfred Jones. The journal claims that a Loyalist captain, James Alexander, was promoted to captain of the Indian Field Company on May 27, 1780, and that he subsequently sought out and killed Felder and John Fry.

## CHAPTER 17

108. Simms, *History of South Carolina*, 158.
109. George Washington address on recruiting and maintaining the army, September 24, 1776.
110. George Washington letter, September 30, 1776.
111. McCullough, *1776*, 188–216.
112. John Adams letter to Elbridge Gerry, June 18, 1775. Also referenced was Horace Kephart, "Birth of the American Army," *Harper's New Monthly* 98 (December 1898–May 1899): 961.
113. "Deliberate, murderous, and accurate fire provided no opportunity to advance." British soldier at the Breach. Colonel Thomson's Rangers were equipped with riflemen, muskets and two cannons.
114. Cornwallis's 1781 letter to General Henry Clinton and similar reflections in the Cornwallis papers, the campaigns of 1780 and 1781, vol. 2. From another fatigued statement to General Clinton on fighting in South Carolina: "I have experienced the distresses and dangers of marching some hundreds of miles in a country chiefly hostile, without one active or useful friend; without intelligence, and without communication with any part of the country." See also Bateman and Pilkington, *Studies in Settler Colonialism*, and the Cornwallis papers (1859), page 102.
115. Militia conscripts varied throughout the war. Initially 30-, 60- and 90-day conscripts were typical, although the number of service days expanded to 180 or more days. A study after the war showed that these men volunteered and then went home to take care of family and farms and to resupply since militia were seldom provided the promised supplies from the Continentals. At latter stages of the war, volunteer inducement included horses, slaves and goods captured from Loyalists.

## CHAPTER 18

116. Russell, *American Revolution in the Southern Colonies*, 165+.
117. Lynch, "Winner or Runner?"
118. Bass, *Swamp Fox*, 46.
119. Bass, *Gamecock*, 84–85.
120. George Washington letter, June 25, 1780.

## CHAPTER 19

121. Reynolds, *Andrew Pickens*, 193; Garden, *Anecdotes of the Revolutionary War*, 287.
122. George Washington was miraculously spared any injury.

## CHAPTER 20

123. Gregorie, *Thomas Sumter*, 157; Sumter letter to Greene, May 6, 1781. Without cannons, Sumter abandoned the siege of Fort Granby's supplies. Lee letter to Greene, May 6, 1781. With field pieces, Marion and Lee began the siege of Fort Motte. Bass, *Gamecock*, 168. Sumter's letter to Greene desperately requested a field piece, and several letters were exchanged. In McCrady, *History of South Carolina…1780–1783*, it is clear that the cannon was promised and possibly en route if Sumter could have retrieved it at the ferry.
124. Bass, *Swamp Fox*, 177. As soon as Greene received Marion's request for cannons, Greene sent a six-pounder; however, Captain Finley got promptly lost in the swamp and returned to Greene.
125. Bass, *Gamecock*, 172. As late as May 8, Sumter repeatedly sent requests, and Greene responded that he would provide a cannon when he received another one from Virginia. However, Sumter received a cannon without permission—apparently a cannon from a local militia.
126. A Revolutionary cannon at White Point Garden on the Charleston Battery clearly bears an interlocked "HF," Henry Felder's trademark initials, over the fuse vent; however, other investigators claim it's a fake four-pound cannon confused with a second cannon, a British cannon from Longitude Lane. The "HF" was claimed to be fake markings of the Hills Foundry in York, which did not make cannons prior to

the American Revolution. From sources, a real cannon and a fake cannon existed; however, the history of the original real British cannon is unknown. Several more probable scenarios exist, but none can be certifiable as accurate, as most writings focus on the controversy in 1933 rather than the source of the British cannon.

127. Bass, *Swamp Fox*, 177+.

128. Bass, *Swamp Fox*, 195. After the hanging, Marion's exchange with Lee's troops left little question that Marion was frustrated with Lee, to add to his existing resentment toward Greene and Sumter.

129. General Greene letter to General Sumter, May 17, 1781, Thomas Sumter Papers, Wisconsin Historical Society, vol. 5 (1986), page 94.

130. Bass, *Swamp Fox*, 188–91.

131. Bass, *Swamp Fox*, 191. While the Quaker General Greene owned slave, he often wrote of the dread of slavery. Marion had continuous issues recruiting and retaining volunteers.

132. See Bass, *Swamp Fox*. Sumter instituted "Sumter's Law" to use captured Loyalist horses, slaves and supplies to induce recruits, which Marion called "plundering" even though he was doing similar things to keep his brigade effective—this explains General's Greene request for horses. In his defense, Sumter provided receipt for captured goods, and actions were approved by Governor Rutledge and General Greene.

133. Sumter's letter to Greene, May 12, 1781, reprint in *Yearbook 1899*, City of Charleston.

134. Greene letter to Washington, May 4, 1781; Johnson, *Sketches of Life*, 2:87. "You frequently hear of great things from Generals Marion and Sumpter. These are brave, good officers; but the people who are with them just come and go as they please. These parties rather serve to keep the dispute alive, than lay a foundation for the recovery of the country. Don't be deceived in your expectations from this quarter; if greater support cannot be given for recovery of these states, they must and will remain in the hands of the enemy."

135. Thomas Sumter letter to Greene, May 6, 1781, reprint in *Yearbook 1899*, City of Charleston.

136. Thomas Sumter letters, May 2, 1781, referenced ten wagons of meal sent to General Greene as an example.

137. General Sumter letters to General Greene, between July 17 and July 22, 1781, Thomas Sumter Papers, Wisconsin Historical Society, vol. 5 (1986), page 111. See also Mayor Smyth's Annual Review, *Yearbook 1899*, City of Charleston.

138. Thomas Sumter letter, July 17, 1782.

139. The Patriots' losses at Quinby and Shubrick's Plantation were seven killed, twenty wounded (Sumter letter, July 17, 1781), although other sources claim higher numbers. After a year of excuses for not following Sumter, the skirmish provided Marion and Lee an opportune to bitterly complain to Greene with an overemphasized sacrifice of men. The actions and letters at the time of this engagement are a sharp disagreement from accounts and memoirs penned years after the conflict. All but one hundred of Marion's militia deserted General Marion the following day (Sumter letter, July 17 and July 21, 1781; Bass, *Swamp Fox*; and a recounted story in Gregorie, *Thomas Sumter*, 179n83, from Draper's papers). Sumter provided his own assessment (letter to Greene, July 22, 1781) when critical of Lieutenant Colonel Lee's hesitation at the bridge, allowing the British to reorganize to defend the bridge.

140. McCrady, *History of South Carolina…1780–1783*, 4:342.

141. Johnson, *Sketches of Life*, 171–77.

142. Johnson, *Sketches of Life*, 176.

143. McCrady, *History of South Carolina…1775–1780*, 3:chap. 14. McCrady provides a compelling assessment of Greene, Lee and Marion's continued contempt of Sumter based on known letters and correspondence rather than secondhand accounts.

## EPILOGUE

144. Governor John Rutledge from Clarence Felder's screenplay for *All for Liberty*, a film that outlines the major events of Captain Henry Felder's life. It has won nine international film awards and two awards for Sons and Daughters of the American Revolution and has seen worldwide distribution from Bridgestone Multimedia Group, BMG-Global.

## APPENDIX I

145. Pon Pon River is sections of the Edisto River.

146. *Journals of Congress of South Carolina*, biographies.

## APPENDIX IX

147. Interview with Felder descendants.

## APPENDIX X

148. Burke and Ormerod, *Genealogical and Heraldic History*, 1:322.
149. Delafield, *Delafield Family History*, vol. 2, chap. 27; *The Ancestor*, no. 11.
150. *Dictionary of English Surnames*, English Ancestral Names references.
151. Although suppressed as fugitives, few Templars were imprisoned, although their orders dissolved due to the damaged reputation and loss influence and property. Many joined Hospitallers or Cistercian orders as the Crusades and the Templars faded into history.
152. European population from 1000 to 1500, multiple sources.
153. DNA technology and European data continues to evolve, with possible stronger inferences, but this is only conjecture.
154. In a curious note, a unique Felder crest located in the Orangeburg archives portrays a fish and an apparent high-neck gorget with plumed hat. A fish symbolizes Christianity, and a gorget represents prominence. Given the first generation of American Felders, Henry's families may have Americanized their crest for their colonial legacy.
155. Many genealogical biographies claim Henry's birth in Wattwil or Zurick. I believe the Zurick reference is inaccurate. The Wattwil reference may be partially confused based on the town that changed names—a present community of Wattwil is four miles north of Ebnat Kappel.
156. "Toggenburg Genealogy Work" (Federle-Frey), Boris Brooks files.
157. In 1762, Ober-Wattwil was renamed Ebnat. In 1965, Ebnat merged with Kappel to form Ebnat Kappel (no hyphen). Ebnat Kappel is a few miles from present-day Wattwil, which is often also claimed as Henry Felder's birthplace.

## APPENDIX XI

158. *Times and Democrat*, December 20, 1893.

# Primary Archives and Sources

Primary archives. *Photographs by the author in Orangeburg, Columbia, and York, South Carolina.*

Charleston County Library Archives, Charleston County Public Library, Calhoun Street, Charleston, South Carolina. Maps, journals and references.

Charleston Library Society, King Street, Charleston, South Carolina. Maps, legislative journals and Sumter and Marion letters.

Orangeburg County Historical Society and A.S. Salley Archives, Orangeburg, South Carolina. Henry Felder folders and related folders.

South Carolina Archives, Columbia, South Carolina. Maps, Congressional journals, Revolutionary War petitions and England land grants.

Southern Revolutionary War Institute, Culture and Heritage Museums, York, South Carolina. Interview with Michael Scoggins, Lyman Copeland Draper's manuscript collection, Draper files and South Carolina legislative volumes.

Adams, John. *The Works of John Adams*. Vols. 1–3. Diary, Debates, Essays, Autobiography and Collective Works, organized by John Quincy Adams until 1839.

*The Ancestor*. No. 11. Archibald Constable & Company, 1904.

Barbour, R.L. *South Carolina's Revolutionary War Battlefields*. Pelican Publishing Company, 2002.

Bass, Robert D. *Gamecock: The Life and Campaign of General Thomas Sumter*. Holt, Rinehart and Winston, 1961.

———. *The Green Dragoon: The Lives of Banastre Tarleton and Mary Robinson*. Henry Holt and Company 1957.

———. *Swamp Fox: The Life and Campaign of General Francis Marion*. Henry Holt and Company, 1959.

Bateman, Fiona, and Lionel Pilkington. *Studies in Settler Colonialism: Politics, Identify and Culture*. Macmillan, 2011.

Burke, John, and George Ormerod. *A Genealogical and Heraldic History of the Commoners of Great Britain and Ireland Enjoying Territorial Possessions or High Official Rank, but Uninvested with Heritable Honours*. Vol. 1. Genealogical Publishing Company, 1977.

Carbone, Gerald M. *Nathanael Greene*. Palgrave Macmillan, 2008.

Chappell, Buford S. *North of the Broad River: The Land and the People*. Chapter 2. Self-published, circa 1980s.

Delafield, John Ross. *Delafield Family History*. Vol. 2. Private printing, 1945.

Dick, Jimmy. "The Gunpowder Shortage." *Journal of the American Revolution*, September 9, 2013.

Edgar, Walter. *South Carolina History*. University of South Carolina Press, 1998.

Ellis, Joseph J. *His Excellency, George Washington*. Alfred A. Knopf, 2004.

Faust, Albert Bernhardt. *Swiss Emigrants in the 18th Century to the American Colonies*. Vol. 1, *1734–1744*. Genealogical Publishing Company, 1968.

Fraser, Walter J., Jr. *Charleston, Charleston!: The History of a Southern City*. University of South Carolina Press, 1989.

———. *Patriots, Pistols, and Petticoats*. Charleston County Bicentennial Committee, 1976.

Garden, Alexander. *Anecdotes of the Revolutionary War*. A.E. Miller, printer, 1822.

Gerson, Noel. *The Swamp Fox: Francis Marion*. Ballantine Books, 1967.

Gilmer, Georgia Muldrow, and Elmer O. Parker. *American Revolution Roster, Fort Sullivan, 1776–1780: Battle of Fort Sullivan, Events Leading to the First Decisive Victory*. Fort Sumter Chapter, Daughters of the American Revolution, 1976.

Gladney, Henry M. *No Taxation without Representation*. A collection of petitions. Xlibris, 2014.
Gordon, John W. *South Carolina and the American Revolution*. University of South Carolina Press, 2007.
Gregorie, Anne King. *Thomas Sumter*. R.L. Bryan Company, 1931.
Helsley, Alexia Jones. *South Carolinians in the War for American Independence*. South Carolina Department of Archives and History, 2000.
Johnson, Paul. *A History of the American People*. Harper Perennial, 1999.
Johnson, William. *Sketches of Life and Correspondence of Nathanael Greene*. A.E. Miller Printing, 1822.
Ketchum, Richard M. *Saratoga: Turning Point of America's Revolutionary War*. Henry Holt and Company, 1997.
Lambert, Robert Stansbury. *South Carolina Loyalists in the American Revolution*. University of South Carolina Press, 1987.
Liell, Scott. *46 Pages: Thomas Paine, Common Sense*. Running Press, 2003.
Lipscomb, Terry W. *South Carolina Becomes a State*. South Carolina Department of Archives and History, 1976.
———. *The South Carolina Lowcountry, April 1775–June 1776*. South Carolina Department of Archives and History, 1994.
Lynch, Wayne. "Winner or Runner?: Gates at Camden." *Journal of the American Revolution* (April 8, 2014).
McCrady, Edward. *The History of South Carolina in the Revolution, 1775–1780*. Macmillan Company, 1901.
———. *The History of South Carolina in the Revolution, 1780–1783*. Macmillan Company, 1902.
———. *The History of South Carolina Under the Royal Government, 1719–1776*. Macmillan Company, 1899.
McCullough, Davis. *John Adams*. Simon & Schuster, 2001.
———. *1776*. Simon and Schuster, 2005.
Ollier, John. *The Swamp Fox*. Da Capo Press, 2016.
Phillips, Kevin. *1775: A Good Year for Revolution*. Penguin Books, 2012.
Purry, M. *A Description of the Province of South Carolina, Drawn Up in Charles Town, in September 1731*. Translated from *Purry's Original Treatise* in French and published for *Gentleman's Magazine* in August, September and October 1732. Reprinted by Peter Force, 1837.
Ramsey, David. *History of South Carolina: From Its First Settlement*. Vol. 1. W.J. Duffie, 1858.
———. *History of South Carolina: From Its First Settlement in 1670 to the Year 1808*. W.J. Duffie, 1858.

Reynolds, William R., Jr. *Andrew Pickens: South Carolina Patriot in the Revolutionary War*. McFarland and Company, 2012.

Russell, David Lee. *The American Revolution in the Southern Colonies*. McFarland & Company, 2000.

———. "Life of Southern Colonies." *Journal of the American Revolution* (February 6, 2013).

Ryan, William R. *The World of Thomas Jeremiah: Charles Town on the Eve of the American Revolution*. Oxford University Press, 2010.

Salley, Alexander S. *The History of Orangeburg County*. R. Lewis Berry, 1898.

Scoggins, Michael. *The Day It Rained Militia: Huck's Defeat*. The History Press, 2005.

Simms, William Gilmore. *The History of South Carolina*. Pantianos Classics, 1860.

Sirmans, M. Eugene. *Colonial South Carolina: A Political History, 1663–1763*. Institute of Early American History and Culture at Williamsburg, Virginia, University of North Carolina Press, 1966.

Snowden, Yates. *History of South Carolina*. Vol. 1. Lewis Publishing Company, 1920.

Tepper, Michael, *New World Immigrants: A Consolidation of Ship Passenger Lists and Associated Data from Periodical Literature*. Genealogical Publishing Company, 1979.

Ward, Christopher. *The War of the Revolution*. Vols. 1 and 2. Macmillan Company, 1952.

# Index

## A



## B



## C

## D



## E



## F



## G

## N



## O



## P



## Q



## R



## S

## T



## W



## Y

# About the Author

Brian Eleazer is a native South Carolinian and a direct descendant of Henry Felder, the protagonist in this work. Brian is also the direct descendant to another book-referenced Patriot, Johannes (Johann) Stephen Eleazer. Johannes Eleazer was a farmer and Spring Hill tavern keeper in the South Carolina Deutsch Fork area, above present-day Columbia, who supplied the Patriots throughout the war. The tavern likely hosted William Henry Drayton in 1775 as Drayton attempted to recruit American Patriots near the Congaree and Broad Rivers, and the tavern remains a family home, possibly the oldest functioning structure on the boundary of Lexington and Richland Counties.

From grade school and through encouragement from his mother, a longtime elementary teacher and family researcher, Brian has visited many Civil War and Revolutionary War battlefields across the Southeast and continuously researches our early American history. In his travels, Brian has built a network of friends and historian acquaintances, including Paul Bartow, previously at the USC history department; the late historian and author Michael Scoggins; and Chris Weatherhead-Felder and Clarence Felder, directors of the Revolutionary War movies *All for Liberty* and *John Laurens's War*. Chris and Clarence are cofounders of the Actors' Theater of South Carolina (ATSC), a multiple international award-winning production company for which Brian serves as a board member.

For the past fifteen years, Brian has written and added material to Henry Felder's story originally for family consumption and has expanded it to document the seldom-chronicled story of the South Carolina militia. Additionally, Brian has written several short stories for his children and grandchildren. He shares historical research pieces on social media and, on occasion, has posted comments and debate on national articles about the Revolutionary militia and South Carolina heroes.